The
Volatility
Machine

The Volatility Machine

Emerging Economies

and the Threat of

Financial Collapse

Michael Pettis

OXFORD
UNIVERSITY PRESS

2001

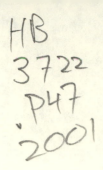

OXFORD

UNIVERSITY PRESS

Oxford   New York
Athens   Auckland   Bangkok   Bogotá   Buenos Aires   Calcutta
Cape Town   Chennai   Dar es Salaam   Delhi   Florence   Hong Kong
Istanbul   Karachi   Kuala Lumpur   Madrid   Melbourne
Mexico City   Mumbai   Nairobi   Paris   São Paulo
Shanghai   Singapore   Taipei   Tokyo   Toronto   Warsaw

and associated companies in
Berlin   Ibadan

Published by Oxford University Press, Inc.
198 Madison Avenue, New York, New York 10016

Oxford is a registered trademark of Oxford University Press

Library of Congress Cataloging-in-Publication Data
Pettis, Michael.
The volatility machine : emerging economies and the
threat of financial collapse / by Michael Pettis.
     p.   cm.
  ISBN 0-19-514330-2
  1. Financial crises. 2. Loans, Foreign. 3. Debts, External.
  4. Capital. 5. International finance. I. Title.

HB3722.P47 2002
336.3'435—dc21   00-049180

9 8 7 6 5 4 3 2 1

Printed in the United States of America
on acid-free paper

Amid the seeming confusion of our mysterious world, individuals are so nicely adjusted to a system, and systems to one another, and to a whole, that by stepping aside for a moment man exposes himself to a fearful risk of losing his place forever.

—Nathaniel Hawthorne

Acknowledgments

This book was written in 1999 and 2000 but incorporates work dating back over four years. A lot of friends and colleagues have helped me in this work, and it is difficult to name them all, but it would be extremely ungenerous not to thank the many contributions made by my good friend and Columbia University colleague Michael Adler. In addition, Jared Gross and Fernando Saldanha read early drafts of the book in great detail and provided an enormous amount of help and advice. Several other people contributed either directly on the book or in the many prior discussions in which I was forcibly educated (or both). These include Craig Blessing, Arminio Fraga, Gary Evans, Frank Fernandez, Carlos Hernandez Delfino, Bob Kowit, David Malpass, Celso Pinto, Lee Sachs, and Robert Wade. Finally, my editor, Paul Donnelly, has made this whole publishing business surprisingly easy and straightforward.

I also owe a lot to my colleagues at Bear Stearns. Thanks to Don Mullen and Peter Herzig, I was able to work part-time for six months so that I could focus on writing the book. The boys on the EM desk— Jorge Cantonnet, A. J. Mediratta, Carlos Vargas, Frederico Gil-Sander and king-of-all-media Fernando Bravo always kept me in the loop. Brian Kim and Bobby Lee, that amazing duo, struggled mightily to maintain the fiction that the Capital Market Strategies group at Bear Stearns couldn't function without me. Economists Carl Ross and Jose Cerritelli were always able to take time from their schedules to give me the advice and information I needed. Jeff Urwin has been an important friend and one of the main reasons I am at Bear Stearns, and of course both things are equally true of *el profesor* Bruce Wolfson.

There are many friends in the market who have contributed knowledge, advice, or drinks. My former partner and supertrader Con Egan is the best source for how bond markets actually work. Hans Humes is both a great friend and a great fount of information on the hazards of debt restructuring. Rudy Amoresano, Bo Bazylevsky, Jon Blum, Enrique Boilini, Rodrigo Briones, Chiao Chiu, Fulvio Dobrich, Alison Harwood, Ken Hoffman, Harry Krensky, Pedro-Pablo Kuczynski, Ricardo Lacerda, George Liberatore, Ross McLaren, Vince and Leigh Perez, Joe Rinaldi, Ian Ross, Susan Segal, Ken Telljohann, Craig Torres, Peter Urbanczyk, Alberto Verme, Tommy Vecchhione, and Richard Watt have all directly or indirectly also had a hand in this.

Finally, a number of students at Columbia University have been very helpful. I spent a lot of time discussing the capital structure framework with graduate students Fabio Bicudo, Steve Kim, Gerrit Koester, and Chi Le. Undergraduate students Sami Mesrour and Ejike Uzoigwe helped out with research while Charles Saliba and Evan Hutchinson participated actively in and out of class. I have only to add the names of John Kim, Dong-Jun Johnny-5 Lee, Kevin Woodson, and Reza Vahid to assure this book a place in history as the first time the names of this amazing group of students have been mentioned together in writing.

Contents

Introduction

In this book I will argue that certain types of financial crises—like the crises that have affected many Latin American and Asian countries in recent years—are problems of sovereign balance sheet mismanagement and not economic mismanagement. In contrast to much of the analysis that has appeared recently, I will argue that these crises do not occur because domestic economic policies are flawed, or because capital flows are excessive, or because international investors behave irrationally, or even because currency regimes are mismanaged. They occur instead for two other, related, reasons. First, emerging market borrowers and investors have consistently underestimated the source and magnitude of volatility in emerging financial markets. Second, perhaps as a consequence, borrowers and investors have permitted and even encouraged sovereigns to put into place capital structures that systematically exacerbate this volatility.

In the world of international finance there is a disconnect between the work of corporate finance specialists and economists. While the former typically attempt to evaluate and quantify the way market risks are absorbed into a company's capital structure, the latter try to understand the development and functioning of the long-term processes that drive an economy. But countries and even regions are subject to market-related risks and shocks that can disrupt their behavior, just as companies are, and these risks are transmitted in the same way: through their capital structures. In fact any economic entity's capital structure can be seen as a sort of volatility machine, one of whose main functions is precisely to manage the way external markets impact internal processes. This volatility machine converts the price swings of the market into greater or lesser volatility inside the economic entity by linking up revenues and costs in a more-or-less predictable way.

This is not just a way of saying that short-term loans subject a borrower to liquidity pressure, or that loans denominated in a foreign currency can change in value in adverse ways, although both of these statements are true. The idea of capital structure as a volatility machine is more general. We begin with the obvious point that the asset and operating sides of a company's balance sheet are subject to a whole variety of factors that can introduce volatility into the company's revenues or asset values. These factors can increase or decrease the value of revenues or assets in a systematic and predictable way, even though we cannot actually predict beforehand which factors will come into play and, consequently, how revenues and asset value are likely to perform. Because these sources of volatility are unpredictable, and unpredictability makes planning more difficult and increases the probability of financial distress, well-managed companies look for ways to reduce these sources of volatility. This usually means that well-managed companies attempt to design their capital structures in such a way that the sum of financing costs is indexed so that the impact of external shocks on revenues and asset values is offset by the impact of these same shocks on financing costs.

To take an example, if a weakening (strengthening) of the euro hurts (benefits) a car manufacturer in the United States, perhaps because it sells cars manufactured in the United States to European consumers, it will seek to hedge this exposure. The easiest way to hedge this exposure is to issue debt in euros. If the euro weakens, the car manufacturer's sales may suffer, but its debt servicing cost, denominated in euros, declines at the same time, so that the impact of the weakening euro is mitigated. The opposite is true if the euro strengthens. In this case, the company's capital structure systematically dampens volatility, but this need not always be the case. Assume a company that provides building materials to the home construction industry decides to fund itself with floating-rate debt. If interest rates decline, home construction is generally positively affected, so our hypothetical company would find itself in the pleasant position of seeing demand for its product increase. At the same time, because its debt is indexed on a floating-rate basis, its debt servicing costs will decline. This will mean that the company's net earnings can rise dramatically thanks to a decline in interest rates. Had interest rates increased, however, the impact would have been the opposite. This company's capital structure acted to increase earnings volatility. For companies who are convinced that future shocks are very likely to be positive, it may seem to make a great deal of sense to put into a place a capital structure that increases volatility. The truth turns out to be actually more complex and we will discuss why in chapter 6.

Corporate finance is, in effect, the study of volatility and how volatility impacts value. There are types of assets whose values increase with *increases* in volatility and other assets whose values increase with *reductions* in volatility. These changes in value do not occur simply because of preferences investors may have for volatility. They occur because changes in volatility change economic behavior. For example, changes in volatility can change the payoff structure for investors, and so affect their decision to invest. They can force managers in search of profit to redirect their attention from strategic issues to financial issues, thereby reducing the output of the whole system. Most important, they can change default probabilities, so forcing a whole series of stakeholders to behave in ways that increase or reduce the economic output of an entity.

Although all economic entities from households to corporations to countries are affected by the impact of capital structure on volatility, it is particularly important for less developed countries, whose small markets can easily be overwhelmed by the macroeconomic shifts that take place in the larger economies. Recently, the high susceptibility to external shocks of the smaller markets in Latin America, Asia, and eastern Europe, combined with very unstable capital structures, has resulted in a series of financial crises that were neither predicted nor subsequently explained by the economists and analysts who cover these regions. Most of the analysis of these crises explained the event by blaming poor domestic economic policies, a sudden change in investors' perceptions of underlying economic fundamentals, the destructive profit-seeking of speculative players, or psychological factors such as investor panic. But none of these reasons provides an adequate explanation for the financial crises, which often seemed to ignore "real" factors and unfolded in an almost mechanical way.

The direct economic impacts of these shocks are clear, of course, but there are also residual impacts on subsequent policy-making. Because it is often difficult to distinguish between economic mismanagement and bad markets, one result of the recent financial crises has been to delegitimatize the various economic policies that preceded the market collapses, much in the same way that the LDC (less developed country) debt crisis of the 1980s delegitimatized the import-substitution policies popular in Latin America in the 1970s. The credibility of economic policies, in other words, collapses at the same time the local markets do.

At the corporate level, the process by which capital structure impacts a company's economic behavior is fairly well understood, and is the subject of a very large and growing literature, whereas country analysts have largely ignored capital structure except when it has already precipitated a market collapse. As a result, the quality of sovereign analysis is much lower than it ought to be, and its usefulness for policy-makers and investors in guiding decisions has been fairly limited. This book integrates a corporate finance approach to risk management with traditional sovereign risk analysis to arrive at a more complete understanding of emerging market risks and the causes of sovereign financial crises. The goal is to understand how volatility is typically transmitted into the less developed economies of Asia, Africa, eastern Europe, and Latin America and what policy-makers should be doing to protect themselves from, or at least mitigate, this volatility. Although there are significant differences from country to country and from region to region, from a corporate finance point of view these markets actually have far more in common than they have in differences, and they respond in very similar ways to external shocks. Because of their similarities I believe that this capital structure framework is applicable to all the so-called emerging markets.

In this book I attempt to do the following, more or less in order:

- Discuss the characteristics of the recent financial crises that have affected emerging market countries
- Propose a model for why capital flows from rich countries to poor countries
- Examine the history of international lending from the 1820s to the present in the context of this model
- Develop a corporate finance framework to explain why financial collapses occur and how volatility impacts the performance of an economic entity
- Integrate the corporate finance framework within the capital flow model
- Develop the concept of a "capital structure trap" to explain destabilizing sovereign financial crises
- Finally, propose a policy approach for less developed and/or smaller economies to minimize susceptibility to financial crises and to protect them from the effects of external shocks

Much of my career has been spent as an emerging markets bond trader and capital markets specialist. Like most other business school graduates of the 1980s I started my career believing that changes in market prices reflected genuine changes in underlying fundamental conditions quickly and efficiently. But later, like most traders, I became more concerned about the structure of the market, the nature of the investor base, the impact of liquidity and changes in volatility, and even, at some point, the sheer unpredictability and seeming irrationality of market behavior.

The Mexican crisis in 1994–95 was for me an eye-opening event, even though my subsequent study of international debt history makes clear that it should not have been. The currency devaluation that set off the crisis had not been completely unexpected, but the virulence of the subsequent market break and the nearly nightmarish logic with which one market in Mexico after another collapsed forced me to reconsider what I thought I knew about how markets responded to changes in fundamentals. The Asian crisis nearly three years later may have been more surprising to most people than the Mexico crisis was, but for me in many ways it was simply a repeat of the logic that had broken the Mexican markets.

Just before the Mexican crisis I had been working on a brief article for the *Columbia Journal of World Business* on the impact of volatility on macroeconomic ratios used to predict creditworthiness. When Professor Michael Adler and I began teaching our course on Latin American financial markets at the Columbia Business School in 1992, one of the points we always made early in the course was how disappointing the ratio analysis of the 1970s had been in predicting the subsequent relative performance of the borrowers. For example, if you had listed the countries of Latin America, Asia, eastern Europe, and Africa on the basis of debt/export ratios in the 1970s, you would have expected to see some strong relation between the weakness of the ratio and the subsequent debt performance in the 1980s. In fact there was nearly none.

Perhaps because of my trading background it occurred to me that the volatility of export earnings might be as important as the actual ratio, since the higher the volatility, the greater the possibility of a sustained payments gap between export earnings and debt servicing. Simple corporate finance theory would predict that because a lender has many of the characteristics of a short seller of put options, debt costs would be higher for borrowers with more volatile export earnings. The combination of higher debt costs and greater volatility would have had a significant impact on the default probability. For my article I recalculated all the old ratios so as to incorporate a simple option format in which the new ratios adjusted the debt/export figures to account for volatility, with higher levels of export-earnings volatility causing deterioration in the original ratios. I was surprised at how much better these adjusted ratios did in predicting the subsequent default history. Volatility itself was an extremely important variable, and to ignore it invalidated much of the analysis.

This study and the Mexican crisis suggested to me that there were flaws in the way analysts understood sovereign risk. Over the next few years I stumbled toward a capital structure framework for thinking about sovereign risk that explicitly incorporated volatility, and I began to focus on the impact of conditions that systematically enhanced or dissipated volatility. The crises of 1997–99 allowed me to test some of the conclusions of the capital structure framework, and I was gratified by how well it explained or predicted some fairly puzzling behavior. The virulence of the Asian crisis in 1997, the post-Asian-crisis boom in Latin American bond issuance in the first quarter of 1998, the rapid recovery of the Asian markets, particularly Korea, in 1998 and 1999, the Russian default in 1999, the inevitability of a Brazilian devaluation and its relatively benign impact on subsequent inflation, the unsustainable debt pressures on Argentina—the capital structure framework predicted and explained all of these long before the explanations became commonly accepted.

The capital structure approach also created in me a great deal of skepticism about the success of the neoliberal model of economic development and an equal reluctance to believe that the Asian crisis "proved" in any way the failure of the Asian development model. I say this for several reasons. An examination of sovereign debt history suggests that there is no obvious conclusion to be drawn about the correlation between, on the one hand, liberal economic policies and sustainable economic growth, and, on the other hand, industrial policies and economic stagnation. During periods of ample global liquidity, most economic policies seem to "work" because of foreign capital inflows, while they all "fail" when liquidity dries up.

Perhaps more important, Latin American countries, contrary to popular belief, actually have a long and not very successful history of experimentation with liberal economic models. On the other hand, successful former emerging market countries like the United States, Germany, France, Japan, Taiwan, and Korea have all followed to varying degrees policies of export encouragement, import substitution, protectionism, industrial targeting, and credit manipulation. Although liberal critics were quick to claim that the recent financial crises, particularly those in Asia, were the consequence of misguided economic policies, in fact, as I hope to show in this book, financial crises are nearly always caused by poorly managed capital structures. For this reason it is useless to look for the roots of the crisis in crony capitalism, state intervention, credit manipulation, or the other various failures of state interventionism.

In 1999 I left the Latin American Capital Markets group at Bear Stearns to run a new group within Bear Stearns that advised domestic and international corporate and sovereign clients of the bank on optimal capital structures. This forced me to reexamine everything I thought I knew about corporate finance theory in an attempt to understand and explain why corporations should care about capital structure and volatility (a more complicated question than I at first supposed). Delving into the basics of corporate finance theory helped me to rethink some of the parts of the capital structure framework and made it a more sophisticated tool.

Finally, I have taught several different courses at the Columbia Business School, but in 1998 I joined up with Bruce Wolfson, senior international legal counsel at Bear Stearns, to develop a new course for Columbia's School of International and Public Affairs. This course was to be on the history of external debt from the 1820s to the present, including the history of sovereign debt restructurings during those years. Wolfson has a great deal of experience in the restructuring and recovery of the Latin American debt markets over the past twenty years, and he and I spent time trying to analyze the general goals and principles of sovereign debt restructurings. I don't know that we have figured out the answers, but the process has certainly helped me to sharpen my own thinking about the role of a country's capital structure in determining its relationship to external shocks.

These then are the ingredients out of which this stew has been made. I have tried to combine corporate finance theory, the history of sovereign external debt, my experience as a bond trader, and the economic theory I have absorbed over the years to propose a finance framework that directly addresses the causes and consequences of financial crises among less developed markets. There is a great deal of debt history in this book, and I think that this is necessary. I have two very strong prejudices: first, that option theory is the best framework within which to evaluate and analyze economic and financial information and, second, that there is very little in the behavior of financial markets that hasn't occurred many times before. The history of international debt, consequently, sheds an enormous amount of light on how markets are likely to behave, and I have tried to use historical evidence as much as possible.

The structure of the book is as follows. The first part of the book, chapters 1 and 2, describes some of the characteristics of the recent financial crises and sets the stage for the development of the capital structure framework. The second part of the book (chapters 3–5) sets up a liquidity model to explain the international lending process. Chapter 3 discusses the various models that seek to explain why capital flows from rich countries to less developed countries. It focuses in particular on a Kindleberger type of *liquidity* model, in which the investment decision is mostly affected by liquidity conditions in the rich country financial centers, rather than the more conventional models that look at domestic factors within the less developed country to explain capital inflow. It also discusses, following Minsky and Kindleberger, what a liquidity expansion might entail.

Chapters 4 and 5, still within the second part of the book, are primarily about the history of international lending since the 1820s in light of the *liquidity* model. They show how the changes in liquidity conditions in the rich country financial centers have depended on domestic factors within these countries and how they created the conditions for the subsequent capital outflows. Chapter 4 focuses on the initial liquidity expansion that preceded each of the international lending sprees, while chapter 5 focuses on the conditions that led to the end of the lending.

The next four chapters—which comprise the third part of the book—build the capital structure framework. Chapter 6 uses a corporate finance framework to discuss the impact of volatility on asset value and on financial distress. It sets out the conditions for stable and unstable capital structures at both the corporate and sovereign level. In chapter 7 I describe the balance sheet conditions that lead to financial collapse as consisting of a kind of capital structure trap. I define a capital structure trap as the position in which a borrower finds itself such that an external shock can force both the borrower's revenue and its debt servicing expense to move sharply in an adverse direction. This occurs to such a degree that it forces an increase in the probability of bankruptcy, which then forces the capital structure to move even more strongly in an adverse direction. The process is self-reinforcing and continues until the initially small shock either forces the borrower into bankruptcy or is resolved by a large lender of last resort. Chapter 8 proposes a sovereign liability management function and outlines the process in which local financial authorities should analyze the risks implicit in the national capital structure. Finally, chapter 9 discusses debt restructuring within the capital structure framework.

Chapter 10, the last chapter and fourth part of the book, presents the conclusions. In it, I argue that the speedy recovery of emerging markets since the 1994 Mexican crisis and the 1997 Asian crises relative to other global debt crises, like the ones that occurred in the 1930s and 1980s, may be leading us to some dangerously optimistic conclusions about the health of the world's financial systems. Specifically, in light of ample global liquidity, the past decade represents what should be considered optimal conditions for emerging market growth and investment. In this light, the "surprising" ease with which recently defaulting countries, such as Russia and possibly Ecuador, will be able to reaccess the capital markets is not surprising at all. (To take one example of this having occurred before, Peru, after restructuring in 1976–77, was able to scoop up new loans during the next few years, also a period of excess banking liquidity.)

Yet in spite of these optimal conditions, emerging markets experienced a near-disaster in the second half of the decade. If the wrong lessons are drawn, either that the world simply needs a little more Anglo-Saxon-style free markets, or that participating in globalization is dangerous and leads inevitably to financial crisis, the conditions that converted a series of small shocks into market collapses will remain in place. When liquidity conditions turn down, as they inevitably must, the capital structure vulnerabilities of emerging market countries will lead again to crisis, but in poor global liquidity conditions these crises will not reverse themselves as quickly as they did in the 1990s. Should that be the case, a major, long-lasting emerging market slump, like the ones we experienced in the 1930s and the 1980s, becomes very likely.

PART I

THE STRUCTURE OF FINANCIAL CRISES

This section, which consists of two chapters, describes the recent financial crises of 1994–99, and lists their major characteristics. Although there were differences among the countries involved and in the way the crises unfolded, in fact they had a great deal in common. We will identify some of these traits and make a distinction between the impact of poor economic policy and poor balance sheet management.

1

Capital Structure and Policy Collapse

The Financial Crises of the Late 1990s

The Start of the Crisis Period

Beginning in late 1994 a near-devastating series of financial crises struck the emerging market countries of Latin America, East Asia, and eastern Europe. Although the sequence of events for each country differed, the crises followed similar patterns. In each case the local currency collapsed, stock and bond markets plunged, the national banking system was overwhelmed by bad debt, and foreign investors fled the region. The afflicted countries all saw imports drop to very low levels as expanding debt, higher import costs, and a breakdown in the economy squeezed local consumers.

In spite of the similarities among the crises, however, it would be hard to find in their economies and political structures much that the afflicted countries had in common. Inflation-ridden Mexico, for example, had recently emerged from one of the most severe debt crises in its history and had become the star performer of the new neoliberal consensus on economic development. Indonesia, though a poor and authoritarian country, had nonetheless astounded the world in the previous two decades with its dramatic "Asian-style" race for growth. South Korea had miraculously transformed itself from abject poverty in the 1950s to an industrial powerhouse, and many less developed countries saw its rapid growth, low inflation, and high savings as a model for their own development. Russia, a fallen superpower with a barely perceptible formal economy and out-of-control corruption, was still recovering from its seventy-year experiment with Leninism. Brazil was an inward-looking potential economic giant whose rigid monetary policies had been credited with ending years of hyperinflation.

Their differences notwithstanding, these countries and several others shared important qualities that made them susceptible to the crises that swept through the emerging markets, and in this book I will attempt to identify and list these qualities. I will also propose policy changes that will protect emerging market countries from suffering as deeply from future crises. The crisis began in Mexico, and it is worth going into some detail on the Mexican crisis since it established the pattern many of the subsequent crises were to follow.

The market collapse in Mexico began on December 20, 1994, when the government of Mexico suddenly announced a 13 percent devaluation of the currency band within which the peso was permitted to trade. In so doing it abandoned a seven-year-old policy that had seemed key to its recent prosperity.[1] This band—a trading range within whose upper and lower limits the peso was permitted to float—was set by Mexico's central bank, Banco de Mexico, and it depreciated, or crawled, every day by an amount that was formally established by the government and known to the market. When the peso traded near the lower end of the band (which meant that it had strengthened against the dollar), Banco de Mexico would sell pesos and buy dollars in whatever amount necessary to keep the peso from trading through the band. The purchase of dollars added to reserves. When the peso traded near the upper end of the band, the central bank would follow the opposite policy in order to strengthen the currency, and reserves would decline.

The currency regime was part of a recent overhaul of Mexican economic policies, and for many years it seemed to have brought stability to the market and helped the government anchor the currency in its fight against domestic inflation. But for several months nervous investors had been aggressively selling pesos and other Mexican assets in order to convert their holdings into dollars. Because Mexico's central bank is ultimately the peso buyer (or dollar seller) of last resort, this had resulted in a drain on the government's reserve holdings of U.S. dollars—reserves had dwindled from nearly $30 billion early in the year to an alarmingly low level of below $10 billion. Because there was clearly a limit to the amount of dollars it could sell, the government felt it had no choice but to devalue the peso in the hopes that this action would protect it from having to exchange more of its dollars to buy those pesos.

1. Mexico fixed the peso's rate against the dollar in 1987 and moved to a crawling peg in 1989. In 1991 it moved to the crawling band regime it had in place until the 1994 devaluation. The band depreciated against the dollar at the rate of 0.0004 pesos a day.

The heavy peso selling during the months before the sudden devaluation had followed several ecstatic years in which foreign capital had streamed into the country. Beginning in the late 1980s Mexico had initiated a series of market-opening reforms aimed at reversing the import-substitution development model that had dominated the thinking of the 1970s. When the country completed the restructuring of its external debt in the 1990 Brady restructuring, market participants began to notice the changes and money started to pour into the country.

By early 1994, however, there had been another change in investor sentiment. Capital flows reversed themselves, and investors began taking money out of the country. At first they did so slowly, but by December the outflow had become a torrent, and the dwindling dollar reserves put pressure on Mexico's ability to continue defending the level of the currency. The strength of the peso within the well-defined band had been the cornerstone of Mexican economic policy for nearly ten years, but this couldn't last in the face of the capital outflows. Five days before Christmas, the Mexican government instructed the Banco de Mexico to shift the upper end of the peso trading band from 3.465 pesos per dollar to 3.975 pesos per dollar. By effectively devaluing the peso it hoped to end the torrential selling pressure.

But instead of drying up the demand for dollars, the policy change only signaled how desperate things were for the country. A large amount of the money borrowed by the government and by Mexican corporations had been denominated in dollars, and the devaluation immediately pushed up the cost of repaying those loans. This caused a sudden and material worsening of the country's economic position, and investor nervousness increased. Two days later, as dollars continued to flee the country, the central bank gave up any pretense of defending the peso peg and permitted the currency to float freely. With that the Banco de Mexico set off the first crisis of the new emerging markets.

The Change in Investor Sentiment

Within a week, the peso had dropped 32%, to 5.075 pesos per dollar, and it continued to fall into the new year. As the peso's value plunged, Mexico's sudden policy reversal stunned international traders and investors who had counted on the security of the crawling band, and within days they began a massive selling of Mexican assets. The selling soon spread to other Latin American assets, and then just as quickly to assets of other emerging market countries. The breadth of the selling astounded everyone. Prices of assets around the world plummeted in a sequence that left bankers and economists bewildered. Because of its close links with Mexico and the implied support of President Bill Clinton and the U.S. government, even the U.S. dollar weakened in international trading. The peso devaluation had set off the beginning of what was known afterward as the Tequila Crisis.

The initial cause of the investor panic was not hard to discern. Mexico's government and its central bank had promised all year that the value of the national currency would remain within a predetermined trading band that set upper and lower limits in U.S. dollars for the value of the peso. The government insisted that it would never consider permitting the currency to trade outside this band, and it was made the cornerstone of the *Pacto*, the agreement between the government, labor, and industry that underpinned a series of reforms begun in the mid-1980s. Until the very last days of the year, a large number of major foreign investors had believed the government. After all, a little more than a year earlier, the U.S. Congress had passed the North American Free Trade Agreement (NAFTA), and in the excitement about the possibilities of a single North American market of over 400 million people, an outpouring of optimism had overwhelmed Mexican markets.

In fact, Mexico was at the vanguard of a new political and economic consensus sweeping the region that would lead, in the hopes of many, to a new chapter in Latin American history. Throughout the region governments were deregulating the banking system, privatizing bloated and inefficient government-owned companies, removing trade barriers, ejecting dictators, and streamlining the economy, and local and foreign investors responded with enthusiasm. For much of the end of 1993 and the beginning of 1994, the Mexican peso was so strong that the Banco de Mexico's biggest currency problem was to prevent it from strengthening through the *lower* limit of its band.[2] Between late November 1993 and mid-February 1994, the Banco de Mexico had reportedly added $11 billion to its reserves, because of interventions to keep the peso from exceeding the targeted value.[3]

Despite the initial promise, 1994 turned out to be a very difficult year for Mexico. A peasant uprising in the poor, southern state of Chiapas, the assassination of Luis Donaldo Colosio, the leading presidential candidate in the 1994 election, and continuous allegations of corruption and drug trafficking had marred the presidential elections scheduled for that year. At the same time, and perhaps more important, Japanese long-term capital, which for years had flowed copiously

2. Pesos are typically quoted in units per U.S. dollar, so a low number implies a strong peso.

3. Michael Adler, "Lessons from Mexico's Roller-Coaster Ride in the First Quarter of 1994," *Columbia Journal of World Business*, Summer 1994: 85.

into the United States, went into a reversal during the last quarter of 1993 and the first quarter of 1994, significantly reducing U.S. appetite for risk assets.[4] When the Federal Reserve Board unexpectedly began raising interest rates early in the year, Mexico saw a tremendous reduction in foreign capital inflows, but with no commensurate reduction in the current account deficit. Central bank reserves began to drop, slowly at first, but more quickly as wealthy Mexicans became increasingly alarmed by the unfinanced trade deficit.

In order to attract more capital and reduce imports, Mexico might have raised local interest rates and depressed the economy. Local interest rates had already increased from single digits (less than 9% in mid-February), to nearly 20% by early summer, but it was difficult to raise them much more in what would be a hotly contested presidential election. At any rate, investors were concerned that, given the large fiscal deficit, which the ruling party was unlikely to tackle during a presidential campaign, any increase in rates might have actually worsened the underlying fundamentals by significantly increasing the government's debt servicing costs. A further increase in rates ran the risk of actually reducing the supply of loans to the government, as fears about the sustainability of the debt servicing payments rose.

The government could have also raised more dollars by increasing the interest it would pay on long-term U.S. dollar external bonds, but finance ministry officials were convinced the investor nervousness was temporary and misguided, and they refused to lock in what they thought were excessively high interest rates.[5] Instead of these options the Mexican government retooled a policy that it had used nearly twenty years earlier. In March 1976, in the face of massive capital flight, speculation against the peso, and declining reserves, the government permitted Mexican banks to accept up to 10% of their total liabilities in the form of dollar deposits. Almost immediately, middle-class Mexicans who had been eager to buy dollars to protect their savings from the increasing risk of devaluation rushed to deposit their pesos into the banking system and redenominate them as dollars.

Although this measure helped to draw badly needed deposits into the banking system and temporarily slowed the sale of dollars by the Central Bank, the transubstantiation of peso obligations into dollar obligations merely increased the cost of devaluation for the government and ultimately served to undermine confidence further. When

4. See Michael Pettis, "What Hit the Emerging Markets in 1994? The Shift in Global Capital Flows," *IFR International Financing Review*, October 1994, p. 7.

5. Conversation with Martin Werner, former deputy minister of finance of Mexico.

the peso collapsed in September 1976, beginning the cycle of *sexenio* devaluations,[6] the dollar obligations of the banking system were a significant cost to the government.[7]

In the spring of 1994, following what was in essence a similar policy for similar reasons, the government increased its issuance of Tesobonos. These were short-term (28- to 364-day maturities) locally issued T-bills whose repayment, although in pesos, was linked to the dollar value of the peso. In other words the government would agree to pay out at maturity enough pesos equal to the nominal dollar amount of Tesobonos. Investors who were concerned about the possibility of an unexpected devaluation would always receive enough pesos to make up the difference in the exchange rate. The advantage of Tesobonos was that as long as the currency did not devalue they were a much cheaper source of financing for the government than peso-denominated bonds, because the interest rate on them was linked to U.S. dollar interest rates, which were substantially lower than peso interest rates. Investors accepted the lower interest rate because Tesobonos protected them from a decline in the value of the peso. Furthermore, since Tesobonos were domestically issued and paid in pesos, not dollars, they did not show up as external debt and did not, in principle, count as a dollar-payment requirement of the Mexican government.

The authorities also thought that Tesobonos were an important signaling device to investors, since the more Tesobonos were outstanding, the more costly a devaluation would be to the government. In a classic central bank strategy, Mexican authorities imagined that by increasing the cost to themselves of a damaging policy shift, they could shore up credibility and convince investors that the policy shift would not occur.[8] Tesobono issuance mushroomed during the year, and by the end of 1994 there was over $30 billion outstanding, maturing at the rate of roughly $4 billion a month. Central bank reserves, however, had gone the other way. After peaking at $29 billion in February, they had declined to $12 billion by the beginning of December, and they dropped a further $5–6 billion in the last, suspicious rush by wealthy Mexicans and Mexican banks to get out of pesos before the devaluation came.

6. Mexican presidents are elected for a term of six years, hence the *sexenio*. Prior to 1976, during the postwar period the peso had been fixed against the dollar and there had been little currency instability. The shock devaluation in 1976 started a series of major devaluations that coincided with the end of the *sexenio* periods, in 1982, 1987, and 1994.

7. Timothy P. Kessler, *Global Capital and National Politics: Reforming Mexico's Financial System* (Praeger: 1999), pp. 38–40.

8. Private conversations with and presentations by government officials. See also Kessler *Global Capital*, p. 107.

When Mexico finally devalued, just before Christmas 1994, the shock was immense. The market for all Mexican assets almost immediately plunged, and it suddenly became clear that investors were going to refuse to refinance the huge Tesobonos maturities coming due. In a hastily organized meeting in New York in January, Jaime Serra Puche, the unlucky newly installed minister of finance, met with panicked money managers to explain the policy change and to beg for tolerance. Investors were furious, however, and the meeting at one point degenerated into a shouting match between major fund managers and Mexican government officials. There *had* been speculation for months that because of capital outflows Mexico might be forced to adjust the band within which the peso was permitted to trade, but the government had never revealed the extent of the problem. Right up to the end most analysts believed that the country could and would do whatever was necessary to maintain the currency peg, and in spite of the warning signals, most investors did not believe that the devaluation would really happen.

The First Financial Crisis of the Twenty-First Century

Although it was clear to everyone that the market would react poorly when the central bank made its unexpected announcement in December 1994, the actual extent of the aftermarket reaction was nonetheless extraordinary. The currency plummeted from 3.46 pesos to the dollar ($0.29 per peso) to 6.35 ($0.16 per peso) before the end of January and to nearly 8.00 ($0.12 per peso) before the end of 1995—a total loss in value of just under 60% for a currency that was believed to be overvalued by 15–25% (see figure 1.1). The stock market also collapsed, and frantic investors desperately called equally frantic traders looking for someone to put out a bid for any Mexican bond. Writing a month after the devaluation, MIT economist Rudiger Dornbusch described it this way:

> Massive selling, redemptions in funds, forced liquidation with price collapse chasing yet further redemptions has been the scene of the past two weeks. The financial chaos, the sheer lack of a market, the inability to raise even a few hundred millions of dollars in new credits conjure up the image of a gigantic fraud—Mexico had never reformed, there was no substance, the other shoe (whichever that might be) was about to fall.[9]

9. Rudiger Dornbusch, "Mexico, the Folly, the Crash, and Beyond," *Garantia Economic Letter*, January 23, 1995, p. 1.

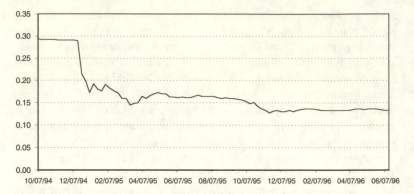

Figure 1.1. U.S. dollars per Mexican peso

For foreign investors the enormous overhang of Tesobonos maturities turned out to be the biggest problem. Investors refused to continue rolling over dollar or peso debt, and investors who had purchased Tesobonos on the assumption that they were almost as good as dollars now realized that they had simply exchanged currency risk for another equivalent risk—convertibility risk. Although they would supposedly get enough pesos to buy dollars at the official rate, if the government did not have enough dollars to sell, it would restrict availability to "necessary" transactions and investors would have to buy dollars in the free market. The free market price of dollars would soar, and the difference would represent a huge loss for investors.

Even worse, because the nominal amount of pesos owed on Tesobonos was exploding as the peso devalued, there was some concern that the government would even be unwilling to print enough pesos to make the payments and so would default on the Tesobonos. For these reasons frightened investors demanded actual dollars and rushed to buy the few that were available. Their purchase frenzy threw the currency into a tailspin, which only increased the cost of the Tesobonos in peso terms. The uncontrollable spiral quickly affected the whole market.

At the same time, it seemed that everything that could possibly go wrong in the private sector was going wrong. Corporations who had borrowed in dollars, of course, saw their equity collapse as the dollar cost of their borrowings ballooned at the same time that revenues were dropping. On the other hand corporations who had tried to play safe and had borrowed in pesos had all borrowed either for short terms or on a floating rate basis, since these were the only terms the market offered. But as peso interest rates skyrocketed, the cost of these borrowings rose even faster than the cost of dollar borrowings. The cash-flow pressures on these borrowers forced many of these corporations to stop or limit payments to their lenders.

Individual Mexicans, meanwhile, were facing similar problems. Those who had borrowed, either to buy homes or to buy high-ticket retail goods, had been forced to borrow on a floating rate basis, and their debt servicing costs more than tripled within weeks.[10] This occurred, of course, at the same time that their wages and jobs were coming under pressure as companies and the government scrambled to cut costs. Between January and February 1995, for example, automobile sales fell by 60%, while restaurant sales, medical services, and hospitals saw revenue drop by 30–40%. As a consequence of rising debt costs and a plummeting economy, many of these individual borrowers were forced to default.

The rapid credit deterioration in banks' loan portfolios caused by financially distressed corporations and individuals forced banks to scramble to raise liquidity to protect their own balance sheets. This meant raising interest rates, calling loans, and cutting back new lending. But that was precisely the opposite of what corporate and individual borrowers needed. In the end the defensive actions of each of the various sectors of the Mexican economy simply added to the burden of other sectors of the economy, and Mexico's markets were consumed in a huge, self-reinforcing loop of disaster. Within weeks of the devaluation the stock and bond markets had gone into free fall, and workers were thrown out of work as investment and consumption shuddered to a halt. Interest rates on local-currency mortgage and consumer loans shot to unmanageable levels, and the newly impoverished middle class was forced into default. By the end of 1995, U.S. accounting standards would have classified one-third of the loans in Mexican bank portfolios as nonperforming. The carnage in the banking system was so great that by 1998 Moody's Investors Services gave Mexican banks an E+ rating, the lowest in Latin America.[11] (See figure 1.2.)

The peso collapse dragged down the value of billions of dollars of securities that Mexican government agencies, banks, and corporations had sold, mostly to foreign investors. As they watched in horror what was happening in Mexico, international money managers began selling their holdings in other Latin American countries in order to meet redemption calls from their own investors, and the crisis quickly

10. This understates the true cost increase to borrowers. In the Mexican environment of high nominal rates, a tripling of nominal rates can result in an increase of real rates by more than ten times.

11. Kessler, *Global Capital*, p. 122.

09/30/94 10/14/94 10/28/94 11/11/94 11/25/94 12/09/94 12/23/94 01/06/95 01/20/95 02/03/95 02/17/95 03/03/95 03/17/95 03/31/95

Figure 1.2. The decline of the Mexican stock market in peso terms

spread. On January 31 President Clinton announced a planned $50 billion rescue package to help Mexico with its short-term liquidity needs, but the desperate surge in optimism that followed did not last long. As the Mexican delegation met with various U.S. congresspeople to explain their position and ask for their support, these congresspeople used the crisis to open up a whole series of concerns—from immigration to abortion to Mexico's relations with Cuba—that were either impractical or that threatened to bog the process down in partisan politics and narrow interests.[12] While the president and the U.S. Congress argued over the funds that would be used to resolve Mexico's liquidity needs, the world held its breath, hoping that the crisis would not destroy all the expectations that had been built up during the decade over Latin America's new prospects.

The Tequila Crisis seemed to signal the end of the new Mexican economic miracle—which had once seemed so solid and destined to change forever the way less developed countries operated. Even more worrying, it had spread extraordinarily quickly throughout the continent and the world as investors rushed to liquidate their holdings in Brazil, Argentina, Venezuela, Peru, and even countries as unrelated as Hong Kong and South Africa.

The most vicious stage of the Mexican market collapse did not end until March when, over the objections of many members of Congress, the United States contributed $20 billion to a $50 billion rescue package supplied by the IMF and various other donor countries.[13] The

12. Conversation with Martin Werner, former deputy minister of finance of Mexico.

13. Because it seemed that Congress would either deny or dither too long over the provision of funds, President Clinton had to draw on the little-used

proceeds of the rescue package were immediately used by Mexico to replenish reserves and to guarantee the ability of investors to withdraw funds as bond obligations came due. It was only as investors became confident that the country's financial structure was no longer likely to collapse that they began reconsidering investment in Mexican securities, and Mexico was able to begin the slow, painful task of rebuilding its capital structure.

The "first financial crisis of the twenty-first century," as the Mexican Tequila Crisis has been called, certainly did seem to be a harbinger of sorts, marking a new, horrible path in the world of international finance. In a few years similar crises hit other emerging market countries. In July 1997, the Thai currency, the baht, was forced to devalue, initiating a startling series of Mexico-like crises that over the next few months engulfed the economies of Thailand, Indonesia, Malaysia, and the mighty South Korea. For a while it looked like even Hong Kong, Taiwan, and China would be swept away by the Asian tidal wave and that U.S. and European markets would be buffeted by the storm. On October 27 the Dow Jones Industrial Average (DJIA) lost 554 points in one day, in the biggest point loss in its history. The New York Stock Exchange was forced to suspend trading that day. In early November, Sanyo Securities, a large Japanese broker, went bust—the first time a Japanese securities house had gone under since the Second World War. Within two weeks Hokkaido Takushoku, one of Japan's top ten banks, also collapsed. In January South Korea was forced to restructure $24 billion of international bank loans.

There were still more shocks waiting. In May 1998, thanks to the currency crisis, Indonesia's dictatorial President Suharto, after thirty-two years in power and amid riots and turmoil, was forced to resign. In August 1998, only months after the investment bank Goldman Sachs had led a hugely successful and popular dollar-denominated bond issue for the country, the Russian currency and markets collapsed, forcing investors and policy-makers to confront the sheer unmanageability of the economy. On the last day of the month, after a great deal of weakness, the DJIA lost 512 points in a single day—its second biggest point loss ever. In September a consortium pushed forward by the New York Federal Reserve provided a $3.5 billion bailout for Long-Term Capital Management—one of the world's largest hedge funds—because of fears that its intricate and highly leveraged arbitrage plays could collapse and bring down with it part of the global financial system.[14]

Exchange Stabilization Fund for a $20 billion line of credit. Although not, strictly speaking, originally intended for that purpose, this fund gave the president discretionary power without congressional oversight.

14. The collapse of Long-Term Capital was an extraordinarily complex

By then, it was clear that Brazil also was headed for a final run on its reserves, and the only thing that saved it was a desperate intervention by the IMF and the U.S. Federal Reserve—the former provided $18 billion of a massive $41.5 billion bailout package while the latter slashed U.S. interest rates. The relief did not last long, though; the run on reserves quickly picked up again. By January 1999 President Henrique Cardoso, of Brazil, finally recognizing that he could not fight arithmetic, accepted the resignation of Gustavo Franco, the president of the Central Bank of Brazil, who had presided over and exacerbated the country's economic deterioration, and let the currency float.

In many ways the crises of the late 1990s seemed radically different from the LDC debt crisis of the 1980s, which was the world's most recent experience of international financial distress in what are now called the emerging market countries. During that time—the "lost decade" of the 1980s—one after another of most of the less developed nations of the world who had been able so successfully to raise international financing in the 1970s fell into payment difficulties and subsequent default. Economists and bankers pointed out that their now-discredited economic policies of import-substitution and central planning had failed to generate sufficient growth to meet their debt payments. In retrospect, everyone agreed, the lending boom in the 1970s that had resulted in the crisis of the 1980s had been absurd and unjustifiable.

This time around, however, many of the afflicted countries had engaged, at least in principle, in what most experts believed was the "right mix" of monetary and economic policies as defined by the evolving "Washington Consensus." Governments of less developed economies were removing trade restrictions, freeing the banking and credit allocation system from government interference, and extracting themselves from managing businesses in a series of huge and highly visible privatizations. Currency reform had been a central part of the plan. At that time the consensus did not seem to account for the dangers of excessive capital account liberalization before the financial infrastructure and banking system stability were in place, so free capital flows were encouraged.

But although there were large differences in the underlying economic and political conditions of the various countries that were affected, there was a striking similarity in the forms of the crises themselves. In each case, a sudden external shock or reversal of capital flows forced an initially small and perhaps necessary readjustment of

---

event that contributed heavily to the sense of market panic. For a recent account, see Nicholas Dunbar, *Inventing Money: The Story of Long-Term Capital Management and the Legends behind It* (John Wiley, 2000).

the currency. In each case, the initial devaluation quickly got out of control and, while investors watched in horror, currency and asset markets began to fall precipitously. And in each case, as the market declines became market collapses, fundamental valuation seemed to disappear altogether as currencies, stock prices, and bond yields reached levels that could not be justified by even the most pessimistic economic analysis. Some analysts go so far as to argue that in many cases the initial currency shift was not even a needed response to misaligned currencies. According to at least one study that measured exchange rates in terms of the yen, the Korean, Thai, and Philippine currencies were correctly valued, the Indonesian currency was undervalued, and only the Malaysian currency was overvalued. In the words of the authors of the study, "The currency falls represented by these countries represent shifts in long-run mean value unrelated to underlying fundamentals."[15]

The Corporate Finance of Crises

How can fundamental valuation ever become irrelevant in financial markets? Although the market consensus has it that investors bolted each market because of sudden changes in economic prospects, in fact a market collapse is nearly always implicit in the structure of the market itself. Market players, in other words, can be forced by the market itself to behave in such a way that asset prices respond to mechanical factors, not to valuation. It is the structure and behavior of market players that systematically undermines the market, not changes in fundamentals. These only set off the crisis.

In such a case, using traditional economic or finance methods of valuing assets can become meaningless. This is not a question of herd behavior, of market failure, of market psychology, or even of the Anglo-Saxon speculators of French and Malaysian nightmares, but rather one of capital structure and its role in transmitting external volatility. The magnitude of the crisis, in other words, largely reflects the capital structure of the affected economy, and to understand how this happens it is necessary to understand not the underlying economies of countries that are breaking down but rather the corporate finance of market collapses. And there is nothing twenty-first-century or even twentieth-century about the recent financial crises—they are not qualitatively different from international financial crises that extend back to the 1820s and probably much further. In an article com-

15. Husted, Steven, and Ronald MacDonald, "The Asian Currency Crash: Were Badly Driven Fundamentals to Blame?" *Journal Of Asian Economics* 10, no. 4 (1999): p. 548.

paring the Tequila Crisis with the Baring Crisis of 1890 (in which Argentina, not Mexico, was the borrower that nearly brought the system down), economist Barry Eichengreen said tongue-in-cheek that the Tequila Crisis was actually the last crisis of the nineteenth century.[16]

But even this overstates its uniqueness. Much earlier, Rome suffered a liquidity crisis as early as 33 A.D. that seems remarkably similar to modern market crises. In what was to become a very familiar sequence, the Roman crisis of 33 A.D. was linked to changes in underlying liquidity conditions caused by shifts in market structure—in this case, real estate lending. During an earlier period of good economic conditions wealthy Romans, eager to deploy the capital tied up in their real estate, began stepping around a Caesarian limit on lending against land. Loan extension, and with it money creation, grew rapidly, along with consumption and speculation on real estate, commodities, and other assets. But since real estate is not easy to monetize, and its value can be highly volatile, there was implicitly a large timing mismatch between the loans and the illiquid real estate claims against which they were backed. As the Roman economy boomed and land-based credit expansion accelerated, Romans consumed huge amounts of imports from the edges of the empire and neighboring countries.

When authorities became concerned by gold and silver outflows from Rome, a magistrate under Emperor Tiberius suddenly began enforcing the lending rules (which acted as a sort of reserve requirement). Because authorities already understood intuitively that a sudden change in liquidity could force a rapid and catastrophic liquidation of the loans, borrowers were given eighteen months to put their affairs in order. Furthermore, in order to protect themselves from the by-then well-known dangers of a collapse in real estate prices, the Roman senate ruled that two-thirds of the previously loaned sums had to be invested in Roman land—it was hoped that this would prop up collateral value. The measure failed. Since the money was tied up, the collateral had to be sold, and the general rush to sell land and pay down loans caused a collapse in land prices.

As land prices fell, many of the loans became worthless, which reinforced the already tight monetary conditions that existed because of the effect of the regional trade deficit on gold and silver in circulation. It wasn't until the emperor, in order to calm the panic, made available 100 million sesterci of his personal fortune in the form of interest-free liquidity loans against real collateral that confidence re-

16. Barry Eichengreen, "The Baring Crisis in a Mexican Mirror," *International Political Science Review* 20, no. 3 (July 1999): 250.

turned and the crisis ended.[17] The speed and mechanical nature of the collapse in land prices and loan values, and the desperate quest to raise liquidity, was perfectly reflected in the plummeting asset values and surging interest rates of nearly two thousand years later. And as was the case during the Mexican crisis, it required a major lender to provide a liquidity facility to end the vicious circle of liquidating assets, plunging collateral value, and more forced liquidations.

Currency Shocks

One of the questions that arise from the recent past is whether or not currency devaluations, which seemed to be the culprit in every one of the recent crises, are necessarily destabilizing. With a number of other countries (including a very vulnerable Argentina) embracing currency boards or even explicit *dollarization*, it is important to understand the corporate finance implications of devaluation in order to consider the effect on the market if these countries are forced off their currency regimes. In classic economic theory, devaluation is generally considered to be expansionary, but recent events have suggested to many that for low-credibility countries, currency devaluations lead inevitably to demand contraction and financial collapse. Mexico's economic collapse in 1994–95 began with the announcement to the Mexican Congress on December 15, 1994, by Finance Minister Jaime Serra Puche that the country was expected to run a $32 billion current account deficit in 1995. He claimed that he expected the deficit would easily be financed, but the market did not believe him. Five days later the Bank of Mexico devalued the band within which the peso was pegged.

The Asian crisis began on July 2, 1997, when the bank of Thailand said it would no longer defend the currency peg—one day after Prime Minister Chavalit Yongchaiyudh said the baht would never be allowed to devalue. On July 11 the Philippine peso devalued, and the Indonesian central bank widened its currency band (on August 14 it abandoned it altogether). By November 17 South Korea stopped defending the won, and the currency plunged in value. Russia's financial collapse the following year, although occurring largely because the government was probably insolvent and the country barely functioning as an economic entity, was also linked to concern about currency devaluations. The Russian stock market broke on August 11, 1998; the government devalued the ruble on August 17 and defaulted on its treasury bills (referred to in the market as GKOs) on August 19.

17. Jean Andreau, *Banking and Business in the Roman World* (Cambridge University Press, 1999), pp. 104–6.

On the other hand, currency breaks are not necessarily a prelude to financial meltdown. It was apparent to some people as early as the summer of 1997 that Brazil would be forced to devalue in the summer of 1998, during the election, but the head of the Central Bank of Brazil refused to consider the possibility. He had an orthodox belief in the importance of a rigid currency policy and was thoroughly convinced that, perhaps because of his more subtle understanding of market dynamics, he could dismiss market concerns. He was also certain that a devaluation would be devastating and would reverse all the benefits of the *Plano Real*—the program implemented under President Itamar Franco that had been credited with ending the hyperinflation of the late 1980s. (So was, in all fairness, nearly every other economic and banking expert.)

The central bank's conviction was so strong that in order to defend the Brazilian currency the government was essentially willing to risk the health of the economy with punishing interest rates. Ironically, because it believed that its policies would restore credibility enough that rates would quickly decline, as part of its defense the central bank also set in place an unstable short-term domestic capital structure. The very short-term interest rates that it relied on ultimately forced the devaluation and may still push the country into economic crisis— as I will discuss later. A $41.5 billion IMF bailout in October 1998 postponed the devaluation until January 1999, with the government still refusing to consider devaluation until an extraordinary loss of reserves forced the issue. However, Brazil did not collapse when Central Bank of Brazil stopped defending the exchange rate. The economy fared poorly in the subsequent months, but it stabilized very quickly, and finally it performed no worse than other emerging market countries. In fact this poor performance was probably more a reflection of poor global liquidity conditions than of anything specific to Brazil.

In spite of its nominal role in "causing" the crisis that was to be called the Asian Contagion, Thailand itself does not prove that all devaluations are so damaging. In the early 1980s, the country was going through a combination of inflation and recession, with declining exports and a banking system near default—conditions that seem very close to the mid-1990s. In November 1984 the central bank devalued the currency by approximately 15% and pegged to the dollar. Instead of destroying the country this turned out to be the turning point for the country's economic performance. The cheaper currency (exacerbated by subsequent dollar weakness) and the flow of Japanese liquidity helped turn the country into an economic superstar within a very few years.

The Role of Capital Structure

How can currency crises have such radically different impacts under what seem like fairly similar underlying conditions? In this book I argue that for the countries that suffered from the recent crises, the main reasons for the sudden market breaks were not overvalued currencies, poor growth prospects, excessive government interference in the economy, weak economic policies, crony capitalism, or even bad banks, although this last was often a contributing factor. The reasons for the market collapses were largely problems associated with an unstable capital structure, of which admittedly banks form an important component. The problem is not the actual shock or its causes but rather the way the shock is transmitted into the real economy. In other words, currency adjustments or other shocks may *reflect* economic pressures, but the mechanism by which a small adjustment becomes a market break is everywhere and always a problem of corporate finance, not economics.

In the case of the recent emerging market financial crises, each collapse was a direct function of the way the local capital structure forced local and foreign players to react to the initial shock. It is generally useless to turn to economic or psychological explanations for financial collapses. What we need to do instead is to understand the *corporate finance* of market breaks, and this means focusing on the way capital is used and repayment is indexed to external prices. Throughout this book I will be making references to "corporate finance," and since this may be confusing, a definition is in order. By "corporate finance" I do not mean the financial behavior of private corporations; I mean the body of finance theory that applies to the relationship between an economic entity, its capital structure, and market risks.

This body of theory refers to issues such as designing an optimal capital structure, the effect of information asymmetries on financing strategies, the effect of capital structure on earnings volatility, the process and goals of liability management, the identifying and indexing of sources of volatility, the hedging process, and so on. In this context, then, I might refer to the corporate finance of a currency regime. This will not necessarily refer to the impact of a currency regime on private corporations but will refer rather to the effect of the currency regime on amplifying or dissipating volatility within the national capital structure. Perhaps at some point it may be useful to introduce the phrase "sovereign finance" to create a concept that is analogous to "corporate finance" but that refers to the capital structure of countries, regions, and groupings of countries such as trade blocs, currency unions, and so on.

Efficient market theorists argue that markets respond quickly and efficiently to changes in information. Implicit in their argument is the suggestion that it is primarily changes in information that change the fundamental valuation of securities, and that market collapses result from a sudden and massive change either in information or in the way the information is interpreted. But this is not the whole story. Markets can be structured in ways that automatically increase or reduce the volatility caused by random information changes. These structures have an important effect on the way market players behave to diminish or exacerbate the initial effect of information changes, so that price changes end up reflecting more than just changes in the underlying prospects and can, in fact, cause additional self-reinforcing price movements.

Figure 1.3 shows the relationship between capital structure and economic fundamentals. On the left are listed the types of shocks that can affect the economy, and these are divided into exogenous and endogenous (by which I mean external shocks unrelated to the country and internal shocks caused by conditions within the country). Exogenous shocks are primarily changes in global liquidity conditions or commodity prices, although they include war, natural disasters, changes in trade agreements, and so on. Endogenous shocks include

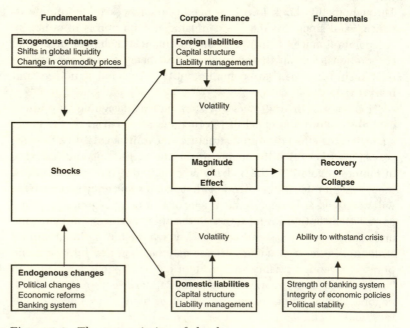

Figure 1.3. The transmission of shocks

domestic social, political, and economic changes. They can refer to a political shift that changes the fundamental economic policies of the regime, or a local armed uprising, or they can reflect a collapse in the banking system because of poor lending practices, and so on.

Whatever the source, external or internal, the shock is transmitted to the real economy through the capital structure. An entity's capital structure is the way a whole series of payments are indexed over time, and the indexation will automatically cause real changes in the value of these payments as external conditions change. This is not to say that *only* capital structure matters—an external shock can be great enough that no capital structure, no matter how well designed, can protect the economy. But depending on the character of the national capital structure, the initial shock can be partially dissipated, if the indexation causes the real value of payments to move in the opposite direction of the effect of the external shock, or exacerbated, if they move in the same direction.[18] Although this may seem complex and even unlikely, the indexation implicit in a capital structure is very automatic and fairly easy to grasp—and it will be explained in some detail in chapter 6. But to continue with the chart, the ability of the country to withstand or recover from the effects of the shock, then, depends on two things. These are shown in the middle and right side of the chart, as the arrows pointing to "Recovery or Collapse." The first is the strength and credibility of the local system, including the banking and political system. The second is the magnitude of the shock as it is transmitted into the real economy via the capital structure.

It is important to say from the beginning that the book is not about economic policy. It is about finance theory and the relationship between capital structure and market volatility, and in it I will argue that the difference between a devastating shock and one that leaves little trace usually has to do with the stability of the country's capital structure. I will distinguish between economic policy and the transmission of volatility, and I will argue that policy-making must be constructed in an environment in which excess volatility is kept to a minimum. By excess volatility I mean those unexpected exchanges and shocks in market conditions that are severe enough to constrain real economic policy.

Although countries and corporations are not always comparable, a corporate metaphor may be useful. In any company, the role of management is to earn profits and maximize equity value by best using

18. "Indexation" in finance refers to the process by which payments are linked to other variables. For example, if payments increase or decrease directly or inversely with the value of a stock market index, inflation, or oil prices, they are "indexed" to those variables.

the firm's assets. In this context it is useful to think about the difference between managing the two sides of a company's balance sheet. For most companies, long-term growth comes about primarily from managing the "left-hand" side of the balance sheet, which represents the assets used for the entity's operations. Optimal management consists of improving the functioning of the underlying business by making appropriate investments, improving the quality of the product, increasing worker and capital efficiency, expanding the marketing of the product, and so on. This is analogous in the sovereign context to making the right economic policy determinations that promote growth over the long term. These include trade and credit allocation policies, investment in education, health and infrastructure, policies on wealth distribution, and so on.

The purpose of managing the "right-hand" side of the company's balance sheet, or its capital structure, is very different, and is primarily defensive. A company's capital structure is the way the company funds itself and indexes its operations to market risks. The most important objectives in managing this right-hand side of the balance sheet are to protect the company from bankruptcy, from disruptions in its ability to raise financing, and from market-related disruptions in its ability to continue managing its operations. The role of the chief financial officer is to build a capital structure that minimizes the volatility of the enterprise and permits management to focus on and implement business decisions. Similarly, one of the main objectives of the ministry of finance, central bank, or other financial authorities in any less developed country must be to put in place a stable capital structure that permits the implementation of development policy. Above all, the capital structure must be one in which the government is able credibly to implement its reform policies and to raise the financing it needs to fund these policies.

A slow-growing badly run company is usually one in which the left-hand "operational" side of the balance sheet is poorly managed, and in such a case the focus must naturally be on improving the underlying fundamentals of the way the company conducts business. From time to time, however, even a rapidly growing company may face financial distress and/or market disruption because of a poorly designed capital structure. A bank run is such an example of a disruption to operations caused by a mismatch between the capital structure and the operations of the bank. In order to prevent the likelihood of such a capital structure disruption, the solution is not to retool the company's operations, refocus the marketing effort, or in any other way to change to underlying business decision. Rather it is to address directly the instability that is introduced through the mismatched capital structure.

The same is true for countries that face financial crises. The success or failure of a set of economic policies to foster growth is a separate issue from the failure of a country's capital structure to protect the country from financial distress or market-related disruptions. When a country's financial markets suddenly collapse, it is more appropriate to look at how the right-hand side of its balance sheet was designed than to second-guess the economic policies that drove its left-hand side. This is not to say that there is no relation between the two sides of the balance sheet. On the contrary, there is an important set of relationships between an economic entity's capital structure and its operations, but the crisis will have been caused by the way the capital structure was able or not able to absorb changes in external conditions, not by the quality of fundamental economic policy-making. It is this subject on which this book focuses—not economic policy, but liability management; not on growth prospects, but on the internal transmission of external volatility.

2

Market Structure Issues

Illiquidity versus Insolvency

Before going on to discuss how changes in global liquidity conditions affect LDC borrowers, there are a few market structure issues worth discussing. First of all, we should make the standard distinction between liquidity crises and solvency crises. A liquidity crisis is analogous to a bank run, in which the bank may well be solvent—and even very profitable—before the onset of the crisis. However, because it normally mismatches its long-term assets and short-term liabilities, when depositors come clamoring for their money the bank may be forced to liquidate illiquid but healthy assets in order to meet the cash needs of depositors. A liquidity crisis, then, is one in which although the value of assets may exceed the value of liabilities when the crisis begins, the liabilities cannot be repaid as they come due by the normal cashflows generated by the assets. If the assets cannot be monetized—or converted into cash—quickly enough to meet liabilities as they come due, the borrower faces a liquidity crisis.

A solvency crisis is different from a liquidity crisis. It occurs when investors realize that the borrower is already in a position in which both the value of his assets is not enough to cover his liabilities and the amount of his current earnings is not enough to cover immediate debt servicing costs. In this case borrowers may refuse to lend or to roll over existing maturities, and the borrower is forced to meet debt-servicing requirements out of insufficient assets and revenues. Liquidity crises can be converted into solvency crises, and there are two ways in which this can occur. If the rate of withdrawal is fast enough and if it coincides—as it often does—with poor economic conditions and great market uncertainty, the borrower may sell his assets into a reluctant market. The forced sale pushes asset prices down and forces losses on the seller. Ultimately, the losses on the sale of assets may be enough to push the bank into insolvency. In this case, the total value of assets is less than the total value of liabilities, the equity holders get wiped out, and the depositors will not be fully repaid. Alternatively if the borrower's capital structure is misaligned such that there is a feedback process in which the liquidity crisis causes debt servicing costs to increase automatically, the liquidity crisis can quickly spin out of control. This occurs, for example, when a country with short-term dollar debt is faced with a "bank run" that puts pressure on its currency. As the currency weakens, the value of the debt increases in real terms, which causes even more pressure on the currency. The process continues until it is either halted by an outside lender of last resort or the borrower becomes insolvent.

Most of the recent sovereign crises in the 1990s were liquidity crises, and these were generally the most surprising of the crises since the affected countries had often seemed in good health before the event. But although they may seem as if they ought to be less serious than solvency crises, liquidity crises can be extremely damaging. As events have shown, liquidity crises can have at least three harmful effects.

1. *Social cost.* The immediate short-term effect on the real economy as local institutions cut expenses, seize assets, etcetera can be devastating, particularly on that part of the population least able to absorb the cost. The high interest rates needed to stabilize currency and bond markets redistribute income away from small companies and low-wage employees, who are usually among the first to be fired as companies cut back spending. In Thailand and Indonesia, for example, the crisis hit hardest at the construction and light manufacturing industries, where low-wage workers are concentrated.[1] High interest rates also force small homeowners with mortgages or small consumers with credit into punishingly high debt payments and, ultimately, bankruptcy, as evidenced by Mexico's banking system, still burdened with an enormous defaulted mortgage portfolio from the 1994–95 crisis. As social and private spending dries up, health and education, the two variables most highly correlated with long-term growth, suffer. Since the benefits of asset inflation–led booms accrue primarily to the wealthy, the asymmetric distribution of the

1. Nancy Birdsall, "Managing Inequality in the Developing World," *Current History* 98, no. 361 (November 1999): 379.

costs and benefits of the cycle can have the secondary impact of reducing the legitimacy and stability of the regime and, possibly, weakening the mandate for reform.

2. *Asset volatility*. The eruption of asset price volatility associated with a liquidity crisis can cause foreign and local investors either to withdraw altogether or to demand a significantly higher rate of return on their investments. If the former occurs and private capital flows dry up, the country is forced to limit its infrastructure and business development to the meager and poorly directed savings it generates domestically and from official institutions. If on the other hand private capital returns, the higher financing cost feeds into slower expected growth for the economy as a whole.

3. *Insolvency*. As we discussed above if it is severe enough a liquidity crisis can so exacerbate the mismatch between the country's "asset" value and its liabilities that the country is forced into insolvency. This occurs because the "value" of the economy, which had been measured with an overvalued currency, becomes significantly lower in foreign currency terms while foreign currency debt payments remain unchanged. This is exacerbated by the "maturity" collapse, as long-term repayment prospects are forced, unsuccessfully, to conform to the short-term obligations that financed them.

Not all the recent sovereign crises were liquidity crises. Solvency crises have occurred recently in Russia, the Ukraine, Pakistan, and Ecuador and will probably occur in Argentina. By this I mean that the amount of external or internal debt is so great and its cost so high that the country simply cannot grow fast enough to continue servicing it and rolling it over. But there is no easy distinction between the two—liquidity crises can become insolvency crises fairly quickly, and even in judging a country to be insolvent it is never obvious that the "assets" of the country are insufficient to repay the debt (which is what defines insolvency). In this book, however, I focus primarily on liquidity crises and on the corporate finance aspect of these crises.

The Structure of Trading Markets

In chapter 5 I will discuss a number of LDC crises that have occurred over the past two centuries, and I will show that, whether they were short-term liquidity crises or long-term debt crises, in either case they were usually set off by external changes. But it is not just their susceptibility to changes in global liquidity that can increase volatility in the markets of LDCs. The structure of the investor base has also, historically, been a huge and costly source of volatility—largely because of the underdeveloped nature of the investor base. It is probably useful in this context to think of investors in terms of their place in the holding-period time line.[2] As a rule liquid securities markets include a wide range of investors with differing holding periods. The shortest time horizons typically belong to market makers, who are usually only interested in providing short-term liquidity and who charge the bid-offer spread for that liquidity. At the other end is the long, several-year time horizon of insurance companies and pension funds that are looking to match the securities cashflows to the long-term obligations they have assumed as part of their business.

As most investors know, the analysis of an asset's underlying value is only meaningful within the context of an investment holding period. If an investor has a very short holding period, he is going to focus largely on the current price and on short-term variables that may drive the price of an asset away from its current level, and he will discount everything else at a very high rate. If on the other hand he plans to hold an asset for a very long time, short-term variables will have little effect on his thinking and he will be more concerned with the long-term outlook and more confident of his ability to discount these variables. So because they can have very different holding periods, investors may value assets and price volatility very differently. This causes them to respond differently to price changes, and their different responses ensure that the market has an appropriate mix of buyers and sellers at all times.

Long-term investors, for example, typically have a fundamental or value-oriented outlook, and in their analyses they attempt to develop a long-term view of the cashflows that are likely to be generated by the security. Because long-term value is highly susceptible to what one considers an appropriate discount rate, these investors also tend to have fairly wide target price ranges for a security that reflect uncertainty about the best discount rate. Long-term investors can usually be counted on to buy the asset if it trades well below its target range or sell it if it trades too high above. Short-term volatility within the target range generally does not affect their investment decision very much. Furthermore, if prices drop sharply because of technical reasons—that is, reasons that may have to do with external market conditions but that do not necessarily affect either the expected cashflow or the long-term discount rate—they see it as a buying opportunity.

Medium-term investors may also have target values, but their shorter time horizons make the target range tighter and make them

2. For an interesting discussion on this see J. Bradford De Long, Andrei Schleifer, Lawrence H. Summers, and Robert J. Waldman, "Noise Trader Risk in Financial Markets," *Journal of Political Economy* 98:4 (August 1940): 703–708.

more sensitive to price swings (see figure 2.1). Although they may sell into large unexpected price drops if their time horizon suddenly shrinks (because of some unexpected market move), they are more likely to *buy* smaller price drops as asset values deviate from their target price. In general, the longer the investment horizon, the larger a purely technical price move needs to be in order to trigger the opposite buy or sell decision, while the shorter the horizon, the more likely it will be to trigger a decision in the same direction as the price movement. As the expected holding period gets shorter, the investor becomes increasingly more concerned with trading patterns and short-term pricing fluctuations.

At the extreme, day traders and market makers have almost no fundamental view of the underlying value of an asset but only a technical view based on its current trading price and short-term demand/supply factors that may cause fluctuations in the secondary market. They are largely trend traders and they try to anticipate pricing sequences. They are also fairly disciplined about selling losing positions quickly. One of the most highly regarded emerging markets traders once told me that "fundamental" information was only useful to him in that it indicated what other traders and investors *might* do. In and of itself it had absolutely no value.[3] In this light a price decline that may seem minimal or even unnoticeable to a long-term investor may represent a significant move in the very short term—it will often trigger a trade by a day trader in the same direction as the pricing break. Shleifer and Summers, in an article on "noise" trading, argue that these sort of traders may be subject to systemic biases.[4] Short-term traders often directly add volatility to a market, but they also provide

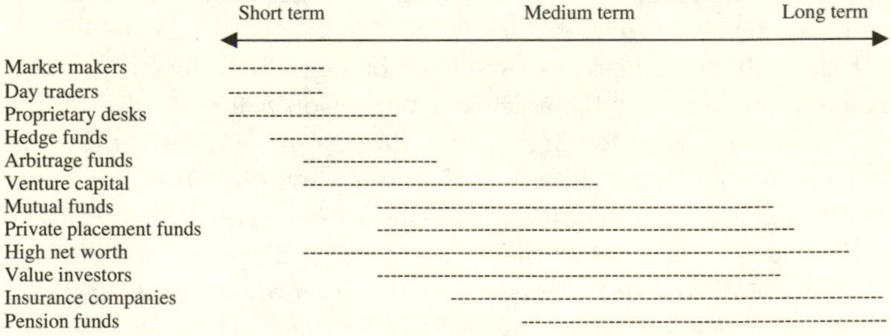

Figure 2.1. Investor time horizons

3. Conversation with Con Egan, DePfa portfolio manager and former head of the emerging markets bond-trading group at Lehman Brothers.

4. Andrei Shleifer and Lawrence H. Summers, "The Noise Trader Approach to Finance," *Journal of Economic Perspectives*, 4, no. 2 (spring 1990): 13–18.

the liquidity that longer term investors need in order to execute their buy and sell decisions, so that in well-functioning markets, they indirectly reduce volatility.[5]

It is important to distinguish the long-term price effect of technical moves versus fundamental shifts. When new information about fundamentals enters the market, it may cause an immediate or gradual reappraisal of projected cashflows, contingent expectations, or discount rates, and the price of the asset will adjust accordingly. But when volatility is introduced for technical reasons, in a market with a mix of long- and short-term investors, the balance of all the various responses to price volatility keeps the market stable. With different types of traders reacting differently to the same price moves, risk is passed back and forth among investors who value the risk differently according to their different portfolio concerns.

LDC Trading Markets

One problem with most LDC securities markets is that there is a very poor balance of investors. Long-term investors in the United States usually ensure that U.S. asset prices do not stray too far from some perception of underlying value, and they can usually be counted on to take on assets for the long haul if they ever become too cheap (based on their fundamental analysis of the asset). But because they cannot make the same legal or accounting assumptions about the value of stocks or bonds in foreign countries with weak regulatory frameworks and inconsistent policies toward property ownership, they cannot play the same role in LDCs. Domestically, the long-term investors who might have the inside knowledge or legal clout are usually too small to make a difference. The result is that the long end of the time horizon spectrum is very thinly populated. To use a phrase common among emerging market investors, there is no "buyer of last resort."

This is not the case with the short end of the time horizon spectrum. On the contrary, the high volatility of LDC markets makes them particularly attractive to short-term proprietary traders and hedge funds, who tend to be hugely important in today's emerging markets. The net result is that most LDC markets consist of an investor base that is too heavily concentrated on the near end of the time-horizon spectrum. Because they tend to act similarly, they exacerbate technical price swings, and there is not enough buying power elsewhere to counteract them. It is not at all rare, then, for volatility to be initiated

5. Edgar Peters describes something similar in *Fractal Market Analysis* (John Wiley, 1994), pp. 42–43.

by a genuine change in fundamentals and then exacerbated by the behavior of the unbalanced investor group. At some point a market move can become so large that it begins to change the underlying fundamentals in a self-reinforcing way. If a currency drops too far below its appropriate value, for example, instead of providing profitable buying opportunities for smart investors, it may exacerbate the currency mismatch in a country's national capital structure and, by so doing, bankrupt the banking and corporate sectors and force interest rates to unmanageable levels. In the end, the country's economy weakens so much that it justifies what was once an irrationally low currency value.

We saw an example of this shortly after Mexico devalued the peso in December 1994. As I discussed in chapter 1, before the devaluation, the Mexican government had promised to maintain the value of the peso within a specified band. However, reserves had run too low by December for the central bank to continue defending the currency, and the authorities finally decided to let it float freely. Before the decision to devalue, most investors believed the peso to be overvalued, so that although the devaluation should have had some impact on relative asset prices, the net effect should have been manageable and even positive for equity prices—at least for those export companies whose costs would now decline relative to their earnings.

But that is not what happened. Short-term traders and investors were forced to exit the market while they reevaluated their assumptions in the new floating rate environment. The value investors who should have been scooping up cheap equity—beginning with export companies—were nowhere to be seen. As prices continued to spiral downward, panicked investors shortened their time horizons even more. The drop in the value of the currency, or the increase in local interest rates, caused the size of a company's debt to expand, which justified further concern. As prices of all Mexican securities fell dramatically, from time to time the market would temporarily stabilize. Each time this happened analysts began recalculating the theoretical levels beyond which prices "could not" fall if value was to have any meaning at all. Nonetheless, a sudden event, such as a small sale of securities or an unfavorable announcement by a U.S. or Mexican political figure, could cause a renewed decline that would in most cases smash through the previous theoretical barrier. There were no investors who were willing to step in to buy an asset that had become obviously "cheap," because no investor was confident enough about his ability to interpret information "inside" his time horizon. For a few scary months the prices of securities seemed temporarily to have lost their moorings and departed altogether from rational valuation.

For LDC policy-makers, then, global liquidity is an important determinant of capital inflows and the amount of volatility their countries must assume, and this is exacerbated by the unbalanced structure of the investor base. External shifts can become reinforced by the distorted activity of investors. In the next three chapters I will discuss the sources of these external shifts.

PART II

GLOBAL LIQUIDITY AND CAPITAL FLOWS

This section argues that the vulnerability of LDC financial markets is due primarily to external factors, of which the most important is shifts in liquidity among major financial centers such as New York, London, or Tokyo. The first chapter in this section lays out a liquidity model that explains why capital flows from rich countries to poor countries. The second chapter examines the history of international lending from the 1820s to the present in light of this liquidity model, and identifies the liquidity factors that set off each lending cycle. The third chapter identifies the liquidity contractions that precipitated the lending crisis.

3

Why Does Rich-Country Capital Flow to Poor Countries?

Models of Capital Flow

Most LDC analysts understand that there is an important relationship between the amount of foreign capital that flows into an LDC economy and the performance of local markets. There are, broadly speaking, two main types of models used to explain the flow of capital from rich countries to poor countries. The difference between them is whether the model posits the *source* or the *destination* of the capital flow as being the prime determinant for the flow. In this chapter, and before I go on to discuss the corporate finance of sovereign capital structures, I will discuss each of these two models, with a particular focus on developing a definition of what liquidity might be. It turns out that the two different models have radically different implications for financial policy. I will discuss these implications and then go on to argue that the conventional model actually does a poor job of explaining the history of international lending. In the next two chapters I will examine this history in some detail before arriving at the financial policy conclusions.

The once-conventional and still dominant explanation of capital flows focuses on what are called "pull" factors. This approach, which I will call the *investment* model, argues that rich-country investors continuously evaluate profit opportunities at home and abroad and, when growth prospects in less developed countries seem favorable, they make the decision to invest—in Mexico, Thailand, Poland, or anywhere else. The focus of analysis is on local economic fundamentals, and the basic assumption is that *improved growth prospects pre-*

cede and cause investment inflows. According to this view, money will flow to and stay in LDCs if domestic authorities eliminate distortions that reduce a country's economic prospects, engage in policies that prepare the country for rapid growth, or structure the economy to reduce expected volatility.

The alternative approach, which I will refer to as the *liquidity* model, focuses less on local economic conditions and more on changes in the liquidity of rich-country markets. It posits that when investors have excess liquidity—more than can be invested in traditional low-risk markets at home—they look elsewhere for investment opportunities. At first money may flow into higher risk local investment opportunities, but at some point some event or accumulation of events causes investors to look offshore into higher risk foreign markets. As these investors begin to invest, the huge size of the investment funds relative to the small LDC markets leads to a surge in capital inflows. In many cases, part of the capital inflow is invested in infrastructure and productive investments, and this leads to some investment-driven growth. Here the basic assumption is that *capital inflows precede and cause growth.*

Other theories have been used to explain why capital flows from rich countries to poor countries, but these mainly fall into the two broad groups just discussed, and, for the purpose of this book, they have the same corporate finance implications, which I will discuss in chapter 6. The *Leninism-imperialism* approach for example, shares with the *liquidity* model a focus on rich-country dynamics but places the emphasis on the inability of internal markets in rich countries to accommodate domestic production. The result is that rich-country capitalists export capital as well as goods and services abroad to make up for limited demand at home. Likewise, *dependency theory*, which borrows heavily from the Leninism-imperialism approach, argues that capital outflows are part of the economic linkage between the developed center and the underdeveloped periphery, so that capital flows are largely determined by rich-country dynamics. In contrast, and focusing on the investment decision and the fundamental needs of the borrower, Christian Suter refers to what he calls the "classic *liberal theory* of international trade" in which capital flows are seen primarily as a response to interest rate differentials and expected exchange rate movements. Finally, the *development economics* approach sees foreign borrowing on the part of poor countries as a function of their stage of economic development and the need for capital imports to bridge the gap between investment needs and domestic savings.[1]

1. Christian Suter, *Debt Cycles in the World Economy: Foreign Loans, Financial Crises, and Debt Settlements, 1820–1990* (Westview Press, 1992), pp. 11–15. For an additional summary of theories used to explain capital flows,

It is the various forms of the *investment* approach that underlie most of the debate on emerging market economies and on the causes of market booms and financial crises. International banks and the multilateral institutions employ an army of economists and statisticians who study central bank statistics, local tax regimes, savings rates and wage pressures, economic reform proposals and the strength of the local opposition, expected global demand for commodities, and a wealth of other data. From these they project fiscal and trade deficits and future inflation and currency levels as variables that cause, not reflect, capital flow decisions, all in the name of understanding how domestic policies and growth outlooks will affect the future market value of assets. A General Accounting Office (GAO) report to the House banking committee on the aftereffects of the Mexican crisis discussed the reason for capital flows into developing countries both before and after the crisis this way:

> Investors have been attracted to the opportunities in the developing world . . . According to the G10, economic liberalization and reform in the developing world have greatly increased the size and volatility of cross-border investments. The G10 has stated that emerging market countries have a firmer grasp on fiscal conditions and, in many emerging market countries, inflation is coming under control. For example, *macroeconomic reforms in the early 1990s in Latin America led to soaring private capital flows,* according to a senior US Treasury official. Financial deregulation by country regulators has led to the opening up of domestic financial markets, to borrowing and lending abroad, to the development of stock markets, and to invitations to foreign investors to participate.[2] (Emphasis added.)

The fundamental analysis practiced by most analysts on the street is not necessarily inconsistent with a belief in the *liquidity* approach, since differences in economic policies, productivity, growth expectations, etcetera may have an impact on differential flows among countries. Fundamental analysis, then, may be successful in predicting the *relative* winners and losers. There is, however, a huge infrastructure dedicated to fundamental analysis and a wide acceptance on the part of investors of the argument that they are making a conscious and specific decision to begin investing in a particular market precisely

---

see the chapter "Theories of Capital Export" in Barbara Stallings, *Banker to the Third World: U.S. Portfolio Investment in Latin America* (UCLA Press, 1987), pp. 11–17.

2. United States General Accounting Office, "International Financial Crises: Efforts to Anticipate, Avoid, and Resolve Sovereign Crises," *Report to the Chairman, Committee on Banking and Financial Services, House of Representatives,* June 1997, pp. 30–31.

because of local conditions that were not in place earlier. Probably because of this, the investment approach dominates the conceptual thinking about emerging markets, even though, as I will argue, there is overwhelming evidence that the capital flow decision is more automatically generated by external conditions than premeditated.

Liquidity Models and Asset Prices

The *liquidity* model, which in its purest form can be associated with the works of Charles Kindleberger and with Hyman Minsky's "financial instability hypothesis," begins with the assumption of a liquidity expansion in the global financial centers, what Minsky calls a "displacement." The displacement or impetus for the liquidity expansion can be fairly complex. In some cases there is an actual increase in the traditional measures of money in a major banking center, but this is not the only cause. It may be the result instead of a change in the structure of the financial markets. Minsky, for example, points out that

> the relations upon which the monetary authorities base their operations are predicated upon the assumption that a given set of institutions and usages exist. If the operations of the authorities have side effects in that they induce changes in financial institutions and usages, then the relations "shift." As a result, the effects of monetary operation can be quite different from those desired.[3]

I will show examples of this in Chapter 4 when I discuss the causes of liquidity expansions in the nineteenth and twentieth centuries. Minsky notes that changes in the set of financial institutions and usages can be brought about because of changes in the regulatory framework, in the operations of financial authorities, or even because of profit-making activities of financial players. Risky structures are usually built up by risky financial practices during periods of financial tranquility—this concept is sometimes summarized as "stability is destabilizing." The point is that at some point the "shift" in usage can have a monetary impact that is hard to predict and that can lead to fragility in the financial system during boom periods so that, in Minsky's words "a slight reversal of prosperity can lead to a financial crisis." When that happens, the previous expansion of liquidity rapidly becomes a liquidity contraction. As English bank reformer Thomas Joplin put it in 1832, "A demand for money in ordinary times,

3. Hyman P. Minsky, *Can "It" Happen Again? Essays on Instability and Finance* (M. E. Sharpe, 1982), p. 162.

and a demand for it in periods of panic, are diametrically different. The one demand is for money to put into circulation; the other for money to be taken out of it."[4]

A related argument—that changes in underlying liquidity are a more important factor to explain booms and busts than aspects of the business cycle such as overproduction, underconsumption, and over-capacity—was proposed by Irving Fischer, who focused primarily on indebtedness and deflation. He believed that credit and liquidity factors—what he called "debt-disease" and "dollar-disease"—are more important than all other causes of booms and depressions put together.[5] One of the points I will make in this book is that the insights about the relationship between monetary shifts and booms and busts in the United States or Europe are even more appropriate in describing the LDC loan market. One consequence of these boom periods is a sharp reduction in risk aversion and risk premiums, so that riskier, high-beta assets tend to perform best, and LDC securities are an extreme example of high-beta securities. During liquidity or credit boom periods, LDC assets are the ones most likely to benefit. Of course during the reversal, these are the assets most likely to suffer.

There are a number of Minsky-type changes in financial structure that I have identified as leading to a form of monetary expansion and that I will describe in the next chapter as creating the liquidity conditions that set off the international lending booms. One type of Minsky displacement that can significantly affect money and credit is simply a change in the legal and regulatory structures that are followed by rapid expansions in bank creation. Since bank notes and deposits are part of the money base, the creation of banks and the expansion of deposits will result in direct money supply growth. As I will show in chapter 4, many of the nineteenth-century LDC lending booms were preceded by an explosion in the creation of joint-stock banks.

In England, for example, the development of joint-stock banking did not occur as a gradual process but rather took place largely during two periods of aggressive bank creation. The first period occurred in the late 1820s and the first half of the 1830s, when the number of banks grew from three, in 1826, to 113, in 1837. The second occurred during the 1860s and early 1870s, when the number of banks grew from 98, in 1857, to 128, by the end of the 1870s.[6] It is not coincidental

4. Quoted in Charles P. Kindleberger, *A Financial History of Western Europe* (Oxford University Press, 1993), p. 273.

5. Ronnie J. Phillips, *The Chicago Plan and New Deal Banking Reform* (M. E. Sharpe, 1995), p. 106.

6. P. L. Cottrell and Lucy Newton, "Banking Liberalization in England and Wales 1826–1844," in Richard Sylla, Richard Tilly, and Gabriel Tortella (eds.), *The State, the Financial System, and Economic Modernization* (Cambridge University Press, 1999), pp. 76–84

that both of these periods—the early 1830s to 1837 and the late 1860s and early 1870s to 1873—were characterized by major lending booms to LDCs.

Another less obvious but nonetheless common Minsky-type displacement involves sharp increases in the turnover of some liquid asset. The first United States secretary of the treasury, Alexander Hamilton, understood this when he argued in the late 1780s for the creation of a unified national debt to replace the fragmented, illiquid, and confusing mixture of obligations generated by the thirteen colonies in the war against Great Britain. "It is a well-known fact," he argued, "that, in countries in which the national debt is properly funded, and an object of established confidence, it answers most of the purposes of money."[7]

Under Hamilton the U.S. Treasury effectively swapped a large number of very illiquid bonds and IOUs owed by the federal and state governments, some trading as low as 5 or 10 cents on the dollar, into a much smaller number of U.S. government bonds. These new "Hamilton 6s"—so called because of the 6% coupon—began trading at 70% and within a few months had reached 93% of face value.[8] With this debt conversion Hamilton created very large, very visible, and very actively traded high-quality assets. Although the total amount of outstanding debt had not changed, investors who owned these new bonds could be confident that they were much easier to value and monetize (i.e., sell for cash) and generally treated them as if they were a form of interest-bearing money. They could be used as collateral for borrowings or could be exchanged directly for other assets in the same way money can. In effect they became near-money.

Money and "Money-ness"

When such a large pool of assets becomes near-money, it can have a direct impact on liquidity in the system, which can lead directly to increases in asset prices as real interest rates decline. Since an asset boom can draw further investment activities from excited investors and so increase asset turnover (which causes liquidity in these assets to increase), it can have a self-reinforcing effect by making a larger amount of assets more money-like. Columbia University economics professor Robert Mundell makes this point when he argues that the

7. From "Report on Credit," delivered to Congress on January 14, 1790. See also Mildred Otenasek, *Alexander Hamilton's Financial Policies* (Arno Press, 1977).
8. Richard Sylla, "Shaping the U.S. Financial System, 1690–1913: The Dominant Role of Public Finance," in Sylla, Tilly, and Tortella, *The State*, pp. 249–62.

addition of very large, highly traded securities can cause a market's liquidity to increase just as if there had been an increase in the money supply.[9] The argument is that all assets can perform some of the functions of money, but their abilities to perform these functions can vary. How easy an asset is to transfer, value, and monetize—or how "liquid" it is—for example, will affect its use as money. As securities move up the liquidity scale, they begin to act more and more "money-like"— not that they cross the line from "nonmoney" to "money" but rather that "money-ness," or liquidity, is a continuous quality, not a static condition.

All types of assets, even cash, can become more or less liquid, and increasing the liquidity of a security can have the same effect as increasing the money supply. As an illustration of the differing "money-ness" of even money, in certain countries in eastern Europe, Deutschemarks circulate along with the local currency. Although dollars are also used as a form of money, a U.S. traveler bringing dollars will find much less appetite for her dollars than she might in Asian or Latin American countries (or even Russia). In a sense, although locals are using foreign currency as a better store of value than the local currency, they are assigning greater liquidity value to marks since the transactional costs are lower (dollars have to be exchanged at a bank or hotel, but most retail businesses will accept marks). In this case marks are in effect more money-like than dollars and are a more important component of the money base. Changes in the amount of marks held by locals will consequently have a bigger impact on the local money supply than equivalent changes in the amount of dollars held.

The process of monetization or "liquification" of assets also occurs when illiquid assets like real estate are used as collateral to back large issues of financial securities that trade readily. An example of this liquidity effect is the "monetization" of U.S. real estate that has occurred over the past fifteen years. During this period, the value of mortgage bonds relative to residential real estate value has increased sharply, effectively making U.S. savings significantly more liquid (real estate holdings are an important component of the typical U.S. savings portfolio). This may be at least part of the explanation for both the stock market and the emerging market booms of recent years.

Another, more interesting example of this liquidity effect was the European stock market boom that followed the French reparation payments of 5 billion francs to Prussia after the 1870 war. In what was at the time the largest financial operation the world had ever seen, France raised the money fairly easily by 1872 following a series of

9. Robert Mundell, "Making the Euro Work," *Wall Street Journal*, April 30, 1998, p. A18.

very successful international bond offerings led primarily by the Rothschild banks. Prussia accepted payments in gold, silver, or the bank notes of a limited number of central banks, including the Bank of England. This massive influx of metallic and high-quality paper money into the German markets, raised from as far away as India, permitted Germany to go fully onto the gold standard, although, probably because of the country's relative lack of financial experience, both consumer-price and asset inflation raged in the next two years.

In France, although there was an immediate negative impact on the real economy, markets quickly recovered and the price of the Thiers *rentes*, as the bonds were called, quickly appreciated by 20–25%.[10] The net effect on the two countries was that the total amount of money and near-money in circulation in Europe was increased somewhat by the amount of the reparation bonds, as these, because of their huge size, visibility, and liquidity, could partially take the place of the money that had been transferred to Germany. Walter Bagehot, writing at the time, claimed that it required "a vast loan in their own securities" to extract "the hoards of France from the custody of the French people,"[11] and it was through the mechanism of the loan that French money holdings were "monetized." This may have partially explained the rather frenzied stock market and international lending booms that spread throughout Europe and the Americas in the early 1870s. The lending boom was short-lived. It ended with the global crisis that began with the Viennese stock market collapse of May 1873, spread to Germany and the United States, and finally ended with massive sovereign and corporate defaults around the world. I will discuss these defaults in greater detail in chapter 5.

The Liquidity Cycle

In sum, there are a variety of ways in which liquidity can be expanded—changes in base money, changes in financial structure, explicit or implicit banking deregulation, increases in the "money-ness" of some asset. Any of these expansions can affect the cost of capital and, by affecting the subsequent return on assets, can increase risk appetite and/or reduce required risk premiums. As this happens, and as asset prices rise and the expected returns on safe assets decline, investors begin to widen their horizons in search of higher returns— they become "yield hogs" in Wall Street lingo—and the horizon often expands to include foreign investment opportunities.

10. Kindleberger, *Financial History*, pp. 235–45.
11. Walter Bagehot, *Lombard Street: A Description of the Money Market* (1873; reprint, John Wiley, 1999), p. 5.

The *liquidity* model for capital flows assumes a direct link between the initial expansion of rich-country liquidity and the boom in capital outflows, in a pattern that includes a great deal of self-reinforcing behavior. The process is usually as follows.

1. From time to time a displacement, such as a large shift in income, money supply, saving patterns, or the structure of financial markets, causes a major liquidity expansion in the rich-country financial centers. This increase in liquidity causes local stock markets to boom and real interest rates to drop.

2. As the rich-country asset markets boom, their trading volume rises and their trading costs decline. Assets begin to act more money-like as they become less volatile, more liquid, easier to trade, and, consequently, more marginable, which continues to reinforce the liquidity expansion. As volatility on risky assets begins to decline, they outperform traditional assets.

3. The pressure to find investment outlets builds, and investors begin systematically to underestimate risk or overestimate growth prospects in nontraditional sectors. Funds subsequently flood into a variety of nontraditional investments. Some of this capital begins to flow into LDC markets, which, because of their small sizes, are quick to react.

4. As consequences of the inflows, the LDCs that are receiving the capital begin to see currency strength and real economic growth, which reinforces the initial investment decision. As more money flows in, local markets begin to boom.

5. A consequence of the sudden growth in both asset values and GDP (gross domestic product) is a seemingly simultaneous move to change or reform the government policies that had "failed" in the past. These initial reforms are often targeted to encourage further capital inflows (by conforming to the dominant theories of development economics), and, because the inflows provide profits and benefits that allow the government to overcome the resistance of the local elite, the capital inflows permit an acceleration of the reforms. This quickly creates positive feedback as foreign investors use the reforms to justify continued capital inflows.

6. One result of the boom is a real appreciation in local currency as inflation differentials between the country and its trading partners, although rapidly declining, fail to keep up with the nominal depreciation. Exports grow because the liquidity expansion in the rich countries is usually associated with rising commodity prices. But because capital inflows are necessarily the obverse of a trade deficit, imports grow even more quickly. The combination of rising international trade and foreign investment often leads to optimistic talk of "globalization."

7. As capital flows in, the local banking system expands. This can be private-sector led and occur in the form of a reduction in "financial repression" (Ronald McKinnon's term)[12] or it can be caused by an expansion of public sector development banks. Credit becomes widely available, and inevitably, given the run-up in asset prices, a part of it is diverted into asset speculation.

8. The combination of a strong currency, asset price inflation, increased trade, and some GDP growth confirms market participants beliefs that the new government policies are "working." A political consensus emerges that the reforms will be continued. Policy-makers, producers, and investors begin to structure their activity on the assumption that, as the reforms are continued, the local economy will continue to grow and capital inflows will be a permanent feature of the economy.

9. After several (or a few) good years, the excess liquidity generation in the rich countries is reversed. This is generally in response to inflationary pressures, excess production leading to credit shocks, banking crises, or (during the gold-standard years) a gold imbalance in the rich-country centers.

10. As the rich-country money supply contracts, money flows to less-developed markets begin to reverse, and commodity prices begin to decline.

11. As the capital flows to LDCs slow down, local asset markets begin to grow more slowly or even to weaken, volatility grows dramatically, and governments and producers belatedly begin to cut costs and increase fiscal discipline—the immediate effect of which is to slow GDP growth. The costs and dislocations implicit in the previous government policies—unemployment related to the deregulation and privatization of state-owned industries, the transfer of ownership from the entrenched elite to a new entrepreneurial class, changes in access to capital—which had been papered over by the abundant capital inflow, start to emerge, and political dissatisfaction increases.

12. At some point, as conditions deteriorate the capital outflows become self-reinforcing and local markets crumble. As international refinancing dries up, if the previous debt buildup has been sufficiently large, international defaults mushroom. Political support for the previous reformist policies quickly diminishes.

This liquidity process occurred during both of the two major twentieth-century LDC lending cycles. In the 1920s, the United States

12. Ronald McKinnon, *Money and Capital in Economic Development* (Brookings Institution, 1973).

ran trade and capital surpluses with a war-torn Europe, one of whose results was, in the words of John Maynard Keynes, "the shipment to the United States of all the bullion in the world."[13] This surge of domestic gold reserves formed the basis of the rapidly expanding money supply. At first, the liquidity growth fueled U.S. stock market and commodity price increases. Following the very successful 1924 Dawes Loan to Germany, however, foreign borrowing from the United States accelerated, and over the next several years the sovereign bond market exploded. In Latin America this explosion of new lending was referred to as the "dance of the millions." The boom ended, however, in widespread sovereign defaults following the sharp reduction in U.S. liquidity that accompanied the collapse of the U.S. banking system in the early 1930s.

In the 1970s, it was a global shift in income and savings patterns that led to the expansion. The OPEC price hikes of the 1970s began when oil prices shot up from around $2 to $10 a barrel following the Yom Kippur War in 1973, with prices continuing to rise to nearly $40 by 1980. These massive price increases caused income to shift from high-consuming oil importers to high-saving OPEC nations, and the money ended up in bloated Eurodollar accounts that were recycled willy-nilly into the LDC lending boom.[14] When the U.S. Federal Reserve Bank under Chairman Paul Volcker contracted the U.S. money supply in 1979–81 in response to inflation in the late 1970s, the liquidity cycle was over. By 1982 many LDC borrowers, unable to refinance, were forced to default, and their economies collapsed into the "Lost Decade" of the 1980s. In chapters 4, 5, and elsewhere I will reexamine these international lending cycles from 1820 to the present in greater detail in light of the *liquidity* model.

I argue in this book that there are roughly two types of externally driven crisis events. One type, like the recent Mexican and Asian crises, consist of sudden exogenous shocks that combine with a collapse in financial margin and a flight to quality—in which investors sell risky assets and buy low-risk assets such as U.S. Treasuries—to cause a temporary capital outflow from LDCs. These shocks may be

13. John Maynard Keynes, "War Debts and the United States" (1921), in *Essays in Persuasion* (W. W. Norton, 1963), p. 57.

14. Charles Kindleberger argues very plausibly that the cycle may have actually started earlier, when Federal Reserve chairman Arthur Burns lowered U.S. rates to help Richard Nixon's 1972 reelection campaign at a time when Germany was running a very tight, antiinflation monetary policy. The inconsistency in monetary policy between the two countries led to a huge outflow of funds from the U.S. into the Eurodollar market, and Eurocurrency banks were forced to find a new loan outlets, including, most famously and disastrously, Third World borrowers. See Charles P. Kindleberger, "Financial Deregulation and Economic Performance: An Attempt to Relate European Financial History to Current LDC Issues," *Journal of Economic Development* 27, nos. 1–2 (October 1987).

brutal, but it is important to note that they usually occur in the context of stable global liquidity conditions—and if the market break does not become a devastating and default-inducing collapse, the recovery can be surprisingly quick. The second type of crisis occurs when there is a major contraction of global liquidity conditions, as occurred in the 1979–81 period. In this case, capital flows to LDCs are slowly squeezed, and to the extent that LDC borrowers require refinancing to service their existing debt commitments, they face the prospect of default or restructuring. Both types of crisis are discussed further in this book, with historical examples.

Implications of the Liquidity Approach

Most economists understand that because LDCs are primarily commodity producers, the volatility of commodity prices is an important source of LDC asset and balance of payments volatility. Even worse, there is fairly extensive evidence that during "good" periods the reliance on commodity exports may lead to a systematic overvaluation of the currency that can slow growth and make the countries more sensitive to currency shifts.[15] What the *liquidity* approach adds to the analysis is the second important source of volatility: changes in global liquidity conditions, which also impact the currency. As global liquidity waxes and wanes, and along with it global risk appetite, the leverage imparted by capital inflows can cause large shifts in LDC economic performance. Morgan Stanley economist Stephen Roach points out the sheer size of capital flows relative to LDCs.

> It may well be that the tiny emerging market economies of the world are literally awash in the turbulent seas of financial capital. For example, the equity market capitalization of large emerging market countries such as Korea, Malaysia, Taiwan and Brazil each totaled about $150 to $200 billion in the pre-crisis period of the mid-1990s. By contrast, the capitalization of the US equity market was about $6 to $7 trillion during that period (and is now closing in on $13 trillion) . . . At today's market levels just a 0.5% move out of US equities into the emerging-market asset class—hardly an unreasonable asset allocation shift for performance-oriented institutional investors—would be worth around $60 billion. Such an increment would equate to fully 6% of the combined market capitalization of the major equity markets in the developing world.[16]

15. Jeffrey D. Sachs and Andrew M. Warner, "The Big Push: Natural Resource Booms and Growth," *Journal of Development Economics* (June 1999): pp. 43–76.
16. Stephen S. Roach, "Learning to Live with Globalization," Testimony

Unfortunately, these two sources of volatility—commodity prices and shifts in global liquidity—have historically been highly correlated, probably because a liquidity boom often results in low real borrowing costs, asset price booms, and consumption booms, all of which can feed into higher commodity prices. As a consequence of this piling on of correlation, it is almost part of the definition of an LDC that its economy is extremely sensitive to external factors. This has important investment implications because it suggests that diversification among different LDC countries and regions has a limited impact on reducing volatility during times of market stress, when it is most needed. This also has important corporate finance implications.

For one, and in contrast to conventional theory, the *liquidity* approach deemphasizes the link between domestic policies and the investment decision of foreign creditors. It argues that the foreign decision to invest, while often justified by perceived changes in economic policy, tends to follow its own exogenous pattern. Probably the strongest evidence most analysts provide against the *liquidity* model and in favor of the *investment* model is the way capital flows seem to be correlated with improvements in local policy-making. Earlier in this chapter, for example, I quoted a GAO report that claimed that "macroeconomic reforms in the early 1990s in Latin America led to soaring private capital flows." The theory is appealing because it suggests that the good (reformers) are getting rewarded.

If reforms and capital inflows are correlated, at first blush it may seem obvious that the causal relation must flow from reforms to capital inflow. It makes intuitive sense to assume that investors only begin to invest in a market when they see evidence that policy-makers are restructuring the market in a way that permits faster economic growth and more profitable investment opportunities. In fact, however, the logic and timing of the sequence between reform and foreign investment can just as easily go the other way. There are at least four reasons that they may do so. First, left to themselves, markets usually evolve in the direction of rationality. If countries do not structure their economies rationally, it is generally because there is a powerful and entrenched elite that benefits at least temporarily from local economic inefficiencies. Capital inflows can permit government officials to implement reform by providing resources and profitable business opportunities to the entrenched elite who might otherwise oppose the reforms.

Second, foreign capital also provides the financing for policies that have a short-term cost and only long-term benefits. These may include, for example, firing employees of bloated state-run companies,

before the Committee on Banking and Financial Services of the U.S. House of Representatives, May 20, 1999.

closing down value-destroying operations, reforming the tax code, building infrastructure and so on. Third, monetary policy has always been a weakness of LDC regimes and has often led to inflation and rapidly depreciating currencies. Large capital inflows alleviate monetary policy by permitting a rapid expansion of the local money base while simultaneously and temporarily strengthening the currency. Finally, because the lure of capital inflows is so powerful, it creates a huge incentive for local policy-makers to implement whatever development policies are currently fashionable among rich-country bankers.

I want to stress the word "fashionable" because there is little historical evidence that previous policy packages that were praised and rewarded by investors were, in the end, successful in generating sustainable wealth. There is usually a well-established consensus among bankers and investors about the sort of reforms that will lead to growth and, consequently, to foreign investment. These reforms are almost always the same package of more-or-less free market, free trade reforms that international bankers and investors tend to promote, largely, it seems, because they facilitate international lending and debt repayment.

The certainty with which these beliefs are held by followers of the *investment* model sometimes leads to surprisingly ideological interpretations of history. One of the most common examples of such a reading is the often repeated claim that the economic success of the "East Asian Tigers" is due at least in part to their open economies, as evidenced by their export successes. For example, *Foreign Affairs* editor Fareed Zakaria, a very knowledgeable international expert, in a review of a book by Cambridge University economist Amartya Sen, argues that the East Asian tigers were "the only countries to move from poverty to near plenty." He cites as a major reason for this that "these countries adopted more free-market policies than other third-world countries did, policies that were widely unpopular until very recently."[17]

Free Market Reforms and Capital Flows

But there are several problems with this assumption. First, there is a very long history of poor countries experimenting unsuccessfully with free market policies: Colombia and Chile in the late nineteenth century, for example, were generally considered models of free market orthodoxy. They were certainly more open than the United States,

17. Fareed Zakaria, "Beyond Money," *New York Times Book Review*, November 28, 1999, p. 14.

with its tariff protection of U.S. industries, significant military expenditures particularly during the Civil War and the Indian wars, and the direct and indirect government role in financing and/or building canals, railroads, and other infrastructure. Second, and more important, one would have to have already decided that only free trade and free markets can lead to the development of wealth before one would hold up the East Asian tigers as models of free markets. It seems more reasonable to credit their success to government planning and to view their famed "openness" to world markets more in a classic mercantilist vein than as an expression of a Smith-Ricardo version of global free trade.

These countries were open to free trade only in that export growth was an obsession, and the openness of the East Asian tigers was really a very mercantilist conviction that production and exporting should be promoted at the expense of consumption and importing. I will refer to this again briefly in chapter 10, when I discuss the history of money doctors, but it is probably worth noting that the free market policy advice that rich countries generally provide to LDCs was, perhaps mercifully, never followed too closely by the best documented cases of LDCs that became rich—England and France in the eighteenth century, the United States and Germany in the nineteenth century, and Japan, Taiwan, and Korea in the twentieth century.[18]

But this digression on fashionable development models can be taken a little further in examining the relationship between policy reform and foreign investment. Although market reforms have been implemented among a variety of countries and at various periods over the past 30 years, the timing of reforms that we have seen in recent years doesn't easily argue that the reform process leads the process of foreign investment. In fact there is a very good recent example of the disconnection between reforms and foreign investment. This is the timing of the so-called neoliberal reforms that were embraced at different times by various Latin American countries during the past twenty-five years. The capital inflow to Mexico beginning around 1990 is usually attributed to the neoliberal reform policies introduced by President Miguel de la Madrid around 1983–84 that dominated policy during the 1988–94 administration of President Carlos Salinas. These reforms included privatization of state-owned enterprises, business deregulation, import liberalization, central bank independence, and a greater emphasis on fiscal discipline. They were an explicit rejection of the import substitution policies followed by de la Madrid's predecessors in the 1960s and 1970s.

18. For a similar argument, see Irma Adelman and Erinc Yeldan, "Is This the End of Economic Development?" *Structural Change and Economic Dynamics* 11 (2000): 95–109.

But Mexico was neither the first nor the last Latin American country to experiment with these reforms. This same basket of market-approved economic reforms had actually been implemented much earlier in Chile, under General Augusto Pinochet, beginning in 1972–74, while Brazil and Argentina began similar reforms in the early 1990s. If capital flows are driven primarily by local market structures, and if these market reforms are indeed the best indicators of future growth, we would have expected to see capital flows to these four countries somehow correlated with the timing of the reform implementations. In spite of the huge timing differences in the reform process, however, the timing of capital flows to Chile, Mexico, Argentina, and Brazil was virtually identical: the massive capital inflows of the 1970s were wholly cut off in 1982–83 and resumed again in 1989–91 to reach their apogee in 1995–97. Although there are marginal differences in the volume of flows, there is little evidence that the market evaluated and responded primarily to policy decisions.

Under these circumstances it does not seem rational to credit domestic policy decisions for foreign investment or to assume that by fixing domestic policies we can ensure stable capital flows. On the contrary, the *liquidity* approach has at least two very different implications. First, preventing externally induced financial shocks is extremely difficult since the investment decision is exogenous and what may seem like small shifts in rich-country capital flows can easily overwhelm less developed markets. Second, if shocks are inevitable, domestic economic policies will have little impact on preventing crises, which means that proposals to prevent future crises by deepening domestic economic reforms, eliminating crony capitalism, improving bank lending procedures, etcetera, although praiseworthy in the long run, are less relevant in affecting the capital investment decision. It is more important to minimize the volatility impact of these shocks directly, and the only available tool with which to do this is the capital structure. In finance theory, a borrower's capital structure is not just the means by which it funds itself, it is also the way it indexes or controls its market risks, domestically or externally. It is a basic tenet of corporate finance theory that market risks should be managed through the capital structure. This means designing a funding strategy that automatically reverses or dissipates the damage caused by unpredictable external shocks. I will discuss what this means in chapter 6.

4

180 Years of Liquidity Expansion and International Lending

The Pattern of Lending

In chapter 3 I argued that global capital flows are less a function of local growth prospects and more a function of independent expansions and contractions in underlying liquidity in rich-country financial centers. Although this *liquidity* approach may at first seem inconsistent with rational investor behavior, it nonetheless provides a better explanation of why capital flows into less developed economies have occurred over the past two hundred years largely in the form of investment waves. In this chapter and the next I will examine these lending waves to argue that the *liquidity* model does a much better job of explaining the history of these capital flows than does the *investment* model. Drawing in part on the work of Christian Suter,[1] we can list these waves as consisting of the periods shown in table 4.1.

What is striking about even a cursory look at the capital flow pattern is precisely that it is so clearly a pattern. In each case within a relatively short period of time, there is a huge expansion of lending and foreign investment to parts of the world that had a little while earlier been largely excluded from foreign investment. More significant, these different parts of the world usually had little in common economically except for their remoteness from international financial centers. The end of the investment boom is also too highly correlated

1. Christian Suter, *Debt Cycles in the World Economy: Foreign Loans, Financial Crises, and Debt Settlements, 1820–1990* (Westview Press, 1992), pp. 53 and 66–67.

Table 4.1. Lending waves to peripheral borrowers

Period	Major borrowers	Primary source	Outcome
1822–25	Spain, Naples, Denmark, Prussia, Greater Colombia, Mexico, Austria-Hungary, Chile, Russia, Brazil, Greece, Peru, Argentina	British	Major international defaults beginning in 1824, representing about 20–25% of total foreign investment
1834–39	U.S. states, Portugal, Spain, Mexico	Mostly British, some French	Major defaults beginning in 1837, mostly 9 U.S. states following the collapse of cotton prices, representing about 20–25% of total foreign investment
1864–75	U.S., Russia, Ottoman Empire, Egypt, Spain, Austria-Hungary, Peru, Romania, Confederate states, Colombia, Tunisia	Mostly British and French, some German	Major defaults across the world beginning as early as 1867, representing about 25% of total foreign investment
1886–90	U.S., Australia, Argentina, Portugal, Brazil, Greece	British	Looms large because of the effect of the Argentine default on Baring Brothers, but a relatively minor crisis period beginning in 1890, with less than 5% of total foreign investment in the form of defaulted bonds
1905–13	Russia, Canada, South Africa, Argentina, various Balkan states, Ottoman Empire, Austria-Hungary, Brazil, Mexico, Cuba	British, French, and German, in that order, with some U.S.	Although defaulted debt represented over 20% of total foreign investment, war and revolution in Russia, the Ottoman Empire and Mexico were to blame. Otherwise high commodity prices caused by World War I ensured a very solid repayment record
1924–28	Germany, France, Argentina, Cuba, Chile, Peru, Australia, Canada, Brazil, Romania, New Zealand, South Africa, Yugoslavia, Greece, Austria, Colombia, Poland, Turkey	U.S. and British, in that order, with some Dutch	Major global default beginning in 1931 with defaulted bonds representing as much as 30–35% of total foreign investment
1970–81	Brazil, Mexico, Spain, Venezuela, South Korea, Argentina, Algeria, Turkey, Yugoslavia, Poland, Romania, Egypt, Indonesia, Philippines, Chile, USSR	U.S., British, Japanese, German, French	LDC loan crisis and the lost decade of the 1980s
1991–present	Argentina, Mexico, Brazil, Korea, Russia, Venezuela, Indonesia, Thailand, various members of Commonwealth of Independent States, Colombia, Panama, Pakistan	U.S., German, Japanese, British, Spanish	Small number of defaults to date, beginning with Russia in 1998

to be determined by chance, when the sudden expansion of lending is even more suddenly cut off.

If the foreign capital flows were simply responding to improved investment opportunities overseas, it seems likely that we would see the distribution of capital outflows behave in a more random way. After all, economic reforms and changes in economic prospects can occur for a wide variety of very specific reasons that have to do with local political conditions, technological innovations, changes in demand or supply of an important locally produced commodity, demographic shifts, etcetera. The pace at which these factors will affect individual countries should be fairly random. When Chile, for example, is benefiting from improvements in these underlying factors, there is no reason to assume that, coincidentally, Turkey, New Zealand, and Austria are also undergoing political and economic changes that suddenly make them better places in which to invest. And yet the flow of funds to all these countries was highly correlated.

Even within specific countries this pattern is clearly visible. A typical relationship between a leading financial center and a volatile emerging market country is that between Great Britain and the United States during the eighteenth and nineteenth centuries, during which period U.S. and British economic cycles were highly correlated for countries with such different economic and political conditions. Part of this is clearly due to the extensive trade relationship—the United States was a primary commodity exporter, mainly to Britain, from whom it imported finished goods. But this isn't the whole story since, contrary to what one might expect, British imports were more highly correlated with U.S. imports than either were with the other country's exports, which is what one would expect if the cycles were driven by trade. But these cycles were also highly correlated with interest rates and specie accumulation in Great Britain. When the Bank of England had high or declining gold reserves, both countries tended to expand. When the Bank of England had low reserves, both countries tended contract. As a rule, then, economic crises and panics in the United States were linked primarily to British market panics and gold imbalances, and it is the liquidity expansion in Britain that seems to have driven both economies.[2]

Before we discuss the corporate finance implications for LDCs of a world in which investment decisions and local growth prospects are primarily driven by exogenous factors, it may be useful to examine these investment "waves" more closely. In the rest of this chapter I will discuss the liquidity conditions that set off the lending waves

2. Burke Adrian Parsons, *British Trade Cycles and American Bank Credit: Some Aspects of Economic Fluctuations in the United States 1815–1840* (Arno Press, 1977), pp. 109–14 and 324–31.

that took place during the nineteenth and twentieth centuries, beginning with the sovereign lending boom of the 1820s. The point will be to identify the causes of the expansion of the money supply in the rich-country financial centers that led to the subsequent lending booms. I will then discuss the sequence of events that followed the initial boom in chapter 5. This will include a description of the subsequent local asset boom, the beginning of capital flows to LDCs, the LDC economic booms, the frenzied lending stage, the unexpected financial break in the rich-country centers, and, finally, the collapse of the international loan market.

The 1820s and the Beginning of the First Lending Boom

I have chosen the international lending boom of the 1820s to start with not because it is the first such surge in liquidity but rather because it arguably represents the first global wave of lending followed by a global financial crisis. Friedrich Engels, writing in the late 1870s, calls it the "first general crisis."[3] As such, it sets a pattern against which we can evaluate subsequent lending booms, and for this reason I am going to discuss it in a more detail than the later periods.

The beginning of the 1820s lending boom was, as I will show, fairly typical in many ways. Following Britain's post-Napoleonic depression, England began a period of rapid economic growth and technological change. This was accompanied by a renewed interest on the part of wealthy English savers, after the difficulties and uncertainty of the war years, to find profitable investment outlets for their savings. These savers began to expand the range of investment outlets, slowly at first and then with increasing speed. Before it ended, the investment frenzy would spread to some of the most far-fetched projects in remote corners of the earth—including at least one successful loan to a country that did not even exist.

If speculative frenzies and loan mania require a liquidity expansion, there were at least four important sources that set off the boom of the 1820s. The first, although perhaps least important, is the 700 million franc indemnity payment imposed on France at the second Treaty of Waterloo, which France was able to pay through the issues of *rentes,* arranged primarily by Baring Brothers. I have already discussed the impact of French reparation payments on the liquidity expansion of the 1870s. Charles Kindleberger makes a similar point about the 1818 loan. He argues that the successful Baring loan recy-

3. Friedrich Engels, *Socialism: Utopian and Scientific*, in Lewis F. Feuer (ed.), *Marx and Engels* (Anchor Books, 1959), p. 100.

cled French indemnity payments into the real economy while introducing British investors to the joys and profits of foreign loans—the *rentes*, initially priced at 67% of face value, traded up to 87% by 1821 and 90% by 1823.[4] In the light of subsequent history one can argue that France's disposition to lose wars in the nineteenth and twentieth centuries may have been an important impetus for economic growth among poor countries during that period.

As an aside I should point out an important innovation in the sovereign loan market that was associated with the financial transactions necessary to resolve the imbalances of the post-Napoleonic period. Following the defeat of the French, Prussia hired the Rothschild bank to arrange a 20 million thaler loan in advance of expected French payments. Nathan Rothschild, the head of the London branch, was able to structure and issue the loan in a way that was radically different from other loans, such as the Baring loan discussed earlier, and that was to have an important impact on the subsequent development of the market.

First, instead of limiting it to one market, Rothschild arranged to issue the loan simultaneously in London, Frankfurt, Berlin, Hamburg, Amsterdam, and Vienna. Second, and much more important, he arranged that the bond was to be denominated in sterling, rather than thaler, so that British investors, who were likely to be the main buyers of the loan, would not have to consider the possibility of a devaluation of the then less-than-stable Prussian currency. Finally, the Prussians were convinced to make principal and interest payments available to investors not just in Berlin but also in London, and in fact anywhere the Rothschilds had a branch. These conditions forced for the first time a non-British sovereign loan to conform to the standards of the all-important London market. It eliminated currency risk while reducing the costs of collecting payments and was a crucial step in the standardization of a fragmented market that had previously been dominated by local investors and bankers. Within a few years most major sovereign financings were to incorporate these innovations, and they paved the way for the British-financed sovereign lending boom of the next decade.[5]

It is worth pausing here again to consider the importance of recycling transactions on the history of liquidity expansions and LDC lending.[6] Besides the recycling of French indemnity payments in 1818

4. Charles Kindleberger, *A Financial History of Western Europe* (Oxford University Press, 1993), pp. 214–15.

5. Niall Ferguson, *The House of Rothschild: Money's Prophets 1798–1848* (Penguin Books, 1999), pp. 123–25.

6. I don't know of anyone better on this subject than Charles Kindleberger. See in particular his short but extremely useful *International Capital Move-*

and the Franco-Prussian indemnity of the 1870s, which I have already discussed, the concept will arise at least three more times in this book. The first time will be in relation to the Dawes loan of 1924, which involved the recycling of German reparation payments after World War I, and its effect on the international lending boom of the 1920s. The second time will be in reference to the role of international banks in recycling the huge treasure chest of petrodollars amassed by OPEC countries in the 1970s and the effect this had on the lending boom of that period. And finally I will discuss the impact the recycling of the large Asian trade surpluses of the 1990s had on U.S. liquidity and the subsequent emerging markets boom.

To return to our story, after the Baring loan there were at least three other sources of liquidity to fuel the 1820s lending boom. In 1822 the British government, whose finances were no longer constrained by the need to finance the war against Napoleon, announced plans to consolidate its debt. As part of the consolidation, which involved converting 5% consols[7] to bonds bearing 4% coupons, investors were permitted to "put" bonds back to the government and receive principal and accrued interest in the form of cash. This operated as a form of open-market purchase and caused a cash injection of nearly £2.8 million into the hands of British investors (compared to total outstanding debt of just over £200 million). Several commentators have pointed out the relationship between the debt repayment and the subsequent need of investors to invest cash proceeds in other financial instruments.[8] This was undoubtedly one of the causes of the increased investment appetite.

The third source of the liquidity expansion was included in the Act of Parliament passed in 1822: as part of its consolidation and rationalization of finance, Parliament permitted provincial banks to issue currency. In the strong economic conditions of the period, banks that took advantage were able to reap large profits by lending the proceeds of the note issuance, so encouraging imitation and a subsequent rapid expansion of the credit offered by banks to British users of capital. The ensuing money growth, according to one commentator, "swamped the whole country with paper money, which found a ready outlet at that time in rising prices and universal speculation."[9] As this

ments (Cambridge University Press, 1987), and, of course, _Manias, Panics, and Crashes: A History of Financial Crises_ (Basic Books, 1989).

7. Consols, also called bank annuities, were British government bonds originally issued in 1751 that paid interest regularly but had no final maturity. They were an important source of government funding.

8. Frank Griffith Dawson, _The First Latin American Debt Crisis: The City of London and the 1822–25 Bubble_ (Yale University Press, 1990), pp. 20–21.

9. H. M. Hyndman, _Commercial Crises of the Nineteenth Century_ (1892; reprint, Allen and Unwin, 1932), p. 29.

money was often used for the purchase of land or other assets, whose subsequent rising prices permitted them to become additional collateral for further money creation, the process was self-reinforcing and led ultimately to excess. This is a process that I will discuss repeatedly in this chapter.

The final source of the British liquidity expansion that is easily identifiable was the extraordinary growth of bullion reserves at the Bank of England, which of course formed the most fundamental base for money during the period. This was caused by the cessation of the government's military expenditures and the rebound in British trade, when, following Napoleon's attempted blockade, the demand in continental Europe for British goods soared. From a low in 1821 of just under £4 million, reserves grew steadily and rapidly to £14 million by late 1824.[10]

Two of the preconditions for the British economic boom of the 1820s—the defeat of the French, and the subsequent development of liquidity in the financial markets—were combined with a third factor that made the age in some way resemble the last decade of the twentieth century. England was, at the time, in the midst of a dramatic technologically led economic expansion, underpinned by the growth of the textile industry, that seemed to augur a new era in the economy. This was, after all, the period that saw rapid technological advancement in the all-important textile industry, the first steam navigation companies, the first passenger railways and gas lighting enterprises, and even, in the United States, the explosion of canal building after the immensely successful Erie Canal, built between 1817 and 1825. Investors were enthusiastic about the opportunities for growth that came out of the combination of technological change and the sudden opening of new parts of the world. They were particularly enthused by the new Latin American countries, with their gold, silver, mineral resources, and, above all, a population just entering, with the defeat of Spain in their wars of independence, into liberal forms of rule and the global economy dominated by England.

This combination of a economic strength, military victory, and domestic liquidity led to a burst in confidence and a frenzy of speculative investing on the part of English capitalists and rentiers. It was also accompanied by about 30% inflation from 1822 to 1825.[11] An observer sixty years later described it like this:

> At the beginning of 1824, therefore, instead of grumbling and discontent, murmurs of satisfaction and gleeful anticipations of

10. Parsons, *British Trade Cycles*, p. 118
11. David Hackett Fischer, *The Great Wave: Price Revolutions and the Rhythms of History* (Oxford University Press, 1996), p. 158.

enhanced gains were heard from the capitalists on every side.
. . . Business was exceedingly brisk. Everybody was making
haste to get rich. Speculation of the most reckless character far
outstripped the limits of the most adventurous trading. . . .
[There was] an accumulation of money in the banks as well in
London as in the provincial centers. A superabundance of capital sought employment of the riskiest of ventures. Projects of
every kind for the construction of canals, tunnels, bridges, tram-
ways, roads, and so forth, were eagerly entertained and accepted.[12]

One result seems to have been a significantly increased willingness
on the part of British investors to take on risk. Even though in Latin
America the final defeat of Spain didn't take place until the Battle of
Ayacucho on December 9, 1824 (news of which took another two
months to reach England), the loan frenzy can be said to have started
in 1822 with the £2 million loan to the Republic of Colombia.[13] Negotiated in London by patriot-later-turned-villain Francisco Antonio
Zea, this loan turned out to be singularly unsuccessful for Colombia.
Approximately half of the issue was immediately exchanged at a 20%
discount against inflated claims on the Colombian government in-
curred during the war of independence from Spain, while much of
the balance was used to pay underwriting expenses and sales com-
missions or suffered deductions for interest and principal amortiza-
tion prepayments. The Republic received very little cash and had to
return to the market fairly soon thereafter, but the loan was a great
success for investors, rapidly trading up, and the newly emerging international loan market took off.

What is important for my purposes is the direct connection between local exuberance in the British capital markets and the subsequent lending boom. Many commentators at the time argued differently, pointing out the tremendous geopolitical changes, to use a
twentieth-century phrase, taking place with the expansion of repub-
licanism throughout Europe and the Americas. These changing conditions, with the huge associated growth potential for international
trade, was, in their opinions, the cause of the perfectly rational investor interest in the region. In retrospect, of course, it is easy to point
out that Europe and Latin America had emerged from the Napoleonic
wars into a period of extreme political uncertainty and long-lasting
civil wars—not much on which to justify the optimism of British investors—and the brutal end of the boom in 1825 made it clear how
unstable conditions really were. What is striking about this episode,

12. Quoted by Hyndman, *Commercial Crises*, pp. 26–27.
13. J. Fred Rippy, "Latin America and the British Investment 'Boom' of the
1820s," *Journal of Modern History* 19, no. 2 (June 1947): 122–29.

and all the ones that followed, is how quickly risk aversion melted away during a period of easy money. Throughout this book I argue that it is the disappearance of risk aversion allied with excess money growth, more than any increase in growth opportunities, that creates the LDC lending boom.

The 1830s and the Second International Lending Boom

The aftermath of the 1825 crisis soured investors on Latin America for decades. But it only took a slight altering of conditions for the lessons of the crisis to be quickly unlearned when, ten years later, the British capital markets entered into another speculative international lending frenzy. The financial boom and crash of the 1830s and 1840s was unlike most others in that it was based primarily on very tight links between one rich-country lender, Great Britain, and a single, rapidly growing, less-developed borrower, the United States. That it is not to say that these were the only affected countries. Although at the heart of the boom and panic was the British speculation in American cotton, British cotton textiles, and American railroads and the American speculation in cotton and land, the boom spread to Europe as well, probably through the rapidly growing U.S. and British import accounts. When the crisis finally came, according to Kindleberger, "it broke out in England in 1836 and 1837, spread to the United States and then, in May 1838 when England was quietly recuperating, erupted in Belgium, France and Germany to spread back again to England and the United States in 1839."[14]

Although the effects were felt broadly, this was largely a case in which the liquidity expansion in one country was mirrored and reinforced by liquidity expansion in the other. Once again, I will focus first on the British liquidity expansion that was the precondition for the international loan boom.

By 1830 England had begun to recover from the 1825 collapse. Bumper harvests in the early 1830s relieved Britain's grain shortage, and the all-important grain prices began declining (which, through its deflationary effect, had an expansionary impact on the real money supply). One aspect of the improving economy was a rapid expansion in the creation of new joint stock banks that were permitted to issue currency. The Bank Act of 1826 had permitted banking companies to be formed with the power to issue notes of a denomination not less than £5. At first, the creation of banks proceeded relatively cautiously.

14. Quoted in John F. Chown, *A History of Money from AD 800* (Routledge, 1994), p. 177.

From 1826 to 1833, thirty-four banks of issue were created. But the process sped up rapidly, and thirty-four more banks was created between 1833 and 1835. By 1836, the trend reached "manic proportions" with fifty-nine banks promoted and forty-two new banks of issue actually established in a single year.[15] In addition, changes in the discounting procedure of the Bank of England, along with a substantial branch expansion, simultaneously increased the importance of the London money markets and, for a few years in the early 1830s, vastly increased the quantity of paper credits in circulation.[16] The rapid creation of money was accompanied by an increase in asset and commodity prices, including, most important for the United States, the price of cotton.

There was another simultaneous source of money growth, which John Chown discusses in his book on the history of money, refering to contemporary accounts by nineteenth-century merchant Thomas Tooke. According to Tooke, at least part of the blame for the money expansion and changes in the Bank of England's discounting procedure may have been indirectly caused by the East India Company. After the Company lost the China monopoly, and probably because of a limited need to invest profits generated elsewhere, there was a rapid increase in the Company's balances held at the Bank of England. As these deposits increased, the Company had been able to negotiate an unprecedented agreement in which the Bank paid 3% on the Company's balances, which reached as high as £4.7 million during this period. Pressure to generate sufficient returns to pay the interest apparently led the Bank of England to an excessive expansion of advances to bill brokers and caused the bank to violate its own set of reserve rules, known as the Palmer rule. According to Tooke, the Bank's irresponsible behavior was a direct cause of the excessive credit expansion among merchants.[17]

The United States, meanwhile, was simultaneously living through an economic boom and one of the most ferocious money fights of its early history. President Andrew Jackson had made opposition to the Bank of the United States one of the pillars of his administration and, on his reelection in 1832, moved to disarm and eventually close down the bank. Although private, the Bank of the United States acted as a sort of central bank and handled fund flows and deposits for the U.S. government. It was by far the largest and most powerful financial in-

15. Hyndman, *Commercial Crises*, pp. 42–43, and P. L. Cottrell and Lucy Newton, "Banking Liberalization in England and Wales 1826–1844," in Richard Sylla, Richard Tilly, and Gabriel Tortella (ed.), *The State, the Financial System, and Economic Modernization* (Cambridge University Press, 1999), pp. 96–97.
16. Parsons, *British Trade Cycles*, p. 219.
17. Chown, *History of Money*, p. 177.

stitution in the country. Under the energetic leadership of Nicholas Biddle, it also took upon itself the task of maintaining monetary discipline in the country by regularly acquiring the circulating notes of banks and submitting them for redemption. This forced the smaller banks to maintain adequate liquidity and to limit the issue of notes to an amount that could be quickly redeemed and was a serious check on inflationary expansion.

By the time the Bank's charter was withdrawn, in 1836, Jackson had shifted the holding of U.S. government funds away from the Bank and toward a group of politically connected smaller banks distributed throughout the country and known as the "pet" banks. The story of the fight over the Bank of the United States is one of the most fascinating in U.S. history; for the sake of brevity I will reduce it to the following points:

- After 1833, when the Bank of the United States ceased to receive public funds, it stopped acting to brake the growth of the money markets. Thereafter there was no institution capable of checking the ferocious growth of circulating bank notes.
- In spite of the government's hard money opposition to banks of issue, the withdrawal of the Bank of the United States intensified the expansion of the state banking system. The number of state banks grew from 329 in 1829 ($110 million of capital) to 506 in 1834 and 788 by 1837 (over $500 million of capital).[18] Bank capital growth was exacerbated by the directing of government funds away from the very conservative Bank of the United States to the frankly expansionary pet banks.
- Both reinforcing and benefiting from the expansion of the state banks, during this period and in order both to finance itself and to encourage the spread of settlement, the U.S. government had been selling huge amounts of public land, the proceeds of which were redeposited in the pet banks. As the money supply expanded, and asset prices in general rose, speculative purchases of public land on credit skyrocketed and added to the money supply excess as these purchases effectively converted illiquid capital (unimproved land) into liquid capital (land loans).

In each country the creation of money drove up the prices of the assets that were used as collateral for additional credit creation and supported the profitability of banking, which supported further bank

18. There are no good records on the number of banks, but these are estimates from Paul Studenski and Herman Krooss, *Financial History of the United States: Fiscal, Monetary, Banking and Tariff, Including Financial Administration and State and Local Finance* (McGraw-Hill, 1952), p. 107.

creation. At the same time the sight of feverish economic activity and skyrocketing markets increased British risk appetite and persuaded British investors to embrace the U.S. "growth story," and they poured huge sums of money into loans and investments. This rush of funds at first underpinned the rapid growth of U.S. gold and gold claims but quickly became the obverse of a U.S. import boom. Between 1830 and 1837, the U.S. trade deficit was an astonishing $140 million, which was necessarily financed by European, mostly British, capital.

As in the previous decade, one sees the same pattern of domestic money growth in England caused primarily by a structural change in the banking system and a rapid increase in circulating notes. A local stock market boom, a run-up in commodity prices, and, ultimately, a huge increase in overseas lending once again accompanied the local expansion of the British money base. What is interesting about the period was that the United States was by then a large enough market for England that its own monetary excesses was able to materially affect British behavior—the two countries were reinforcing each other's money expansion. The marvelous growth experienced by the U.S. economy during this period was initiated by monetary changes across the Atlantic in the same way that its subsequent collapse was. Again, I will leave the story with the beginning of the lending boom and discuss the aftermath in chapter 5.

The Third International Lending Boom and the First World Debt Crisis

The international lending and trade boom of the 1860s and the early 1870s is arguably the first time the world experienced a modern "globalization" cycle, although smaller versions of this characterized earlier international lending booms. Like the subsequent ones—including the 1890s, the 1920s, and the 1990s—this version of globalization was tied to the investment and trade expansions that followed the previous liquidity expansion. And also like subsequent ones, it was accompanied by an internationalization of academic and artistic culture, a spreading of a dominant ideology, and a widespread recognition of the interrelatedness of the world economy. Carlos Marichal lists the expansion of world markets during the 1860s and the easy availability throughout Europe, the Americas, and even Asia and Africa of consumer products from all over the world—and calls the 1873 crisis the first world debt crisis.[19]

19. Carlos Marichal, *A Century of Debt Crises in Latin America, from Independence to the Great Depression 1820–1930* (Princeton University Press, 1989), pp. 68–98.

In discussing the dynamics of this particular capital cycle, I will begin as usual by attempting to identify the liquidity precondition. I have already discussed the huge success of the Thiers *rentes* used to finance the Franco-Prussian indemnity, and it is hard to over-emphasize its effect both as a sort of money creation and on its impact in whetting British, French, and German appetite for foreign securities. Of course the impact of the Thiers loan was felt only during 1871–72, and it is probably no coincidence that it came during the final speculative frenzy of the 1870–73 period.

Up to that period Europe was in the midst of what was a long and extraordinary expansion in European trade and economic performance. This had begun shortly after the largely U.S. crisis of 1857, and it was not in the least dampened subsequently either by the U.S. Civil War or the various Prussian wars. In fact, by generating a huge demand for manufacturing products and developing financial innovations to raise the necessary money, the U.S. Civil War may have been an important spur to European economic activity. During this ten- to twelve-year period, imports and exports more than doubled in Great Britain, the United States, France, Austria, and Belgium and shot up in most other countries. There was an enormous expansion of railways, steamships, and telegraph cables, while the United States was leading a revolution in the production of agricultural commodities.

As usual it is also important to mention innovations in banking that changed the nature of money and dramatically increased the system's liquidity—particularly in the United States, Germany, Austria, and France. One of the great innovations of the time, for example, was the new market of middle-class American savers that financier Jay Cooke was able to access so efficiently to help the North raise funds during the U.S. Civil War. In order to finance the war, Treasury Secretary Salmon P. Chase, along with financiers like Cooke, expanded the financial system to incorporate larger numbers of Americans.[20] This period also saw the creation between 1859 and 1864 of the first deposit banks in France, Crédit Industriel et Commercial (1859), Crédit Lyonnais (1863), and Société Générale (1864). The net effect of the creation of the deposit banks was a radical improvement in the efficiency with which the banking system was able to collect, mobilize, and channel French savings, and I should point out that this is one of the common forms liquidity expansions have taken. According to

20. Richard Sylla has argued that in fact U.S. government needs—particularly during wartime—have been the major impetus for financial innovation in the United States. For further reading on the topic see Bray Hammond, *Sovereignty and an Empty Purse: Banks and Politics in the Civil War* (Princeton University Press, 1970), and John Niven, *Salmon P. Chase* (Oxford University Press, 1995).

Kindleberger, the real innovation was perhaps not in the *idea* of the banks but rather that after an initial period of investment in the manufacturing industry, they turned away from manufacturing and toward commerce and, especially, to speculation in foreign bonds.[21]

This eagerness to trade in foreign bonds was later encouraged by the huge success of the *rentes* issues used to finance the Franco-Prussian indemnity, but already by the mid-1860s Paris was beginning to rival London as a market for new international loans. France was also the beneficiary of the creation in 1865 of the Latin Monetary Union. One of the earlier attempts at European monetary union, it was created by France, Italy, Belgium, and Switzerland (later followed by the Papal States, Greece, Rumania, and some shadowing by Spain) to bring about a common bimetallic currency system. The Union functioned well in its first few years—as monetary unions always seem to during periods of easy capital flows—and one of its results was a significant buildup of gold reserves at the Banque de France. Ultimately, though, the Union was unable to survive the wars and financial crises of the next several years, and although it was not formally disbanded until 1926, its importance was eroded by the end of the century.

Financial innovation was not limited to France and the United States. Germany also saw a similar expansion of its banking system and in the creation of joint-stock corporations. During the 1866–73 period, so many joint-stock companies were created that the period is known as the *Gründerzeit*, or the founders' era. Most of the new German banks had been created in the 1850s, but as a financially backward and fragmented market, it took nearly two decades for them to develop and unify the provincial money and credit markets. Of course, the Franco-Prussian indemnity payment was a huge spur to money creation and to the establishment of these new banks, particularly since the German authorities decided to issue new gold coins with the proceeds of the payment but had mistakenly issued them before the old silver ones had been withdrawn.[22] In Austria, similarly, bank capital, which had amounted to 190 million gulden in 1866, had exploded to 508 million gulden by the end of 1872. In the first three months of 1873, fifteen new banks were established with additional paid-up capital of 72 million gulden.[23]

The international lending boom started out reasonably enough. It was spurred largely by the need to finance trade activities between the European powers, primarily Great Britain, and the peripheral

21. Kindleberger, *Financial History*, p. 113.
22. Charles P. Kindleberger, *Historical Economics* (University of California Press, 1990), pp. 310–17.
23. Hyndman, *Commercial Crises*, p. 104.

nations, although Great Power rivalries had an important effect on loan flows, particularly in France and Germany. In Latin America, local governments had finally worked out their loan problems during the thirty years following the 1825 crisis. Thanks to Latin American export revenues from booming commodity prices and the shipping of Peruvian guano, the region had also become an increasingly important export market to British and other European countries.

As the payment record on the merchant advances against imports rebuilt confidence, the region began returning to the capital markets in the 1850s, although many of the early transactions were done largely to refinance or restructure older defaulted debt. During this time the gold booms in California and Australia were responsible for an expansion both in international gold holdings and in human migration as workers and miners traveled in huge numbers from Europe, the east coast of the United States, Chile, and even Asia to the gold mining centers. The large migrations and enthusiasm for gold brought with them the need to develop an enormous transportation infrastructure that tied regions in Latin America, the Pacific, and North Africa into the first global economy (the Suez Canal, for example, was built during 1859–69). Most of these projects were financed profitably by the growing European capital markets, and a truly world trade in consumer goods ensued.

Asset prices rose steadily during the 1860s, particularly toward the end of the decade, as the long, largely uninterrupted economic boom that began in the 1850s solidified confidence. The Dutch and Germans, and to a lesser extent the English, had bought huge amounts of low-priced U.S. government bonds during the U.S. Civil War, and with the victory of the booming, self-confident North, the success of these bonds as investments whetted appetite for further adventures in international lending. The period was not without crises—the 1866 collapse of a major British bank, Overend, Guerney, which brought down several English banks, had some knock-on effects in other markets, but world markets recovered and stabilized fairly quickly.

Market behavior accelerated during the 1860s until, between 1870 and 1873, during the period of French reparations, the markets seemed to change and speculative activity stepped up markedly. World commodity prices, which had been rising but generally steady over the previous decade, suddenly shot up. An *Economist* article from December 30, 1871, lists the price increases *during the year* for a number of commodities, including 67% for wool, 16% for cotton, 24% for iron, 27% for copper, and 6% for wheat.[24] In Germany and Austria, a sudden explosion of new banks dedicated to the mortgage

---

24. Reprinted in Walter Bagehot, *Lombard Street: A Description of the Money Market* (1873; reprint, John Wiley, 1999), p. 140.

market helped finance a construction boom that, combined with the frantic run-up in securities prices, plunged the country into a series of notorious stock swindles that came close to bringing scandal to Bismarck's government.[25]

In the United States, the New York Stock Exchange was engulfed in a speculative frenzy surrounding railway stocks and bonds, and stock market operators like Jay Gould and Diamond Jim Brady quickly became leading players and notorious figures in what had become a deep, dishonest market. In England the stock market skyrocketed, and British investors, after buying £57 million of Latin American bonds during the whole of the 1860s, scooped up £59 million in the first three years of the decade.[26] Marichal writes that during this period

> all the Latin American states were besieged by the European moneylenders, who urged them into the financial fray. Under the circumstances, it is not surprising that few politicians or bankers took precautions to deal with a possible abrupt change in the international economic climate.[27]

At the risk of becoming tedious, it is worth identifying once again the same sequence in the lending cycle. The sudden expansion of international lending was accompanied and preceded by a burst of speculative activity in the local markets, all of this preceded by sudden rapid European money creation. Although international lending to LDCs grew throughout the 1860s, most of the lending (over half) occurred during the very short period after 1870.

The Baring Crisis and the Lending Booms of the Twentieth Century

Peru was the biggest Latin American borrower in the 1870s, and the subsequent crisis of 1873 was devastating for the country, so much so that it remained on the sidelines fifteen years later during the next Latin American lending boom. Pride of place, in this case, belongs to Argentina, whose borrowings were so great that when it found itself unable to repay its debt in 1890, the crisis threatened to bankrupt England's largest merchant bank, Baring Brothers. Although this lending boom is limited and perhaps less of a typical LDC boom then some of the others, Argentina being a fairly rich and credible country at the time, it nonetheless was the recipient of a standard liquidity expan-

25. Kindleberger, *Financial History*, pp. 126–27.
26. Marichal, *Century of Debt Crisis*, pp. 243–45.
27. Ibid., p. 97.

sion in England. Kindleberger credits a major conversion of British government obligations in 1887 under Viscount George Joachim Goschen, chancellor of the exchequer, for setting off the loan boom, although interest rates had been very low throughout the decade.[28] The Goschen conversion, similar to the one associated with the Bank Act of 1822, resulted in a partial payment of the debt and a significant reduction of coupons. The conversion, by lowering the yield on British Treasury instruments, forced investors to look elsewhere for yield and resulted in an almost immediate rise in the value of French and Prussian bonds.

Although Argentina had borrowed from the London markets in the 1820s and 1860s, it was economically insignificant for most of this period. It wasn't until it had completed the conquest of the wheat-growing pampas and strengthened federal rule by putting down in 1879 the last Buenos Aires insurrection that the country began to emerge as a major exporter to Europe of wheat and leather. The sailing of the ice-packing *Frigorifique* in 1876 also began its highly profitable export of chilled meat, and over the next few years Argentina grew rapidly as an important exporter of agricultural commodities. By 1881, the country had reformed its currency and banking sector and, under the leadership of General Julio Roca, began to borrow heavily for a variety of infrastructure and military expenditures. By 1889, between 40% and 50% of all British funds invested outside the United Kingdom went to Argentina.[29] I will discuss the aftermath of the Argentine loan boom in chapter 5.

It is unnecessary to go into great detail on the subsequent Twentieth-Century international lending expansions to LDCs since they have been much discussed by historians and economists and the literature on the subject is well known. It is enough to summarize the key liquidity events that preceded the booms. The boom in the first two decades of the twentieth-century, which was really an extension of the good liquidity conditions prevalent under the gold standard period, was preceded, again, by significant innovation in the banking system. This included a very rapid growth in industrial borrowings and the expansion of an increasingly important and liquid banking system based in New York. It was in the 1910s, after all, that U.S. commercial banks established their first overseas branches, in Argentina. That cycle ended with the beginning of the First World War of 1914–18.

In the 1920s, as I discussed in the previous chapter, the huge accumulation of gold in New York following the First World War set the

28. Kindleberger, *Manias, Panics, and Crashes*, p. 255.
29. Barry Eichengreen, "The Baring Crisis in a Mexican Mirror," *International Political Science Review* 20, no. 3 (July 1999): 252–54.

stage for the boom. An explosion of margin lending and call loans in the New York stock markets exacerbated this growth in high-powered money. Finally, the decision by the New York Federal Reserve Bank, under Benjamin Strong, to lower U.S. interest rates in 1927 in order to accommodate the Bank of England's attempts to raise gold set the final stage for the euphoria. The investing frenzy drove up the prices of assets as diverse as Latin loans, ships, major commodities, and of course U.S. stocks.

The next major twentieth-century LDC lending boom, as I also discussed in the previous chapter, was the LDC loan frenzy of the 1970s, often attributed to the explosive growth of the Eurodollar market. The Eurodollar market was the name given to the market surrounding the dollar accumulation in the banking system outside the United States during the "dollar glut" period of low U.S. interest rates in the 1960s. It consisted for the most part of dollar deposits in commercial banks, which funded dollar loans to international entities. Originally centered in Geneva and Zurich, the market eventually migrated to London, where major U.S. and foreign banks set up important lending operations.

The Eurodollar market developed in the late 1950s and 1960s largely because of the need by certain entities—notably the USSR, concerned about possible confiscation of its dollar assets by the United States in case of hostilities—to hold dollar deposits outside the U.S. banking system. Its importance was strengthened by the passage in 1964 of Lyndon Johnsons's interest equalization tax, which was passed as part of the effort to slow down the flow of dollars abroad. The tax, along with capital controls imposed at approximately the same time, was designed to reduce foreign borrowing in the United States and U.S. lending abroad by taxing U.S. purchases of foreign securities. This created a strong incentive to push the lending process offshore, and U.S. and international banks began setting up operations in Europe for this purpose.

In 1970–71, Federal Reserve Chairman Arthur Burns, during a period of tight German monetary policy, decided to loosen U.S. monetary policy; critics later claimed that this was done primarily to help Richard Nixon's 1972 reelection campaign. "I hear all about the balance of payments and nobody worries about 8% unemployment," Nixon angrily said during a 1970 meeting with his advisors.[30] The Fed decision to loosen, perhaps a way of addressing the 8% unemployment, may have helped the Eurodollar market take off by encouraging a large outflow of dollars out of the low interest rate environment of the United States into Europe's higher interest rate environment. As

---

30. Danniell B. Mitchell, "Dismantling the Cross of Gold: Economic Crises and U.S. International Monetary Policy," *CIBER Working Paper Series* 99–25 (1999), p. 14.

dollars flowed into Europe, European central banks began exchanging them with the United States for U.S. gold reserves. One of the consequences of the dollar outflows that occurred during this period was the decision by President Nixon in August 1971 to end the 1944 Bretton Woods agreement by closing the gold window by which the United States was committed to buy and sell gold at $35 an ounce. With the subsequent OPEC price hikes beginning in 1973, in which the price of oil rose from $2 to nearly $40 a barrel in the course of the decade, oil-exporting countries were flooded with dollars. Given their small economies, they were unable to spend the money quickly enough, and the balance accumulated in the Eurodollar deposit market. The accumulation of dollar deposits in the world's major banks was mirrored by the growing trade deficits typical of oil-importing LDCs.

As confidence in the import-substitution economic policies practiced by many LDCs grew, it seemed natural to recycle OPEC surpluses into balance-of-payment loans to LDCs. The initial loans were very successful and, after surviving the difficulties of the oil price hike, LDC economies began responding to the capital inflows with local GDP growth. Within a few years bank lending to LDCs mushroomed to insane proportions. Even a near-crisis in 1975–76 involving, among other countries, Mexico and Peru, only slowed growth down temporarily, and by the end of the decade many of the world's largest banks had lent multiples of their equity base to developing countries.

The Current Lending Boom

Every international lending boom seems to be preceded and accompanied by the same economic phenomena. I have discussed this in chapter 3, and the description of the cycles in this chapter bears it out. First, some structural event significantly expands the definition of money and leads to a rapid credit expansion. Second, an asset boom in the domestic markets encourages increasingly risky behavior by successful investors. Finally, some event sets off the fashion for foreign securities, and money pours into LDCs. In the next chapter, I will discuss the outcome of this process as it occurred during the international lending booms of the last 180 years. Before doing so, it is worth discussing some of the possible causes for the most recent LDC lending cycle—the emerging markets boom of the 1990s. Are we seeing a global liquidity expansion today, or is something else driving the asset inflation in the emerging markets?

How much money is flowing into these countries? Table 4.2 shows the World Bank's calculations for capital flows to LDCs during the 1990s. Official flows declined from $37 billion in 1991 to a $1 billion

Table 4.2. Capital flows to LDCs

US$ billions	1991	1992	1993	1994	1995	1996	1997	1998
Net official flows	37	22	20	2	26	−1	24	42
Net private flows	124	119	182	153	193	212	149	64
Net direct investment	31	36	57	83	97	116	143	131
Net portfolio	37	51	114	106	41	81	67	37
Other net investment	56	33	11	−36	55	15	−60	−103
Net capital flows	160	142	202	154	219	211	173	106
Change in reserves	−62	−52	−76	−67	−120	−109	−61	−35

Source: World Bank

outflow by 1996. During this period, however, total flows increased by more than 30% annually to $211 billion, powered mostly by expansions in private sector debt and FDI (Foreign direct investment).

Optimists may believe that the current round of foreign investment reflects a new reality of triumphant capitalism, globalization, and the abandonment of failed state-driven economic policies. There is little evidence, however, that the world is more hospitable to capital today in a way that is radically different from any previous historical period. It is more reasonable to believe that the world is simply undergoing another major liquidity expansion. At least three things are probably responsible for the current expansion—and they resemble some of the factors I have identified in the past. First, and most important, U.S. savers seem to be going through a transformation in which, whether or not they are marginally saving more, they are switching their savings out of low-velocity real estate and into high-velocity stocks and bonds. As evidence, the ratio of total residential mortgages to total residential real estate value was more or less constant from the early 1960s until around 1982–84, when it began to rise sharply. This suggests that American savers are saving less in relative terms in the form of the equity in their homes and, presumably, more in other forms, primarily stocks and bonds.

This increase in mortgages has been combined with one of the big recent innovations in finance, the development of an active and liquid market for mortgage securities. The net effect was that the capital "imbedded" in U.S. real estate was increasingly monetized in a way that resembled the land speculation frenzy of the 1830s, when speculative investment in stocks, commodities, and real estate was funded by loans collateralized by the real estate.

The second factor that may be a cause of the liquidity expansion is the recycling of trade surpluses. Japan (along with other Asian countries) has been running a huge trade surplus, which began growing rapidly in the early to middle 1980s. The Japanese typically recycle this surplus by investing in foreign securities, primarily highly liquid U.S. Treasuries and large cap U.S. stocks. The effect is as if U.S. consumption were transformed through the trade account into a huge increase in total savings.

Finally, a third factor in the liquidity expansion, although much more difficult to quantify, is the tremendous flight of capital out of Russia that has occurred in the past decade as Russians loot their country's export earnings and place the money in banks in Europe. It is too early to get much of a historical overview of the current period, but each of these factors is of a sufficiently large magnitude that it will have had some measurable impact. The combination of these three events, and possibly others, seems to have resulted in a market awash in liquidity and one in which investors are searching for new investment opportunities.

5

The Contraction of International Lending

Liquidity Sequence

It would have been useful for my argument to measure expansions and contractions in global liquidity conditions in some objective way and to correlate these directly with expansions and contractions in international lending. The difficulty in doing so is that monetary expansion is a dynamic process, and it is extremely difficult to point to a single variable or group of variables that identify the expansion in each of the different cases. Liquidity is a complex enough concept, that there is no easy way to quantify it, and liquidity expansions can come about in many forms. I have identified in my 180-year history and discussed in this book a variety of ways they can occur, such as direct expansions of gold reserves, the sudden rapid creation of banks and joint stock holding companies, large money transfers and recyclings, the creation of large, actively traded bond issues, securitization of real estate, etcetera. For this reason I have tried to list the expansionary events associated with each of the lending cycles.

In this chapter I will pick up the story of the LDC lending process of the last 180 years from the beginning of the international lending booms described in the previous chapter. Once again, the point of this account is not simply to recount the history of international lending but rather to identify the major liquidity components of the lending sequence and to confirm that it is primarily changes in global liquidity, not in local growth prospects, that determine the lending cycle. And once again there is no obvious variable that represents a collapse in liquidity, although the evidence of such a collapse—sharp rises in real interest rates and the hoarding of liquidity by the banking system—is more straightforward. Whereas liquidity expansions can happen for a variety of reasons, all sharp liquidity contractions seem to occur in a very limited number of ways.

I showed in chapter 4 that the expansionary sequences have the following form:

1. A banking innovation or other change in financial structure in a capital center causes an expansion in the money base. Bank lending to local borrowers increases.
2. A period of economic growth and asset price growth follows.
3. Asset price growth and the easy availability of money causes an increase in investor risk appetite, and investment behavior becomes speculative.
4. Some event turns attention to international loans, and the market for international lending quickly takes off.

I will argue in this chapter that the end of the international lending boom is, like its beginning, determined primarily by a change of conditions in the world financial centers. The point I want to make is that although the decisions to invest or to withdraw from LDCs may be couched in terms that refer primarily to growth and profit opportunities in the LDC markets, in fact they too seem to be driven largely by external events. As in chapter 4 I will discuss the first three cycles in greater detail since these establish the basic patterns and are generally less well known.

The Panic of 1825

In chapter 4 I ended the discussion of the 1820s with the Colombian loan of 1822. At that time, England was in the midst of a speculative binge, with a wide variety of companies coming to the local markets to raise capital. A few very successful European loans associated with the French reparations following the Napoleonic wars had whetted investor appetite for foreign adventures, and the Colombian loan was one of the first to tap into this. For Colombia the loan was not a great success, since its novelty and the uses of the proceeds ensured that Colombia was saddled with a large debt from which it derived little in the way of actual proceeds. For the capital markets, however, the Colombia loan was an unqualified success. Bankers made very large profits on limited risk. Investors who were receiving 4% on their British government consols were eager to purchase debt obligations at initial prices ranging from 80% to 84% of face value, bearing 6% coupons, from a country that, as many investors and journalists pointed out at the time, seemed really no different from the United States forty years earlier. The Colombian bond quickly traded up in the secondary market.

Thanks to the success of the Colombian loan, that year, 1822, saw several other sovereigns borrowers come to market. Chile issued £1 million in bonds, Peru issued £450 thousand, Denmark put in for £2 million (at a very similar yield when the coupon and issue price is adjusted), and Russia, which had been a major player in the defeat of Napoleon, raised a whopping £6.5 million.[1] The most astonishing transaction was the £200 thousand offering by the Kingdom of Poyais. This was a fictitious Central American country whose self-appointed king, Sir Gregor MacGregor, was a Scottish adventurer who had fought at the side of Simon Bolivar during the independence wars (and to whom a statue in Caracas is dedicated). After its issue the bond actually traded up before brokenhearted investors realized that there was no such country—at least not one ever capable of or intending to repay any debt.

Over the next three years several other foreign loans came to market. In order of descending size Austria and Portugal issued £5 million between them in 1823. Colombia, Mexico, Naples, Brazil, Buenos Ayres (as it was then called), Greece, and Peru sold nearly £15 million in 1824. In 1825, the biggest and last year of the boom, Denmark, Mexico, Brazil, Greece, Peru, the city of Guadalajara, and Guatemala— all repeat borrowers except the last two—collectively issued more than £15 million of new bonds. Over fifty stock companies were organized in 1824 and 1825 for the sole purpose of operating in Latin America. Their authorized capital was more than £35 million, although most of this had not yet been put up when the crash came. Most of these companies were very optimistically created to mine the Andes, or other regions of the continent, even though there were no roads or engineers, few workers, and not even fuel in many of the selected places. Other projects included fishing for pearls, building steam lines, cutting canals, establishing farming colonies, selling furs and warming pans, creating butter locally, and so on. The boom was not limited to countries that issued bonds in the London markets. The United States, for example, was also experiencing an economic boom,

---

1. Frank Griffith Dawson, *The First Latin American Debt Crisis: The City of London and the 1822–25 Bubble* (Yale University Press, 1990), gives statistical tables on pp. 246–49. The list of loans and investments here and further hereafter comes from two other sources besides Dawson. These are J. Fred Rippy, "Latin America and the British Investment 'Boom' of the 1820s," *Journal of Modern History* 19, no. 2 (June 1947), and Carlos Marichal, *A Century of Debt Crises in Latin America, from Independence to the Great Depression 1820–1930* (Princeton University Press, 1989), pp. 12–41.

driven largely by sharp increases in cotton prices caused by speculation and the easy availability of credit in both countries.[2]

At first things went well for both investors and borrowers. The
lending, investment, and silver booms combined to pump fuel into
the newly emerging economies of Latin America, the United States,
southern Europe, and elsewhere. In Latin America they strengthened
the hands of the new governments who believed that the combination
of independence, republican forms of government, and integration
into the world economy would allow the region to grow as rapidly as
the United States had. Latin American consumption grew strongly,
while imports from England by 1825 were double their levels of only
four yeas earlier. But by 1825 problems were already beginning to lay
themselves out in a pattern that would later become very familiar.
First, it became clear that many of the investments were of very ques-
tionable value, and the extent of speculative activity began to worry
some bankers and government officials. In the spring of 1825 England's Lord Liverpool, chancellor of the exchequer, went so far as to
publicly warn the market that speculators had gone too far and in
case of problems the government would not save them.

The unraveling of the market started in early 1825, as it often does,
with a central bank response to gold depletion and subsequent weak
commodity prices. After a several-year period in which Bank of England bullion reserves had risen steadily, reserves experienced a dramatic decline from £14 million in 1824 to £2 million by late 1825.
This occurred largely because of the rapid expansion of British imports over the 1822–25 period combined with the capital exports associated with foreign investment. This loss of reserves began to worry
Bank officials and forced them to raise the discount rate so that they
could begin to reaccumulate gold. Their gold hoarding severely interrupted the outflow of funds until 1827, when reserves stabilized at
around £10 million.[3]

The break in commodity prices was caused partly by overproduction, partly by the recovery of inventories after the great wars,
and partly because of the selling of excess stock due to speculative
hoarding. The rise in interest rates increased the financing costs of
holding stock and put selling pressure on hoarders. As prices declined, several English banks that had lent against coffee, tin, iron,
sugar, and cotton began to experience problems with their loans. By
October, both the domestic and foreign loan markets were trading

2. Burke Adrian Parsons, *British Trade Cycles and American Bank Credit:
Some Aspects of Economic Fluctuations in the United States 1815–1840* (Arno
Press 1977), p. 209.

3. Parsons, *British Trade Cycles*, p. 118.

poorly in London. A number of failures among cotton-trading firms in November caused the Bank of England to tighten credit, which worsened overall economic conditions and caused further asset price declines. In mid-December, two major London banks that acted as agents for dozens of provincial banks, mostly in the Yorkshire textile region, collapsed. This set off the general panic.

Over the next few weeks as panic selling hit commodity prices, several more London banks and over sixty provincial banks were forced to close. Altogether seventy-six of the 806 banks in England and Scotland closed their doors permanently during the crisis period, and Walter Bagehot says that the Bank of England itself was nearly forced to suspend payments.[4] The remaining banks, of course, in order to protect their balance sheets, began calling in loans and raising liquidity as rapidly as they could, which forced industrial companies to cut back production and lay off workers. By February 1826 there were riots among weavers at Norwich, and these spread throughout the country in the next three months. By the summer of 1826, the crisis had spread to Berlin, Amsterdam, St. Petersburg, Vienna, Rome, and Paris. In the general panic, as banking houses fell one after the other, the remaining solvent European banks desperately hoarded money and in so doing forced the a general collapse in liquidity conditions worldwide.

The effect on the smaller sovereign borrowers, including Latin American borrowers, was nearly immediate. After mid-1825 there were no more new foreign loans in the British market until 1828, when Spain, using its substantial mercury production as collateral, raised £600 thousand for British compensation claims that had originated during their civil war. The drying-up of financing was combined with the accelerating decline in commodity prices caused by the collapse of European demand. These two events ensured that the new republics of Latin America were completely unable to raise the gold necessary to make interest and principal payments on their debt, and beginning in 1826, payments were halted on one loan after the other. By 1829, every Latin American borrower except Brazil had defaulted, although even Brazil, in 1829, required an emergency "new money" loan of £800 thousand, arranged by Rothschild at an issue price of 54%, to make its interest payments. The losses to British investors were huge, and the pages of the British press were filled with anger, bluster, and threats. It would take a full generation before Latin American borrowers would be able fully to regain the international markets, but only a decade before a new international loan mania swept through Great Britain.

4. Walter Bagehot, *Lombard Street: A Description of the Money Market* (1873; reprint, John Wiley, 1999), p. 39.

The Second Loan Crisis and the Panic of 1837

In chapter 4 I discussed the events leading up to the English lending spree of the mid-1830s, in which a domestic speculative frenzy and a new infatuation with U.S. prospects, combined with the chaotic expansion of the U.S. banking system, created the conditions for an expanding liquidity pool. English investors poured money into a wide variety of ventures, including significant lending to several U.S. states, which were considered, in those pre–Civil War times, to be quasi-sovereign borrowers. Money poured into railroads and canals, and the price of cotton and other commodities boomed. In the United States, land speculation reached levels unprecedented in the country's history, as the government sold off large plots of remote land.

The frenzy raged during the 1830s, but by 1836 it was clear to cooler heads on both sides of the Atlantic, and particularly at the Bank of England, that the markets were at risk of being seriously overextended. In May, J. Poulett Thompson, the then-president of the British Board of Trade, complained that the only difference between the current market and that of 1825 was that investors were throwing their money away mostly on worthless domestic schemes as opposed to foreign ones. Nicholas Biddle, at the bank of the United States, worried about the uncontrolled money creation in the U.S. banking system. In France and Belgium, government warnings against speculation became fairly regular.[5] For a while none of these warnings seemed to matter, but eventually the money creation had to reverse itself.

The collapse started on both sides of the Atlantic at roughly the same time. In July 1836, in what Bray Hammond, in his indispensable account of early U.S. banking history, calls the only administrative act that was actually consistent with his hard money beliefs, President Andrew Jackson changed the rules of the land speculation game: he issued the "specie circular," which required that all land purchases be paid for in gold or silver. If banks had to lend to land speculators in the form of gold or silver, rather than with their own promissory notes, their ability to lend was sharply constrained by the actual gold and silver deposits they had on hand. Without easy credit, most speculators did not have the means by which to buy the land, so the specie circular effectively eliminated the credit expansion that had fueled the land boom.

Coincidentally, by 1836 the Bank of England had started to become nervous about the possibility of a repeat of the 1820s speculative excess and about the flow of gold to the United States, and it began to rein in money creation. Bullion reserves, which had climbed up to

5. Charles P. Kindleberger, *Manias, Panics, and Crashes: A History of Financial Crises* (Basic Books, 1989), pp. 109–11.

£11 million in the early part of the decade, had by 1835 dropped to £6 million, and to £4 million in 1836.[6] In order to replenish its gold reserves the bank raised the discount rate from 4% to 4½% in July, and then again to 5% in August. At first the increase in rates and reduction in deposits in the private banking system had little effect, because English banks simply increased their money creation to compensate for the Bank of England's tightening by increasing the ratio of outstanding loans, notes, and currency to gold reserves. However, when news of the specie circular reached the Bank, it understood the consequences sufficiently that, in an unfortunately clumsy and scaremongering way, it let it be known that it would not accept for discount the notes of banking houses with excessive U.S. exposure. The credit contraction began fairly quickly after that.[7]

As merchant-banking houses with U.S. business sold off cotton inventory to meet their liquidity needs, the price of cotton, the major U.S. export commodity, declined sharply, from 8 shillings to 5 ½ shillings within the first three months of 1837—a drop of more than 30%.[8] The drop in value of primary export earner and an important collateral asset accelerated the liquidity contraction in the United States. Banking houses in New Orleans and New York began closing in 1837, and the British, beginning to suffer from their own economic slowdown, cut off all further lending.

With private banks rushing to raise their own gold holdings to protect their ability to pay back depositors, the Bank of England continued to lose reserves and had to apply for an extraordinary £2 million gold loan from the Bank of France. Even with the loan, reserves dropped to £2.4 million.[9] Nicholas Biddle, president of the former Bank of the United States, now-renamed United States Bank of Pennsylvania, began a public-spirited but doomed attempt to hold up cotton prices by single-handedly cornering the cotton market. The attempt ultimately failed and like the rest of the U.S. banking system the Bank was forced in 1839 to suspend payments, finally closing in 1841, to great European consternation. For many of the European houses the Bank of the United States was seen as the U.S. equivalent of the Bank of England. Its suspension came as enough of a shock that it was part of the reason for the Rothschilds' subsequent reluctance to open a bank in the United States—probably the biggest strategic mistake in the history of the Rothschilds.

6. Parsons, *British Trade Cycles*, p. 118.

7. Bray Hammond, *Banks and Politics in America from the Revolution to the Civil War* (1957; reprint, Princeton University Press, 1985), pp. 455–58, and Douglass C. North, *The Economic Growth of the United States, 1790–1860* (W. W. Norton, 1966), pp. 199–203.

8. Parsons, *British Trade Cycles*, p. 301.

9. Bagehot, *Lombard Street*, 1999, p. 179.

The loans made by British investors in the United States were never made to the federal government (which had actually retired the entire U.S. federal debt with the substantial fiscal surplus generated throughout this period under the conservative Jackson). They had been made, instead, to a variety of private borrowers and to several states. The state governments were the most burdened, particularly since tax revenue was generally low and most revenues consisted of land sales—now sharply reduced because of the specie circular—and various forms of import revenues, now on a collapsing import base.

When these borrowers were simultaneously faced with lower import earnings, slowing economic activity, and a standstill in refinancing, they were wholly unable to raise sufficient amounts of gold to make the required payments. The result was predictable. By 1842, at the bottom of the depression, Pennsylvania, one of the richest states and heaviest borrowers, suspended interest payments. By then, Arkansas, Florida, Illinois, Indiana, Maryland, Michigan, and Mississippi had already defaulted, along with much of the U.S. banking system. Pennsylvania eventually resumed interest and principal payments, but Mississippi, Arkansas, and Florida, with "carefully rationalized arguments" simply repudiated the debt outright.[10]

The international loan crisis was not exclusively an American crisis, but given its huge wealth, promise, and the amounts lent, it was perceived primarily as a U.S. crisis. States governments, just by themselves and excluding private borrowers, defaulted or rescheduled $120 million of loans.[11] The European reaction to American perfidy was outrage. By the end of the decade James Rothschild, the head of the French branch of the House of Rothschild, was reported to have told a visiting representative of the U.S. Treasury, in typical Rothschildian pomposity, "you may tell your government that you have seen the man who is the head of the finances of Europe, and that he has told you that you cannot borrow a dollar, not a dollar."[12] The fury and sense of betrayal of English investors led to an outpouring of hatred and scorn for the American rascals, and English literature is the richer for the many scathing diatribes that followed. But it should

10. Paul Studenski and Herman Krooss, *Financial History of the United States: Fiscal, Monetary, Banking and Tariff, Including Financial Administration and State and Local Finance* (McGraw-Hill, 1952), p. 118. For an account of the reasons for the state defaults, see Richard Sylla and John J. Wallis, "The Anatomy of Sovereign Debt Crises: Lessons from the American State Defaults of the 1840s," in *Japan and the World Economy 290* (Elsevier, 1997).

11. Christian Suter, *Debt Cycles in the World Economy: Foreign Loans, Financial Crises, and Debt Settlements, 1820–1990* (Westview Press, 1992), p. 69.

12. Niall Ferguson, *The House of Rothschild: Money's Prophets 1798–1848* (Penguin Books, 1999), p. 374.

be noted that Spain and Portugal also participated in the loan cycle both on the way up and on the way down.

The Loan Crisis of 1873

I listed in chapter 4 the sequence of financial events, beginning with a series of banking innovations that led to a rapid expansion of currency and culminating in the French indemnity payment following the Franco-Prussian war, that preceded the speculative frenzy of the 1860s and early 1870s. Once again, the boom followed the pattern established in the previous crises—first, rapid money expansion in Europe, followed by an increase in speculative activity among European investors and an outburst of enthusiasm for "new" prospects in foreign countries. As in earlier cycles, the contraction of lending also began in Europe. In this particular case the crisis of 1873 began in Vienna.

I have discussed the rapid expansion during the first years of the decade of the Viennese stock and land markets, with prices reaching unprecedented levels. Kindleberger claims that by the beginning of 1873 there was a general sense that the Viennese market was overvalued and unsustainable, but investors were looking forward to the World Exhibition to be opened in Vienna on May 1. They were irrationally hoping that the Exhibition would change the underlying situation and somehow justify the high asset prices. During April of that year, in response to a period of weak and declining stock prices, the local banking authorities became concerned about the position of banks and made a series of attempts to support the market. As a precaution, however, nervous banks were contracting credit and attempting to raise liquidity by calling in loans. When the Exhibition opened on May 1 and, not surprisingly, nothing really changed, investors lost heart and began selling.[13]

The selling pressure in the market built steadily. On May 5 and 6 the market began falling, and on May 8 it suddenly crashed. With the crash a full-blown panic began in Vienna that was almost immediately felt throughout the country as banks and investors rushed to dump assets. The panic spread quickly to the German money markets, but these were able at first to shrug off the bad news, and the equity markets held on reasonably well. In New York, however, news of the Viennese crash unnerved investors, who had been swamped with railway securities over the previous months and years. These railway securities were extensively used by speculators as collateral against loans whose proceeds were invested in additional securities. When a

13. Charles Kindleberger, *A Financial History of Western Europe* (Oxford University Press, 1993), p. 270.

bank that had extended too much credit against southern railway bonds was forced to close in early September, the nervousness spread further until, in a tremendous shock to confidence, the house of Jay Cooke & Company—America's largest private bank, financial agent to the U.S. government, and one of the leading innovators in financing the Civil War—was forced to close on September 18 because of its holdings of Northern Pacific Railway bonds.[14]

The news of Jay Cooke's closing was enough to break the New York exchange. That day and the next, sellers poured into the market, and as prices spiraled downward, the value of land, railway bonds, and anything else that had acted as loan collateral plunged as forced liquidations threw them into the market. Within a very short time banks around the country were forced to suspend payments as their ability to raise liquidity to pay depositors evaporated. The panic was so deep that in mid-September, for the first time in its history, the New York Stock Exchange closed, not to reopen till the end of the month (perhaps the first circuit breaker in the history of the exchange). The United States subsequently entered five years of what was then called the Great Depression.

In October the crisis returned across the Atlantic as the German markets crashed. England was hit in November and had to fend off the rush for gold by raising the discount rate to rebuild its gold reserves—all in all it changed the discount rate twenty-four times during this period. Russia and the Scandinavian countries were very quickly sucked into the panic. France too was affected, although only partially, since the war had pretty much kept it out of the general prosperity and the market boom. Bank after bank around the world collapsed, and as the survivors liquidated assets and hoarded gold, the familiar pattern of a sharp global liquidity contraction led to the equally familiar international inability to raise the gold necessary to make debt payments. Middle Eastern and European countries defaulted on their loans. In Latin America, none but the three wealthiest nations, Argentina, Brazil, and Chile, was able to avoid default, thanks to huge commodity export revenues even after the fall in global commodity prices. Chile's struggle was so great, however, that she lost much of her banking system and all her gold, and by 1878 the country's main bank was forced to declare its currency inconvertible.

The Baring Crisis

It is important to point out that the major international debt crises discussed so far in this chapter are not the only types of financial

14. H. M. Hyndman, *Commercial Crises of the Nineteenth Century* (1892; reprint, Allen and Unwin, 1932), pp. 99–127.

crises that can occur. Throughout this period there were also a large number of smaller, less generalized crises that could and did often leave LDC markets reeling. It is in this context that we should see the famous "Baring" crisis of 1890.

I discussed in chapter 4 the rapid expansion of international lending to Argentina in the 1880s. Because it had escaped the 1873 crisis relatively unscathed and had subsequently enjoyed an economic boom that made it one of the wealthiest countries in the world, Argentina was the darling of investors during much of the decade. It absorbed at one point over 40% of British savings invested outside the United Kingdom. Sovereign, provincial, public works, railroad, and several varieties of corporate bonds and stocks had been issued in Europe, primarily in London and Berlin, and eagerly taken up by investors. Around 1888, however, German investors, an important source of lending to Argentina, stopped buying new Argentine issues—in part because of a politically driven investment shift among Germans toward Russian bonds and the domestic markets. British lending began increasing even more rapidly as British banks and investors absorbed German holdings.

But things were beginning to get unstable. In Argentina, President Miguel Celman's inflationary policies were creating strong political opposition and nervousness about the sustainability of the currency. When British investors became concerned about political instability in Argentina in the late 1888 and 1889, the government tried to ensure confidence in the currency by converting the peso-denominated cedulas (mortgage bonds that were the largest component of foreign financing) into gold-backed cedulas. As I discussed in chapter 1 in the Mexican Tesobonos example, this is a popular central bank strategy. The government believed that if it increased the cost of devaluing to unacceptable levels, its credibility with British investors would soar. It didn't work. The biggest sign of impending trouble began when Baring Brothers, Argentina's leading banker, arranged a large £2 million offering for the Buenos Aires Water and Drainage Company and was only able to place £150 thousand. It had to take the rest onto its balance sheet.[15]

On October 8 of that year, the Bank of England, concerned by excessive outflows of gold and excessive speculation (for reasons largely unrelated to Argentina), raised its interest rate to 6%. This was the culmination of a series of rate hikes that had brought rates up from below 3% just six months earlier. Capital outflows from London slowed, and Argentina found it had difficulty raising money to continue supporting its currency. New loans declined from £23 million

15. Niall Ferguson, *The House of Rothschild: The World's Bankers: 1849–1999* (Viking, 1999), p. 340.

in 1888 to £12 million in 1889 and only £5 million in 1890.[16] In July 1890, Argentina's finance minister resigned because of his opposition to President Celman's inflationary monetary policies and, in so doing, precipitated the much-feared exchange rate crisis. In the ensuing uproar, Argentine naval officers stepped in and forced President Celman to flee. When the currency broke, the suddenly expanding cost of the gold backing on cedulas, combined with the panicked selling of pesos for gold and hard assets, forced the country into payment difficulties. As news of the devaluation, the political crisis, and Argentina's inability to make interest payments spread, the price of Argentine securities dropped to below 40% of face value.

The plunging value of Argentine securities, including the unsold Buenos Aires Water and Drainage Company bonds, nearly bankrupted Baring Brothers, whose balance sheet included several million pounds of Argentine securities (against a capital base of £2.9 million).[17] As the New York Federal Reserve Bank was to do in 1998 when it rescued Long Term Capital, the Bank of England was forced quickly to put together a consortium of private banks to rescue the Baring bank because of fears that its collapse would bring down the British financial system. The near collapse of Baring and the desperate need of the Bank of England to raise gold reserves as quickly as possible to protect itself from a full-blown banking crisis caused a rapid contraction in British and European monetary policy. New loans to LDCs declined further.

In the immediate aftermath, Argentina was the only major defaulter, but several other countries came under pressure. As the Mexican crisis was to do 105 years later, the Argentine crisis sharply reduced British lending worldwide and contributed to a series of international panics around the world for the next three years.[18] Although the crisis was fairly short-lived as far as Baring brothers and the European banking system were concerned, it was several years before Argentine borrowers would be able to access the market again.

The Crises of the Twentieth Century

It is probably unnecessary to go into great detail into the sequence of events that ended the subsequent twentieth-Century loan booms, since these events are fairly similar to the earlier breaks and far more familiar to most analysts today. The lending boom of the 1910s, which was actually the continuation of expansion in the 1880s and 1890s

16. Barry Eichengreen, "The Baring Crisis in a Mexican Mirror," *International Political Science Review* 20, no. 3 (July 1999), pp. 257–58.

17. Ferguson, *The World's Bankers*, p. 341.

18. Kindleberger, *Manias, Panics, and Crashes*, p. 147.

once the Argentina crisis had been resolved, ended, for obvious reasons, with the beginning of the First World War. Interestingly enough, the huge increase in commodity prices that accompanied the war was a major boon for the commodity-exporting LDCs. The rapid increase in export revenues that they enjoyed thanks to the war needs of the belligerents replaced capital imports as a source of foreign exchange, and so this became one of the only major international lending booms that did not end in large-scale LDC defaults. The countries that did default—Russia, Mexico, and the Ottoman Empire—did so primarily for political reasons: all three countries suffered bloody revolutions and/or political collapse during the 1910s and 1920s.

Because of the huge increase in U.S. liquidity during the period, U.S. investors largely drove the lending boom of the 1920s. The end occurred before the Great Crash of 1929, when the final, dizzying ride on the New York Stock Exchange, beginning around May 1928, along with the popularity of call loans and stocks bought on margin, sucked up all available investor money. The Great Crash and the subsequent collapse of the U.S. banking system in 1930–31 nailed shut any hope of a resumption of international lending.[19] Rather than loosening reserve requirements, the Federal Reserve System tightened on top of an already contracting money supply. There was a sudden temporary explosion of international lending in the first half of 1930, but it was too little to help. LDC countries that found themselves simultaneously unable to raise new money in the United States and unable to earn much in the way of export revenues from the depressed commodity markets after the crash faced payment difficulties and, once again, massive LDC defaults.

Finally the LDC lending frenzy of the 1970s was also killed by a sharp and brutal monetary contraction in the United States—engineered by the Federal Reserve System in 1980–81 as Federal Reserve Chairman Paul Volcker sought to crush the high inflation of the 1970s. As a result of his tight policy, interest rates soared, with the London Interbank Offer Rate (LIBOR), against which most bank loans were indexed, rising at one point to above 20%. At the same time, thanks again to the tight monetary policy, bank deposits were declining. LDCs consequently saw debt servicing costs rise at the same time that banks became unwilling to finance new loans. The result was predictable— at some point the net outflow of funds was too great for the LDCs to maintain, and, beginning with Mexico in August 1982, they began asking their creditors for debt relief.

19. The banking collapse was probably exacerbated when the French, along with to a lesser extent other European gold bloc countries, converted about $750 million of their dollar holdings into gold in 1931 in order to protect their own liquidity needs.

Long-term Liquidity Contractions versus Short-term Collapses in Margin Lending

The pattern across the seven lending cycles, from the 1820s to the 1970s, is fairly consistent. The beginning of each lending cycle was correlated across countries and associated with asset expansions in the rich-country financial centers. This can only be explained if we assume that the decision by investors to lend to LDCs is driven by rich-country factors rather than by conditions in the recipient country. In chapter 4 and this chapter I have tried to identify the major stages of the LDC lending pattern following the *liquidity* model of capital flows. Although these are described more formally and in more detail in chapter 3, I can summarize them as consisting of two exogenous shocks, each followed by local consequences. In each case, first there is some displacement that sets off a liquidity expansion in the major capital exporting countries, which is followed by the lending and investment boom in the LDC markets and, usually, a spurt of growth. At some point there is the second, usually external, shock that causes a rapid tightening or a sudden collapse in market liquidity in the major money centers. The local LDC boom quickly ends, and payment difficulties begin.

Although each of the crashes had certain similarities, in general it is necessary to distinguish between the two types of financial crises:

- *Long-term liquidity contractions.* These are periods, such as those of the 1870s, the 1930s, and the 1980s, in which rich-country financial centers undergo a long-term and severe contraction of liquidity. In these cases, the reversal of the rapid liquidity expansion that had taken place over the previous years causes an increase in real interest rates and a long-term reduction in the availability of risk capital. Sovereign borrowers that are unable to service their obligations without the high export revenues and refinancing ease typical of the liquidity expansion years can be forced into defaults and restructurings. These are the crises that are generally referred to as global debt crises since the refinancing pressure affects all high-risk assets and borrowers.
- *Short-term collapses in financing at the margin.* In these cases a sudden shock may cause a temporary collapse in margin lending that may feel like a liquidity contraction but is really nothing more than a sudden "bank run" on an international scale. There are literally dozens of examples of these types of crises in the last two centuries. They include the Overend, Guerney crisis of 1866, the Baring crisis of 1890, and the U.S. stock market crisis of 1907. More recent examples are the 1976 loan crisis in Peru and Mexico, the 1987 worldwide stock market crash, the Tequila Crisis of 1994–95, and the Asian Con-

tagion of 1997–98, when sudden shocks combined with very unstable capital structures to cause market collapses.

The latter crises do not generally lead to global defaults, whereas the former usually do. This was a point that was missed during the trough of the Asian crisis, and it is easy to confuse this. As severe as these crises were, they were not caused by a major rich-world liquidity contraction initiated by the monetary authorities or caused by market forces. The Asian crises actually came about during an "optimal" time in which U.S. and European liquidity conditions were stable or expansionary. One of its undoubted consequences was a temporary "flight to quality" as investors around the world withdrew loans and cut trading lines.

Although this may have felt like a severe liquidity contraction, it was different from most of the crises I have described in this chapter (except the 1890 crisis) and really represents a quickly reversible margin collapse, not a collapse in underlying rich-country liquidity. It was in effect a sort of "run on the bank" in which investors temporarily withdrew funds because of concerns about the instability of the Asian borrowing structures. Conditions in the Asian markets stabilized once liquidity facilities were reestablished, although the pain experienced by the Asian working and middle classes was very real and persisted.

It is worth noting that one consequence of the Asian crisis was actually an increase in the accumulation of liquidity among international funds available for investment elsewhere. Table 5.1 shows why. As the Asian countries found themselves facing very sharp reversals in capital flows, their current accounts were forced to respond, and they all made major adjustments, usually by contracting imports, from current account deficits to large, in some case massive, surpluses. South Korea, for example, transformed deficits of 4–5% of GDP into surpluses exceeding 10% of GDP. In all, the five countries most afflicted saw a $124 billion *annual* swing in their current accounts between 1996 and 1998. These surpluses were recycled to the outside

Table 5.1. Net capital flows: Indonesia, Malaysia, Philippines, South Korea, and Thailand (US$ billions)

	1995	1996	1997	1998
Current account	−41	−55	−26	69
Private flows	80	102	0	−28
Equity investment	15	19	4	14
Private creditors	65	84	−4	−41

Source: Institute for International Finance

world in the form of loan repayments or purchases of U.S. Treasury instruments as bank reserves were rebuilt, and so were made available for relending into other markets. The Asian crisis, ironically, led indirectly to a major buildup of liquidity, primarily in the United States., which may have contributed to the strong stock and high-yield markets and undoubtedly helped subsequently power the Latin American debt markets to record new issuance in the first quarter of 1998.

As I will discuss in the next three chapters, when these temporary crises are combined with capital structures that amplify the effect of external shocks, they are dangerous and can lead to individual sovereign and corporate defaults. In such cases, the borrowing LDC may simply be unable to absorb the impact of the shock as debt servicing costs rise quickly against rapid declines in debt-servicing capabilities—a common enough phenomenon, as I will show later in this book. When this happens, even though overall liquidity conditions may be favorable for capital flows, the individual borrower may find itself in the position of a bank that has mismanaged its asset-liability structure and breaks down. Unlike major liquidity contractions, margin collapses should not lead to sovereign defaults. If a country has designed a risky capital structure, however, these temporary phenomena can overwhelm LDC borrowers and force them into suspending payments—much as an otherwise healthy bank can be forced to suspend payments during a bank run.

The major conclusion that arises from the *liquidity* model is that as far as the LDC recipient is concerned, the important turning points in the investment decision are largely exogenous, although domestic shocks can also cause short-term investor withdrawals. For the most part, however, they do not reflect local activity and performance as much as external and even global events. This is actually a more general point. Charles Kindleberger has complained about commentators who describe the financial crises that have occurred within their countries as if they were primarily of local origins and consequences. Many of these crises, he argues, were clearly international in scope and occurred in different forms simultaneously across borders.[20] Whereas most crises have proximate causes that may be domestic, the underlying conditions that cause the local shock are often global in scope and reflect changes in international monetary conditions. This is even truer of LDCs, with their relatively small economies.

20. He specifically mentions the U.S. crises of 1873 and 1829, the Overend, Gurney crisis and the Italian *corso forzoso* crisis, both of 1866, and the Baring crisis of 1890. See Charles P. Kindleberger, *Historical Economics* (University of California Press, 1990), pp. 310–11.

PART III

THE CORPORATE FINANCE OF CRISES

In part II I established the liquidity framework for international lending. I argued that because international investment is driven largely by short-term and long-term exogenous factors, LDCs have little to no control over the overall size of capital flows except, at best, in influencing the relative direction of flows among themselves during liquidity periods.

This has very important implications for liability management policies. For one, since short-term shocks in which foreign capital surges into or abruptly withdraws from an LDC are inevitable, the national capital structure must be explicitly designed to defend national economic policies from the impact of these disruptive shocks. There is a wide body of corporate finance literature that discusses how to protect economic entities from market shocks at the corporate level, but it has not been applied to economic management at the national level. In chapter 6 I review the corporate finance framework and show how it can be applied to sovereigns. In chapter 7 I discuss how unstable capital structures can result in an almost mechanical process of financial collapse, and I introduce the concept of a capital structure trap that leaves a country vulnerable to such a collapse. In chapter 8 I propose a liability management function at the sovereign level and discuss what its obligations should be. Finally, in chapter 9, I discuss the consequences of debt crises and the debt restructuring process within a corporate finance framework.

6

The Theory of Capital Structure and Financial Risk

Managing Shocks

In this chapter I will discuss the corporate finance implications on sovereigns of external shocks. Although much of the following discussion may be easily understandable to readers with strong backgrounds in finance theory, parts of it may be rougher at first for those without. For LDCs, external shocks usually mean one or both of two things—a sudden collapse in commodity prices or a sudden contraction of global liquidity. Because of the huge volume of international capital flows, the latter, in particular, can be very large relative to the size of most LDC economies. In table 6.1 I list the magnitude of certain capital flow reversals experienced by LDCs in recent decades. The reversal reflects the difference between inflows and outflows, as a percentage of GDP, over the indicated years. As the table shows, the size of these reversals can be extremely high.

Because LDCs are primarily commodity producers, both the volatility of commodity prices *and* the volatility of global liquidity are important sources of LDC shocks. Furthermore, as I discussed in chapter 2, the composition of the investor base can act to amplify the effect of this volatility by changing the trading characteristics of the market. Because these three sources of volatility have historically been highly correlated, it is almost a part of the definition of an LDC that its economy is extremely sensitive to external factors.

There are other kinds of shocks, of course. For oil importers, for example, the balance-of-payments impact of the oil price increases of the 1970s was actually analogous to a collapse of commodity prices.

Table 6.1. Selected capital flow reversals

Country	Period	Reversal as % of GDP
Argentina	1982–1983	20
Mexico	1981–1983	12
Malaysia	1993–1994	10
Turkey	1993–1994	10
Venezuela	1992–1994	9
Chile	1990–1991	8

Source: Private Capital Flows to Developing Countries 1997[1]

A war in another country or a significant increase in international tensions can cause a flight to quality in the asset markets, and this may feel a lot like a global liquidity contraction. There are also other shocks that are less market linked and so harder to hedge—a foreign invasion, for example, or domestic political instability. In this chapter I will examine how capital structure affects the way external shocks impact local operations for corporations as well as sovereigns. In order to do so I will discuss the role of corporate finance in maximizing value, analyze the relationship between volatility and asset value, and examine how volatility affects the probability of financial distress.

Before I discuss the capital structure and corporate finance implications of this volatility, it is worth repeating my discussion in chapter 1 of what I mean by corporate finance: a reference to the "corporate finance" implications of the model does not mean the effect of liquidity on private corporations. Instead it refers to the relationship between any entity, private or public, and its capital structure, and encompasses issues such as the effect of capital structure on earnings volatility, the process and goals of liability management, the identifying and indexing of sources of volatility, the hedging process, etcetera. My discussion concerns the transmission of volatility through the capital structure.

One of the important corporate finance implications of the *liquidity* model is, in contrast to conventional theory, its reduced emphasis on the link between domestic policies and the investment decision of foreign creditors. At this point it probably makes sense to make a distinction between the policy implications of *preventing* shocks versus those of *minimizing* their impacts. Most of the literature on the recent crises has implicitly or explicitly proposed ways to prevent crises from occurring again in the future by attacking the source of

1. Quoted in Jaime Sabal, "Financial Decisions in Emerging Markets," manuscript.

the shocks, for example by changing the capital allocation process or by trade liberalization. This is generally the object of the analyses that have poured out from government agencies, bank research departments, and journalists.

But because of the huge disparity between the size of capital flows and the size of LDC economies, and because these flows respond to exogenous factors, the *liquidity* model downplays any expectation that shocks can be prevented or that their causes can be eliminated, or even controlled, from within the LDC. On the contrary, the *liquidity* approach argues that preventing externally induced financial shocks is virtually impossible, since what may seem like small shifts in rich-country capital flows can easily overwhelm less developed markets. Certainly the financial history of the world leaves us with little room for optimism on this front.

If financial shocks arising from external conditions are inevitable, then obviously domestic economic policies aimed at limiting shocks will have little impact on preventing crises. This means that proposals to *prevent* future crises by deepening domestic economic reforms, eliminating crony capitalism, improving bank lending procedures, etcetera, although praiseworthy in the long run, are irrelevant, that is, they are not useful in preventing crises. They may increase future growth prospects by improving productivity and the credit allocation process, but they do not address the way shocks are transmitted into the economy and they cannot reduce the occurrence of these shocks. This doesn't mean, however, that there is no scope for policy action. If shocks cannot be eliminated, then official policy must focus on controlling the impact of external shocks. The objective of crisis management must be to *minimize* the volatility impact of these shocks directly, and the only meaningful place in which to do this is the capital structure.

The Role of Capital Structure

In finance theory, a borrower's capital structure is not just the means by which it funds itself. It is also the way it indexes or controls its market risks, domestically or externally. This includes all direct and contingent inflows and outflows that are indexed in a predictable way to external variables, such as hedge instruments, commodity- and currency-related cashflows, and certain components of its operating earnings. Even the tax regime is part of a borrower's capital structure, since changes in earnings can have a predictable impact on tax payments. At the extreme, it is possible to think of a company as nothing but a portfolio of instruments, all of which constitute part of the capital structure. Although extreme, this is a conceptually useful exercise for a liability manager. It forces him to evaluate the way all payments are indexed, and it permits him to think about the sources and extent of volatility in each cashflow, as well as correlations and the implicit risk premium associated with each component of a borrower's cashflow. By treating a company as a portfolio, he can then "construct" a liability structure that minimizes portfolio risk.

Corporate entities, in other words, attempt through their capital structures to minimize the impact of the market risks they do not want to assume. In minimizing the impact of market risks, corporations must develop a clear idea of how their assets and revenues are indexed or correlated to the price of some other market asset. At its simplest level, for example, a German company with an investment in Japan has some direct exposure to the yen. If the yen weakens, the nominal value of the investment will decline. There are also, however, a whole series of secondary impacts on the company. A weaker yen may increase or decrease the value in yen of the investment itself. A weaker yen may affect the pricing ability of Japanese-based competitors. It may have an impact on disposable income of Europeans and other consumers outside Japan by changing the price of Japanese inputs. It may affect the price of some other commodity input of which Japan is a big producer or user. In short, there are a whole series of asset value and cashflow impacts that flow from a change in the value of the yen.

Once the German company has developed a clear understanding of these impacts (often no easy thing to do) it must hedge two separate types of impacts—asset value impacts and immediate cashflow and earnings impacts. By this I mean that the company needs to put into place positions with long-term yen exposure such that their market values vary relative to the change in the price of the yen in an equal but opposite way to that of the German company's basic underlying assets. This protects the company's equity value from changes in the net asset value of the company. The company must also put into place short-term hedges that mirror the earnings and cashflow impacts of yen changes. This protects the company from earnings volatility and, more important, from an unexpected cashflow gap that may become difficult to finance.[2]

Before I go on to discuss the correct corporate finance strategies for sovereigns, it is worth looking briefly at the corporate finance and capital structure decision at large corporations to develop an insight into the liability risk management process. A typical marketing doc-

2. Some academics may argue that if asset value is hedged, a cashflow gap can always be financed, so that it is unnecessary to hedge cashflow directly. But as long as there is uncertainty about net asset value and about future changes in cashflow, investors may be reluctant to provide financing or will do so only on terms that are suboptimal. Consequently, the company may find itself unable to finance a cashflow gap.

ument for a New York investment bank lists what specialists believe to be the four primary goals in developing the capital structure and deciding on financing transactions:

1. *Flexibility.* The balance sheet should be sufficiently liquid to meet the changing needs and strategies of management in the short term. This includes:

   • The ability to meet current obligations easily, even in difficult market conditions.
   • The ability to raise cash quickly for strategic purposes.

2. *Stability.* Over the medium term, potential market disruptions or changes in financing costs should never be capable of forcing management to discard or change its existing strategy. The borrower should be protected from:

   • The possibility of large maturities coming due during periods in which market conditions are unsettled or chaotic and credit spreads are extremely high.
   • Significant duration mismatches in which in a rising rate environment the value of assets fall much more quickly than the value of liabilities.
   • Other currency or commodity price mismatches in which large shifts in the value of a currency or commodity can cause the value of assets to fall relative to liabilities.
   • Unexpected cashflow gaps caused by real or financial price changes.

3. *Minimizing of volatility.* Leverage ratios, the short-term/long-term debt mix, the duration of liabilities, and currency and commodity-price exposure should be structured so as to minimize overall portfolio volatility by aligning them with the market risks inherent in the company's assets.

   • Decreasing the volatility of earnings will increase the total value of assets and, consequently, will indirectly increase the equity value of all but the most highly leveraged or earnings-volatile companies.
   • Reducing volatility directly increases the value of debt and so reduces credit spreads.

4. *Relative value.* Depending on current market conditions, debt can be structured to take advantage of market inefficiencies, such as excessive relative demand for a particular maturity or currency.[3]

3. Bear Stearns and Co., Inc. Reprinted in a variety of internal marketing documents in 1999 and 2000.

It is a basic tenet of corporate finance theory that market risks should be managed through the capital structure. Of the four goals listed here in designing an optimal capital structure, the first three have to do exclusively with managing the relationship between risk and asset value or earnings volatility. The specialist sees the role of the chief financial officer (CFO) as adding value in two different ways. He adds value indirectly by creating a stable and flexible structure that permits management to develop and implement business strategies without disruption, and he adds it directly by matching up the risks of the revenue and asset side with the expense and liability side.

Although the fourth goal, timing the market to take advantage of specific *relative value* opportunities to lower funding costs, is one of the CFO's responsibilities, most specialists consider this to be the least important of the goals and only worth pursuing when the other are three are in place. I will argue later in this book that when managing the capital structure of a country, most sovereign finance teams focus mostly on the fourth goal and not enough on the first three.

There are constraints on the ability of a borrower to design its capital structure, and models of imperfect information explain an important source of these constraints when signaling effects can adversely affect the demand for the instrument to be sold. One of the points that is relevant to my discussion of sovereigns is the impact of perceptions of creditworthiness on debt issuance. If a borrower issues debt in enough quantities that the debt servicing burden can force deterioration in the perception of creditworthiness beyond some level, instead of simply forcing the required borrowing cost upward it may have two other effects on the borrower. First, lenders may shorten the tenor of new debt, as it is rolled over, to maturities that are not optimal for the borrower and may increase the risk of some adverse event forcing the borrower into greater distress. Second, they may ration credit by refusing to roll debt over altogether because of the perception that an interest rate high enough to justify any existing level of risk may push the riskiness of the borrower even closer to default. The supply curve for new loans, in other words, may bend backward as the borrowing cost increases.[4] I will discuss the effect of these constraints in chapter 8.

4. Bruce Greenwald, "International Adjustments in the Face of Imperfect Financial Markets," *Annual World Bank Conference on Development Economics* (IBRD/World Bank 1998), pp. 273–89, and Joseph Stiglitz and A. Weiss, "Credit Rationing in Markets with Imperfect Information," *American Economic Review* 71 (September 1981): 393–440.

Does Volatility Matter? The Cost of Financial Distress

In order to determine the best corporate finance policy for a borrower, we should not just assume that volatility is necessarily harmful for a borrower. It has been shown elsewhere that under certain conditions increases in underlying volatility can actually improve the value of certain debt obligations.[5] Because the question of whether volatility matters is actually a difficult one whose answer depends on underlying conditions, it is important to develop a conceptual framework that explains exactly how it is damaging and when, if ever, it is beneficial. Moreover, this must be done from the point of view of users of capital as well as of providers of capital. I will look at volatility from both points of view.

Do increases in underlying asset volatility hurt the value of a company's securities? In finance theory there is a concept of *financial distress* that is a key factor in deciding on corporate leverage and capital structures. Financial distress imposes certain costs that reduce the total enterprise value of an entity, and the higher the probability of financial distress, the more the value is reduced. More important, a reduction in value can ultimately feed directly into borrowing costs.

The cost associated with financial distress may not at first be obvious. What we mean by this term is the amount of value lost by a corporation when it is engaged in debt restructuring or bankruptcy procedures or when the likelihood of debt restructuring or bankruptcy becomes high. It is important to differentiate financial distress costs from the actual bankruptcy. A company that is entering into bankruptcy has obviously seen the value of its assets erode to the point where the value of its business can no longer cover the debt servicing costs—but this is just a question of a decline of normal market value. In itself it is not qualitatively different from any other decline in an asset's market value, whether or not there is a high debt burden being supported by the assets.

In fact, two companies in the same business with the same assets can have dramatically different enterprise values (market value of equity plus market value of debt) if one of the companies, because it has more debt in its capital structure, is facing some probability of bankruptcy materially greater than zero. This is because there is a secondary, more important, impact of the bankruptcy process itself. As the

---

5. Michael Pettis and Jared Gross, "Delta, Kappa, and the Equity-like Features of Speculative-Grade Debt," in Michael Pettis (ed.), *The New Dynamics of Emerging Markets Investment: Managing Sub-Investment-Grade Sovereign Risk* (Euromoney Publications PLC, 1997), pp. 37–50. A revised version of this appears as an appendix to this book.

likelihood of bankruptcy rises, lenders may change the form in which they are willing to lend because of the need to reduce their risk. Competitors may engage in predatory behavior in the expectation that the distressed company will be unable to respond. Distributors, employees, and suppliers may reduce their commitments in order to protect themselves from the consequences of a bankruptcy. Customers may be concerned about the continuing ability of the company to service their needs over the long term and so switch their purchases to other companies. Even the behavior of equity investors can be adversely affected, since the returns on new investment are likely to be shared among debt and equity investors in a way that is suboptimal for the equity investor. All these stakeholders may change their behavior in ways that may be suboptimal for the company and may actually exacerbate the problems the company is already facing.

This can harm a company's ability to maximize the profitability and value of its assets and operations. Furthermore, when a company is actually undergoing bankruptcy, its normal operations—which have a value, even if it is lower than it used to be—can be disrupted by a number of additional factors. These include legal restrictions, the unwillingness of investors to finance even "safe" operations, inefficient sharing of the payoffs from new investments, poor information disclosure, personnel losses, and other types of uncertainty. The value of the company as a going concern, in other words, is reduced to less than what it should in principle be *because of the bankruptcy process itself*. In corporate finance the important point about financial distress is that it imposes a significant cost that is borne by the lenders and owners of a company, and this cost, along with the probability of its having to be "paid," is always included in the valuation of the company's assets.

If the costs of financial distress are high, then it seems that investors should adjust their valuation of debt and equity as the probability of entering into bankruptcy changes. In fact they do. When a firm takes on more debt relative to its asset value, the market value of the company as a whole—which in principle would not be affected by the leverage ratio if there were no financial distress costs—can be reduced. Investors begin to include the probability of default—and the costs associated with it—in their value calculations, and the greater the costs or the greater the probability of financial distress, the more the value of the company is reduced. From this it follows that to the extent that the company's CFO can reduce the risk of financial distress, the value of the company's stock and bonds will increase commensurately.

There are two ways to do this. The first and most obvious way is simply to reduce leverage. By reducing the amount of outstanding debt, the company reduces the likelihood that at some time in the future there will be such a large mismatch between its operating revenues and its debt servicing costs that it will be unable to pay of its obligations. The second, less obvious, way is to reduce directly the mismatch between revenues and expenses by lining up debt servicing costs with operating revenues. This is a very important point in finance and worth repeating. For any given asset value and leverage ratio, the greater the likelihood of a mismatch between revenues and expenses—and thus the greater the probability of a gap—the less the value of the company as an operating entity because of the increase in the probability of financial distress.

Sovereign Capital Structure and Financial Distress

The same is true of a country, except that the costs of financial distress are even greater, and the probability of financial distress for equally rated countries is probably much higher.

- The costs of sovereign financial distress are greater because they tend to take longer to resolve than corporate bankruptcies and they affect human lives in a way that corporate bankruptcies do not. During a period of financial distress no new financing is likely to be raised by the distressed country—and for capital-starved countries that need to import capital goods and technology, this can have a devastating impact on growth prospects. Furthermore, local politics tend to be polarized around the debt issue, so that necessary fundamental reforms are ignored or postponed. Finally, the uncertainty surrounding the debt restructuring process can impede local entrepreneurs from building businesses while encouraging the flight of capital.
- Although it is not clear why default probabilities for sovereigns are higher, countries seem more likely to enter into financial distress, or to default, than equivalently rated companies. One possible reason is that rating agencies tend to focus primarily on *expected* debt servicing ratios and fail to include volatility projections around those expectations—on the assumption that changes in ratios are roughly similar between corporations and LDC sovereigns. However, if most sovereign capital structures systematically magnify volatility, and I will argue that they do, then for any given level of debt servicing ratio, the probability of a significant improvement or a significant deterioration in the ratios will necessarily be higher. Increases in the volatility of outcomes have a tendency

to push the probability of any particular outcome towards 50%, so that a low-probability event, such as a default, is more likely to occur with high-volatility LDCs than with lower volatility corporations.

It should of course follow from all this that *as leverage increases, the correlation between revenues and expenses must also increase* so as to reduce, at least in part, the financial distress impact of increasing leverage. The cost of financial distress is not an abstract issue. Those who experienced the "Lost Decade" of the 1980s know implicitly the cost of the restructuring process. For many years during the 1980s the restructuring countries of Africa, Asia, Eastern Europe, and Latin America were simply unable to participate in the then-booming global economy because investors were unwilling to invest even in profitable ventures—the uncertainty surrounding the restructuring was too great.

The most important cost of sovereign financial distress probably arises from systematic underinvestment in the local economy. "Bankrupt" or restructuring countries implicitly impose a sort of tax on new investments that discourages new investors. This is because any increase in total export revenues caused by a successful new investment must be "shared" by all creditors, who have a claim on any increase in export revenues. They effectively split the proceeds with the new investor. For a creditworthy country, on the other hand, the marginal claim of lenders on additional revenues is very small since total claims are capped by the amount of the loan. In that case, new investors are not taxed, or are taxed to a much lower extent, making the investment hurdle significantly lower.

This point is worth exploring in more detail. For countries in distress, because the amount of the obligations exceeds the ability to repay, any improvement in repayment prospects increases the value of all debt at the expense of the new investment. If a country lacks sufficient export revenues to service its external debt, for example, an investor may be reluctant to invest in a "profitable" project that increases export revenues since a large part of the additional export revenues may be appropriated (or expropriated) to service the existing debt. The *cost* of the investment is borne only by the investor, while the *benefits* are shared. Good investments, in other words, increase the value of all assets, but the share "taxed away" by existing investors may make even very profitable opportunities unprofitable for the new investor. This obviously makes it very difficult for a country to attract positive investments.

An options framework makes this conceptually clearer. An equity investor can be seen as being long a call option on the assets of a company, and a lender can be seen as being short a put option. In option theory the way option positions effectively "share" increases in asset value is defined as the *delta* of the respective options. The delta of the two implicit positions[6] must add up to unity, which is just a way of saying that all the increase in asset value goes to debt-holders and equity investors in the company. Because this is a fairly well understood insight, I will not attempt to demonstrate here why— the proof can be discovered in most option textbooks.

But how is the increase in value actually shared? For very highly creditworthy companies, the equity option is implicitly highly in-the-money, while the debt option is highly out-of-the-money. The delta for equity owners, consequently, is very close to unity, while the delta for debt holders is close to zero. This is just a way of saying that almost all the increase in asset value goes to equity holders. If the equity holders determine that there is a profitable investment oppor-tunity for the company, the company will probably undertake the in-vestment because equity holders, who implicitly make the invest-ment, get close to the full return on the additional investment. Remember that equity investors receive delta times the increased value, and in the case of a highly creditworthy borrower their delta is close to unity. But as credit quality declines, the equity delta also declines while the debt delta increases by an equal amount (the rate of decline is known among option specialists as *gamma*). For com-panies just on the edge of bankruptcy, both debt and equity positions have a delta of close to 0.50.[7] This means that equity holders and debt holders share any increase in value almost evenly.

How does this affect investment? Assume that equity investors see a profitable opportunity to invest $100 and immediately increase the value of the company by $150. Normally, equity investors would jump at this opportunity. In this case, however, although a $100 investment by equity holders increases the total value of the company by $150, half of this value, or $75, goes to debt holders, while the remaining half goes to equity holders. In spite of the profitability of the invest-ment, in other words, equity holders would actually take a 25% loss on their $100 investment if they decided to invest. Clearly they will not do so. In fact they will not invest in any project unless the profits are large enough even after sharing them. This is even truer, by the way, for companies that are actually bankrupt, since the debt delta continues to increase while the equity delta tends toward zero.

---

6. That is, equity, or the long call position, and debt, or the short put po-sition. The delta is technically the first derivative of the price of an option with relation to the price of the underlying asset. The option price, in other words, moves by an amount equal to the price movement in the underlying asset times the delta. This is described further in the appendix to this book.

7. Again, this is a well-known condition explained in most beginning op-tions textbooks.

Although countries do not have "equity" in the same way as companies do, the mathematics of value sharing is the same. Countries that are facing payment difficulties are in a similar position to nearly bankrupt companies in that the value of their debt is highly sensitive to changes in the country's ability to increase export earnings (the delta of debt is significantly greater than zero). Any investment project that increases a country's ability to add value increases the creditworthiness of the country at the expense of the investor in the project. Intuitively one can think of it as the ability of the country to expropriate dollar earnings in order to make debt payments. In such a condition, not surprisingly, foreign investors will refuse to invest in a distressed country even if the project in and of itself is very profitable.

We saw this most dramatically during the LDC debt crisis, when U.S. investors, flush as they were with cash, refused to buy or invest in assets in Mexico and other restructuring countries even though the assets were extremely cheap by almost any fundamental measure. And because there were few new investments in productive capacity, the restructuring economies of the 1980s fell behind the rest of the world in economic growth and in many cases are only now catching up to their per capita income levels of the late 1970s. Private sector estimates suggest that Latin America's GDP is as much as 20% lower than what it should otherwise have been if the underinvestment problem caused by the debt overhang did not exist.

As bad as they were, it is worth pointing out that the debt restructurings of the 1980s may have been relatively easy as debt restructurings go, since the creditors consisted largely of a fairly homogenous group of international commercial banks that had similar goals and were subject to home government pressure. With most LDC indebtedness today held by a diverse group of creditors with differing and even conflicting goals and tactics, if a sovereign were forced to restructure its debt today, many analysts believe that the restructuring process would be messier and the bankruptcy costs absorbed by the borrower even greater. I will address the corporate finance of financial distress and its relationship to the sovereign debt restructuring process in greater detail in chapter 9.

The Cost to Lenders

Of course it was not just the borrowing countries that were hurt by the restructuring process. The international commercial banks that had made most of the loans that financed the 1970s boom were also badly hurt by the long, drawn-out restructuring. First, because there was a moratorium on new capital inflows, borrowers found it difficult to grow their way out of their debt burdens, and this reduced the potential value of the debt owed to the banks. Second, the uncertainty associated with the restructuring process resulted in very wide bid-offer spreads in the secondary market, illiquidity, and valuation uncertainty. This caused the prices of loans in the secondary market to fall even below their perceived economic value, and the low market values put equity valuation pressures on the banks.

Third, because of the virulence of the LDC loan problem, bank managers were unable to focus on developing and implementing profitable business strategies even in their home markets. During the 1980s, for example, U.S. money center banks with LDC exposure fell far behind the growth rate of the U.S. regional banks—most of whom had little to no LDC exposure. Bank analysts argued at the time that this was largely because the primary strategic focus of the money center banks was to resolve the terrifying LDC crisis, which threatened to bankrupt them, rather than to discover and exploit new profit opportunities.[8]

Most investors, for all their short-term memory, do remember the high cost of financial distress during difficult market conditions. The very large credit spreads on LDC bonds, for example, demonstrate that they implicitly include this cost in pricing their loans and bonds. LDC bond credit spreads, which measure the amount of return investors require before they will take on the risk of investing, are notorious for increasing dramatically during periods of increased uncertainty—far more dramatically than equivalently rated U.S. corporate bonds. If increases in the probabilities of distress have a much higher impact on sovereign credit spreads than on U.S. corporate credit spreads, this must reflect investors' concerns that the costs of distress are much higher for sovereigns than for U.S. corporations.

As with corporations, it turns out that there are two main components in determining the likelihood of financial distress. First, most obviously, the higher the level of debt, the more likely a borrower is to find itself unable to meet its debt servicing requirements. This is simply because high levels of debt absorb a high fixed portion of income and permit little variation in that income. Second, and perhaps less obvious, the more volatile the relationship between income and debt servicing costs, the greater the risk of financial distress of any given borrowing level, since there is a greater likelihood of a debt servicing "gap." This greater risk should feed directly into borrowing costs, and in fact there is a great deal of empirical evidence that for corporations, volatile cashflows are correlated with higher borrowing costs.[9] I am going to define volatility as the magnitude of the mismatch

8. Conversation with Chris Kotowski, former bank analyst and head of equity research at CIBC World Markets.

9. See, for example, Bernadette A. Minton and Catherine M. Schrand, "The

between expected revenues and expenses, or inflows and outflows. One way of thinking about this is that the more the expected variation in the *net* flows (i.e., inflows minus outflows), the more volatile a capital structure is. Given the components that determine the likelihood of financial distress, one of the primary responsibilities of the finance ministry of any LDC should be to quantify a reasonable overall debt servicing capacity and to reduce the volatility of net flows.

To put the second point another way, the financial managers of an LDC should seek to increase the direct correlation between outflows and inflows. The higher the correlation between inflows and outflows, or revenues and expenses, the lower the likelihood that some unexpected event can force contracted outflows to be greater than expected inflows. As the likelihood of a sustained gap between revenues and expenses decreases, the likelihood that a borrower will be unable to meet its debt servicing costs also decreases. This is what was meant when, earlier in the chapter, I argued that risk management specialists attempt to minimize volatility. By reducing volatility—which is the same as saying increasing the correlation between inflows and outflows—financial managers reduce the probability of distress and, with it, the cost of borrowing.

The Value of Volatile Revenues

Volatility hurts a borrower in another way. A fundamental rule of finance is that the value of an asset is the sum of future expected cashflows discounted at an appropriate yield, and the appropriate yield depends on the expected volatility associated with the cashflows. More volatile flows must be discounted at a higher yield, so that a reduction in volatility is usually associated with greater value. When an entity borrows, the volatility of its "residual" cashflows after debt servicing costs usually increases because leverage increases residual volatility in a linear way.

By this I mean that when revenues have a certain level of volatility, borrowing against those revenues will normally increase the volatility directly and in proportion to the amount of leverage, since a fixed payment must be subtracted from the revenues. When a fixed debt payment is subtracted from revenues, this "bunches up" all the original revenue volatility into a smaller residual amount, so that the same amount of volatility has a much greater percentage impact on the

Impact of Cash Flow Volatility on Discretionary Investment and the Costs of Debt and Equity Financing," *Journal of Financial Economics* 54 (1999): 423–60, and Rene Stulz, "Managerial Discretion and Optimal Financing Policies," *Journal of Financial Economics* 28 (1990): 3–28.

owner of the residual flows. It is possible, however, to borrow and hedge some of the volatility implicit in the revenue stream, so that the hedged debt payments increase or decrease in line with revenues. When this happens, the value of the residual will actually increase since it will have become less volatile. Although this may sound excessively theoretical, in fact valuation exercises are explicitly or implicitly very sensitive to changes in expected volatility.

For those readers interested in a more rigorous theoretical framework, I will once again consider an option framework to analyze the impact of changes in volatility. Within the framework, as I pointed out earlier in this chapter, equity in a company can be seen as a call option on the assets of the company struck at a price equal to the value of its debt plus bankruptcy costs (the "exercise" price). [10]It may not literally be the case that equity is a call option, but this closely approximates economic value and it can provide valuable analytical insights into valuation issues. Once again, because this is a fairly well understood insight, I will not attempt to demonstrate here why—the proof can be discovered in most option textbooks.

As we know from pricing options, the value of an option, hence the value of equity, can be usefully divided into two components. The first is its intrinsic value, which is equal in this case to the market value of real assets minus its contractual obligations, including debt. The second is its time value, which generally represents the excess of the market value of a company (debt plus equity) over the market value of its real assets—this can show up as goodwill, the value of brands, other intangibles, et cetera. The intrinsic and time value components of an option are shown in Figure 6.1 for options with a variety of different strikes.

Increasing earnings volatility reduces the market value of assets— partly by increasing the probability of financial distress and partly by requiring a higher rate against which to discount earnings. If the market value of the asset decreases, of course, the intrinsic value of the option decreases since it consists of the difference between market value and the "exercise price" of the option. The graph shows how the time value and the intrinsic value combine to create the net value of these options as a function of changes in volatility (we assume a constant *nominal* amount of debt). As the graph shows, an increase in volatility causes a decline in the "intrinsic value" of the option. Increasing volatility, however, has the opposite effect on time value, as is also shown in the graph. This is because time value is proportional to the probability that the value of the asset will be higher than

10. The option is only "exercised" during bankruptcy, so that the remaining value of the assets must be reduced by bankruptcy costs before debt holders are paid out. This can be though of as an additional senior claim on assets.

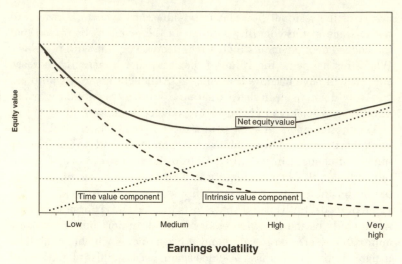

Figure 6.1. Volatility and equity value

the exercise price, and the greater the volatility, the higher the probability of an increase in the asset's value.

The net effect on equity value depends on where the company lies on the "net equity value" curve. For most companies, an increase in earnings volatility is associated with a reduction in equity prices. This is shown on the left side of the graph. For these companies, which have high intrinsic values, the reduction in intrinsic value associated with an increase in volatility is greater than the increase in time value, so that overall value, shown here as "Net equity value," declines. This is not always the case, however. Companies that are very highly leveraged (like near-bankrupt S & Ls in the early 1980s) or with extremely high levels of volatility associated with future earnings (like Internet companies) may see their stock prices actually benefit from increases in volatility. These companies have a low intrinsic value, and they are to be found on the right side of the graph. When volatility increases, the negative effect on the already low intrinsic value is less than the positive effect on time value. As volatility increases, consequently, equity value increases.[11]

11. This, incidentally, formally explains why established media companies with Internet operations are better off isolating their Internet activity into a separate subsidiary and partially or wholly spinning them off. By combining the operations directly, the effect of the increased volatility of Internet earnings on the larger, more established operations of large media companies reduces equity value. For a fuller discussion of the option framework, see Michael Pettis and Brian Kim, "Where's the Value in Dot Coms: Volatility-Loving Companies in a Volatility-Hating Environment," *Global Finance*, July 2000.

Sovereign Value

The story is the same at the sovereign level—for a high-intrinsic-value country, which most countries are, increases in volatility always reduce the country's "value." It is difficult to think of sovereign countries as having a low intrinsic value, and most countries are actually bunched up on the left side of the scale, so that increases in volatility almost always reduce the value of the country's net inflows. I should point out, though, that the argument that certain highly risky countries can actually increase value by increasing the riskiness of their outcomes is not as crazy as it might seem. A Brazilian economist and fund manager has argued to me that during the early stages of the Brazilian crisis, after the January 1999 devaluation, the Central Bank under Arminio Fraga, a very sophisticated trader, perhaps unwittingly engaged in precisely such a maneuver. At that time, according to his reasoning, the risk inherent in the very short duration of Brazil's local debt structure was so great that the country faced a domestic financing crisis. Any further increase in interest rates would feed immediately into higher debt servicing costs because the debt was all short-term or floating, and this would have caused the fiscal deficit to mushroom. As the deficit mushroomed and investors' nervousness grew commensurately, there was a real risk that investors would stop rolling over their debt and the government would be forced either to inflate its debt away or to default.

At first it might seem that the "proper" risk management strategy in this case would have been immediately to extend the duration of the debt, no matter what the cost, and so reduce volatility. But the country was on the verge of insolvency (and so the "intrinsic" value of the option was low). Any reduction in volatility would have simply locked in an impossible situation and forced the government to "bleed" to death through the high interest payments on its debt. For this reason, and because any increase in volatility would also increase the likelihood that it would survive, the Central Bank implicitly decided to gamble—which is the same as systematically increasing volatility. It is unlikely, by the way, that the Central Bank consciously employed this reasoning in deciding on its strategy. It simply made the same rational choice that the option framework predicted it would have made. By maintaining the short-term structure of the internal debt, the Central Bank bet heavily that rates would decline since any other bet would have almost guaranteed a "loss." Rates did decline, and the Central Bank "won."[12]

The option framework can give us important insights into how a sovereign's interest can vary as the intrinsic value of the implicit op-

12. Conversation with Fernando Saldanha, international research analyst at Tudor Jones.

tions increases or decreases. For lenders, on the other hand, the insight is even simpler. As long as the borrower is not a "basket case" country with no reasonable hope of repaying its external debt as originally contracted, increases in volatility almost always reduce value. This is because increases in the underlying volatility increase both the intrinsic value and the time value of the option. Since lenders are effectively short the put option, they almost always lose from increases in volatility. The exception is when the asset value of the borrower (country or company) is so low that the short put option is transformed into a long call option struck at zero. In this case, lenders actually benefit by increases in volatility, but this is admittedly a rare case limited to a very few highly indebted poor countries.[13]

The purpose of this exercise comparing corporate and sovereign risk appetites within an option framework is not just to point out that volatility matters. Of course it does, but there are more important conclusions that can be drawn from the analysis, although they are for the most part only touched on here. For one thing, the interests of lenders and the interests of the country are structurally different—in some cases their interests coincide, and in others their interests are at odds. What matters is how changes in underlying value are shared (the delta of their exposure), and how their respective appetites for volatility can increase, decrease, or even invert, depending on the optionality implicit in their relative positions. Furthermore, the option framework can show how hedging can change bankruptcy probabilities and how both the costs and benefits of hedging strategies are shared. The framework even shows how different types of hedging strategies have different relative impacts on lenders and borrowers. It is important to remember that all contingent claims are like options and, as such, all are affected by the various sensitivities that affect option valuation.[14] These issues have important policy implications both in designing an optimal sovereign capital structure and in driving a default or debt restructuring strategy.

13. The impact of volatility on sovereign lenders is fully explained in Michael Pettis and Jared Gross, "Delta, Kappa," pp. 37–50. A revised version of this appears as an appendix to this book.

14. These valuation sensitivities are often called "the Greeks" by option traders, since they are symbolized by Greek letters. Of the most important, delta is the sensitivity of an option's value to changes in the value of the underlying asset; gamma is the rate of change of delta; kappa (or, less correctly, vega) is the sensitivity of an option's value to changes in volatility; theta is the sensitivity of an option's value to time decay; and so on.

Credibility and the Relationship between
Assets and Liabilities

There are two initial conclusions we should draw for sovereign borrowers from this admittedly theoretical and excessively brief analysis
of volatility. The first is that any reduction in the probability of financial distress will have a large impact both on the likelihood of significant costs to the local population and on the returns that investors will
demand. And second, for all but the most insolvent and risky of countries (for whom revenue increases will automatically go to pay debt),
most systematic attempts to hedge market risks will increase the value
of a country's revenues and export earnings, which will automatically
feed into lower borrowing costs, although it may take time before the
market assigns value to the lower volatility. To the extent that a country
can reduce its expected volatility by managing and hedging market
risks, the country benefits both immediately by an increase in "equity"
value and in the future by a reduction in financing costs.

This bears repeating. One of the commonplaces of LDC analysis is
that "credibility" is a key factor in permitting an LDC to take advantage of foreign capital to develop and implement its policies. A country with low credibility must pay a higher yield to investors, and these
investors are generally unwilling to face temporary downturns with
any confidence that they are only temporary. When a low-credibility
country experiences a market shock, the first reaction of investors is
to withdraw from the market—thereby exacerbating the problem—
until its impact can be understood. Of course this makes a long-term
policy commitment difficult because without long-term backing by
businesses and investors, it is very difficult for policy managers to
implement reforms whose benefits accrue over a long time frame. The
threat is that short-term problems—generated from inside or outside
the country—can result in capital flight that derails the program before the country can receive the payoff.

But what is "credibility"? Most economists use the word to refer
to the likelihood that a government is willing and able to maintain
the integrity of its policies, even in the face of shocks. A credible
government is one under which investors and businesses can count
on a clear and consistent framework within which to operate and
plan. When external conditions change, the impact of the change in
a country with high credibility is limited to the direct consequences
of the change in conditions, which can be calculated and even previously hedged. In a country with low credibility, however, the impact
can be incalculably higher because the consequences of the shock can
force a policy shift, which may itself lead to additional and unpredictable changes that cannot be hedged. Low credibility countries suffer from policy "gapping."

An example of the different ways shocks impact credible and non-credible countries is the difference between what happened to England in 1992 and Mexico in 1994. When Germany's government kept interest rates high to defend the country from inflation following the reunification in 1989, there was tremendous and ultimately unsustainable pressure on other European currencies, including the British pound and Italian lira. It was difficult for the United Kingdom to continue to maintain the high value of the pound, and sure enough on "Black Wednesday," September 16, 1992, under intense speculative pressure, the United Kingdom—along with Italy—left the European Exchange Rate Mechanism and devalued its currency. Mexico's problem in 1994 was similar—its currency was clearly overvalued, which was hurting Mexican exporters, and it had to keep interest rates exceedingly high to protect the currency, which was depressing the economy. In December of that year, unable to withstand the capital outflows, it devalued the peso.

The sudden devaluation of the overvalued pound was a major policy shift, but because of the government's credibility, investors assumed that except for the change in the currency regime, there would be no other major policy shift or breakdown in the underlying economic framework. Investors, in other words, expected that there would not necessarily be an immediate explosion in inflation, regulations and property rules would not change, residual values could be calculated with some certainty, foreign investors would not be penalized, etcetera. Most important, the country's banking system and capital structure were not so vulnerable that the devaluation would cause a financial collapse. The informational content of the devaluation was fairly specific and easy to evaluate. Since the market believed that the devaluation was in response to a condition in which the need to protect an overvalued currency was undermining economic growth, the country's improved growth prospects following the devaluation encouraged investors and businesses to participate in the improved domestic circumstances, and the stock market quickly rose.

On the other hand, when Mexico devalued its equally overvalued peso in 1994 after an even more costly attempt to defend it, instead of a rush by investors to take advantage of Mexico's more competitive industries, there was a rush out of the country, and the market collapsed. This was because it was difficult to evaluate the full informational impact of the devaluation. Mexico's leaders were just as determined to maintain their record of economic reforms and to regain growth as England's leaders were, but no one believed them—they had no credibility.

I would argue that the word "credibility" has a fairly important corporate finance component, and that in evaluating a country's credibility, the focus should be on the ability, rather than the will, to maintain the integrity of the proposed government policies. Here is where the corporate finance component of credibility is important. Although most evaluations of a country's credibility focus on the determination of policy-makers to maintain their policies (and on the strength of domestic political support for these policies), it is easily possible that even where an overwhelming political consensus seems to exist, credibility can nonetheless be low. In this case policy "gapping" can occur not just because political will is weak but because a misalignment in the underlying market or political structure can systematically exacerbate shocks in such a way that even the sternest of administrations are overwhelmed by the shock.

Since low credibility equals high uncertainty and high required yields for events that are in the medium- or long-term future, and since it forces investors to reduce their time horizons, low credibility is very expensive. But in order to increase credibility, it is not enough to increase political support for a policy framework—it is just as important to reduce the perceived impact of shocks. In fact I believe that the importance of the "political will" component of credibility is usually overstated. What really cause changes in policies are not changes in political will but the recognition that a policy mix has suddenly become unsustainable—and it is because of structural changes that a previously "good" policy suddenly becomes unsustainable.

For this reason the volatility imbedded in a country's capital structure has an important impact on its credibility, and in fact I would argue that the stability of the country's capital structure is and should be the main factor in assessing credibility. Because they are less susceptible to destabilizing shocks and so incorporate a lower probability of financial distress, countries with very stable inflows and outflows are more credible than countries with unstable inflows and outflows, but that is not the whole issue. Countries in which inflows and outflows are highly correlated will also have higher investor credibility because the residual flows will tend to be less volatile; they will have low credibility when the inflows and outflows are both volatile and poorly correlated. Because of the increased probability of financial distress, it is the mismatching of inflows and outflows that increases the risk of market gapping, and a country with a heavy mismatch will have lower credibility.

Matching Inflows and Outflows

I have argued that the probability of financial distress is reduced when inflows and outflows are correlated, and I have pointed out that market risks are managed through the capital structure. This means that credibility is increased when a borrower designs a funding strategy that correlates payments and revenues, thereby dissipating the damage caused by unpredictable external shocks. The capital structure, in other words, should be designed to hedge unwanted market risk in the assets and operations of the borrower. The borrower does this by designing the cashflows associated with financial obligations to mirror real changes in revenues and costs. If a stronger euro is associated with an increase in export revenues, for example, the country should borrow in euros and hold dollar and yen reserves. If a drop in copper prices reduces the cost of a major input, the country should consider borrowing in such a way that interest payments are inversely indexed to the price of copper so that its financing cost increases. In both cases, the volatility of net earnings declines.

This can get more complicated than simply matching up financing costs to commodity prices. If a country's fiscal credibility—and consequently local interest rates—is highly sensitive to the federal debt service, instead of "saving" money by borrowing short-term, the government should be willing to pay more to lock in debt servicing costs that are less sensitive to changes in interest rates. This may seem counterintuitive. If a high debt servicing burden is a problem, then surely it would make sense to do whatever is necessary to reduce the debt servicing cost, including borrowing on a floating-rate or short-term basis.

But the corporate finance and option frameworks show why this common mistake is in fact just that—a mistake. As long as the government borrower is perceived to be relatively solvent, the "low cost" borrowing option actually reduces value. It does so in two ways. First, by increasing the impact of interest rate changes on fiscal credibility (i.e., speeding up the fiscal impact of changes in short-term rates), the short-term borrowing strategy adversely affects the impact of capital structure on the stability needed by policy-makers. "Stability" was one of the liability management goals I listed in the beginning of this chapter.[15] As the experience of Brazil in 1997–98 showed, the impact of rate changes on fiscal credibility was so great that during much of this time too much government attention was focused on dealing with and reacting to the interest rate environment rather than attending to on more fundamental reforms.

The second way this option reduces value is by increasing the probability of financial distress. There were several periods in Brazil during 1997–98 when investors spent most of their time estimating how long it would take before debt servicing costs became unsustainable. Because the market believed that there was a probability signif-

---

15. "Over the medium term, potential market disruptions or changes in financing costs should never be capable of forcing management to discard or change its existing strategy."

icantly greater than zero that at some point the government would be unable to refinance or repay its debt, they required a huge risk premium to continue lending. High-risk premiums increase borrowing costs, which reinforce concerns about bankruptcy, and so on. For much of 1998, for example, Brazilian interest rates were above 40% even while inflation was substantially below 5%. Of course rates this high were unsustainable, and eventually the Brazilian government was forced into a major policy shift, and in doing so it finally did the unthinkable—allowed the currency to float freely, which was tantamount to devaluation.

Designing a funding strategy that correlates payments and revenues is actually a straightforward process, even though most LDCs get it backward and unwittingly design capital structures that automatically *increase* volatility. To explain why they tend to get it backward I have to revert to my models for capital flows. Unlike the *liquidity* model, the conventional *investment* explanation of capital flows implicitly encourages risky capital structures. It proposes an optimistic financing strategy. If foreigners invest because growth prospects are promising and the government's policies are "working," and since these policies are likely to be continued, it is logical that borrowers would take advantage by structuring their funding in a way that allows them continuously to lower their borrowing costs as conditions improve. In other words, there is no need to correlate revenues and expenses since the assumption is that revenues can only increase. The risk of a decrease in revenues, or in other measures of "well-being," is very low.

Under these conditions it makes sense to structure borrowings so that expenses simultaneously decrease. This type of funding is implicitly an *inverted* structure, one in which there is an inverse correlation between the flows associated with the asset and liability sides· of the national balance sheet. An *inverted* capital structure, in other words, is one in which conditions that cause or lead to *improvements* in the "asset" or revenue side will lead automatically and immediately to reductions in borrowing costs and to improvements in the "liability" side. Conversely, conditions that lead to *deterioration* in revenues and operations will lead to higher borrowing costs and deterioration in the liability side.

Correlating Capital Structures

An example of *inverted* funding would be an airline company who decided to borrow in a way such that its financing costs varied directly in line with the price of oil. For airlines, oil prices are a key risk measure since fuel costs are an enormous component of their total operating costs. As fuel prices rise, airline operating profits (i.e., profits before financing costs and taxes) usually decline, and as fuel prices decline, operating profits rise.

Let us assume that an airline's CFO decided to fund the company in an *inverted* way. If the airline funded itself in such a way that its financing costs decreased when oil prices decreased (which is easy to do), it would find itself in an enviable position if oil prices were actually to drop. Its operating profits would rise as the fuel-cost component dropped, and its financing costs would decline since they were directly indexed to oil prices. The growth in its net income would be substantially greater than that of its airline peers.

The problem arises if oil prices were unexpectedly to rise. As oil prices rose, the cost of the debt would simultaneously rise, and the airline would find itself squeezed between declining operating profits and rising debt servicing costs. Mismatching the revenues and expenses, in other words, would increase the probability of financial distress and so would immediately result in a lower overall value for the company's debt and equity. Because these risks are obvious, investors would never permit an airline to make such a foolish financing decision. Were it ever to do so, investors would quickly sell stocks and bonds until the price were low enough that either management would be forced to change the strategy or new management would be imposed by rebel shareholders.

In this case an appropriate funding strategy would be a *correlated* capital structure. A *correlated* capital structure, as its name implies, is one in which debt servicing costs move in the same direction as revenues. They are directly indexed, in other words, to conditions that are associated with improvements or deterioration in the operating performance of the borrower. In the airline example, if the CFO borrowed in such a way that debt servicing costs increased when oil prices declined and declined when oil prices increased, financing costs would vary with revenues in such a way that the residual income would show a low level of volatility.

The effect of inverted and correlated structures on residual payments is demonstrated in figure 6.2. Here, there are two different types of debt payment schedules. The darker dotted line represents that of an *inverted* capital structure in which improvements in revenues are met with reductions in debt servicing costs, and vice versa. The lighter dotted line represents the opposite, debt payments associated with a *correlated* capital structure.

As the schedule shows, improvements in revenues are matched with higher debt payment costs and vice versa. This involves a partial hedge. Over time the expected servicing cost for either structure is identical, and it is easy to see that on average the two debt payment lines are the same. The volatility of the residual, however, is markedly different, even when the average is also expected to be the same.

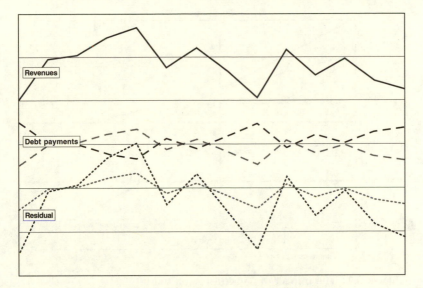

Figure 6.2. Impact of debt payments on residual value

"Good" outcomes are much better for the *inverted* structure, represented by the darker line, but "bad" outcomes are also much worse. The *correlated* structure, shown as the lighter line, is always less volatile.

Let us be clear about the lack of symmetry between the two different outcomes involving *inverted* and *correlated* capital structures. In an *inverted* structure, improvements in external conditions can lead to a sort of "doubling up" of the benefits, while deterioration in external conditions can lead to an equivalent "doubling up" of the costs. This doesn't mean, however, that the expected outcome for a company with an *inverted* capital structure is the same as that for a company with a *correlated* capital structure (i.e., that the costs and benefits are symmetrically distributed, as they are shown in figure 6.2). The expected value of the two companies is different even though one company might simply seem to be a leveraged version of the other company. This is because of the addition of financial distress costs. Figure 6.3 lays this condition out visually. In the graph, the downward-sloping lines show the "value" of an entity as underlying conditions improve or deteriorate, beginning at the center of the graph on the "Conditions today" line.

Improvements in underlying conditions—moving toward the left—correspond to an increase in value, while underlying deterioration corresponds to a reduction in value. As the graph shows, for the levered (more volatile) company, the effect of a change in underlying conditions is simply a multiple of the effect on the unlevered com-

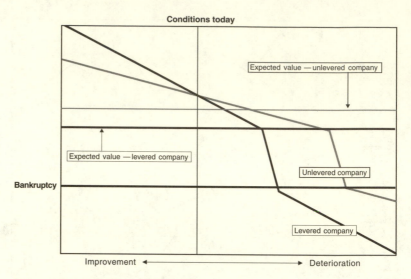

Figure 6.3. The impact of bankruptcy on value

pany. This is a standard finance theory condition. At some point, though, if conditions deteriorate beyond some level, value has declined enough that the entity falls into payment difficulties and possibly default (signaled by the "Bankruptcy" line). When this happens, the value of assets drops discontinuously as the process of financial distress causes a sharp reduction in asset value. We are assuming that the cost of financial distress is the same for both companies. Obviously, the difference between the levered and unlevered companies is that the value varies more quickly in the former case, and, if conditions deteriorate, bankruptcy occurs at an earlier stage.

As the graph shows, excluding the effect of bankruptcy, which immediately causes a one-off reduction in value, the values of both the levered and unlevered companies are symmetrical as of the "Conditions today" line. Whether conditions improve or deteriorate, the expected outcome for an investor is the same, and in fact an investor can use a combination of leverage (or deleverage, that is, by buying risk-free bonds) and any one company to mimic the result of the other company. When we introduce the possibility of bankruptcy, however, with its associated financial distress costs, because of the value "gapping" caused by the bankruptcy process, the expected value shifts, as is shown with the two horizontal "Expected value" lines. These lines represent the possible outcomes multiplied by their probabilities, and the greater probability of bankruptcy losses associated with the more levered company means that it has a lower value to investors.[16] This is the primary effect of volatility on the value of a company—because more volatility corresponds to an increase in the default probability, the asymmetry of the process reduces the expected value of the more volatile entity. All other things being equal, more volatile entities have a lower expected value.

Sovereign *Inverted* Financial Structures

All of this is true not just for corporations but also for countries, except that given the copious default history of sovereign borrowers, default probabilities for sovereign borrowers are usually higher than they are for equivalently rated corporations. This higher probability can easily be explained if sovereigns have systematically more *inverted* capital structures. I discussed earlier as an example of *inverted* funding an airline that borrows in a way such that payments are indexed directly to oil prices. At the sovereign level a corresponding type of *inverted* funding might be short-term debt denominated in dollars (and throughout this book by "dollars" I mean any currency other than that of the LDC borrower).

Why is this form of funding *inverted*? The answer lies in the inverted relationship between inflows and outflows. In this case as the economy improves, the local currency strengthens in real terms and, along with it, presumably, asset values and local revenues increase. Because the borrowings are in dollars, whose value in real terms is declining if the local currency is strengthening, the real cost of the borrower's existing debt continuously drops as conditions improve. The debt payments, which are a function of interest rates and the borrower's credit spreads at the time the loan was made, may remain constant in dollar terms, but because the value of dollars is depreciating in local currency terms, the cost to the borrower drops. Short-term dollar borrowing also ensures that the borrower sees its financing spreads decline quickly as debt comes due since, presumably, the borrower's credit quality is improving. Every time the debt is refinanced it is refinanced at a lower rate as lenders reduce the risk premium they charge for the higher credit quality.

But as in the airline example, there is a cost to this type of *inverted* capital structure. It results in increased exposure the borrower has to market risks and volatility. If external conditions deteriorate, debt

---

16. Because it may be confusing I should point out that although the "Expected value" lines spread horizontally across the graph as I have drawn them, they are not meant to vary as underlying conditions vary. They simply represent the value of the companies *today*.

servicing costs on existing loans automatically increase for the same reason that they decrease in improving conditions. Specifically, deterioration in global conditions can cause a weakening currency and a decline in both asset values and revenues. Debt costs, however, be cause they are fixed in dollars, increase in relative terms. In addition, as the debt is refinanced the weaker conditions can cause lenders to demand a higher risk premium. This type of borrowing ultimately adds instability to the balance sheet by "doubling up" the effect of both good events and bad events.

In domestic U.S. markets, debt and equity analysts are extremely sensitive to these types of unstable capital structures and will severely penalize a company whose balance sheet incorporates too much market risk. Whenever this happens, the total enterprise value of the company will be reduced, with most of the reduction occurring as a reduction in equity value. A part of the reduction, of course, shows up as a reduction in the market value of outstanding debt, and the closer the company comes to bankruptcy the greater the sensitivity of debt— this is all explained within the option framework by examining the changing delta of debt. For some reason, however, analysts and investors don't respond as negatively to unstable capital structures for emerging market countries, even though the consequences of market instability can be much worse. This is perhaps because the corporate finance framework has not been rigorously applied to what most analysts believe requires a primarily economic framework. Sovereign analysts, usually economists, generally ignore the volatility consequences of specific capital structures and tend to miss the impact of capital structures on transmitting external volatility.

A typical example of *inverted* funding was the structure of Mexico's local capital markets during the peso crisis of 1994–95. In Mexico at that time, as in most LDCs, local financial markets consisted (and still do) largely of short-term or floating-rate instruments—the peso yield curve barely extended out to one year, with most of the market indexed to twenty-eight-day rates. As I discussed in the Brazil example, there was consequently no lag or "stickiness" between changes in market conditions and changes in debt servicing payments, so that the borrower immediately assumed all the risk of changes in market conditions.

Investors, who normally share market risk with users of capital, were not able to assume any of the interest rate risk, even when they were eager to do so. As a result, when things were going well and inflation was declining, as it was in the 1990–94 period, borrowing costs declined immediately, and the borrower's financial position automatically improved just as its "real" economic condition was also improving. When things went badly, however, the reverse occurred, and interest rates immediately rose because in a primarily short-term market, rising rates feed automatically and immediately into higher debt servicing costs.

Following Mexico's December 1994 peso crisis, inflation fears and capital flight caused peso interest rates to shoot up. Mexican corporations suffered from the sharp fall in economic activity and, simultaneously, saw interest rates suddenly rise to unmanageable levels. Mexicans with consumer or mortgage loans were also affected, as their interest costs soared just as their real wages or jobs were being cut. The *inverted* funding resulted in a condition in which the pain that Mexican borrowers were feeling on their asset side was heavily reinforced on their liability side in the same way that the previous improvements in the economy were matched by continuously declining borrowing costs. The cost of the devaluation was, consequently, much greater than anyone had predicted because of simultaneous deterioration of both sides of the national "balance sheet."

The *liquidity* approach leads borrowers to take the opposite funding strategy. Since lending conditions reflect shifts in a wide range of unpredictable variables, borrowers can make no a priori assumptions about future market conditions no matter how certain they are about the value of their current economic reforms. Consequently the liability management strategy is necessarily focused on minimizing the combined "portfolio" volatility of both the asset and liability side. Minimizing portfolio volatility means that in order to limit potential damage, borrowers must structure their borrowings so that the cost of the debt is correlated with underlying conditions. In corporate finance this is considered ordinary hedging. The consequence is that although when underlying conditions *improve*, the real cost to the borrower immediately and automatically increases, it does so when the borrower is best able to handle the higher cost.

When conditions *deteriorate*, on the other hand, the cost automatically declines. This reduces the volatility of the borrower's overall performance by allowing the borrower to "share" upside and downside risk with investors. There are many obvious forms of *correlated* funding structures—for sovereigns dependent on foreign capital they include medium- or long-term fixed-rate local currency borrowings, equity sales and project financing, borrowings indexed to commodity prices or inversely indexed to U.S. interest rates, and so on. A large body of work in corporate finance theory can be applied to sovereign entities, which makes clear the volatility implication of different asset-liability strategies.[17] In the next chapter I will expand my dis-

17. During the sovereign debt restructurings of the 1980s a few farsighted analysts—like Frank Fernandez, then at Manufacturers Hanover, and Gary Evans, then at Bank of America—tried to incorporate *correlated* instruments into the restructuring agreements. The "Value Recovery Rights" attached to

cussion of inverted capital structures. More specifically, I will discuss the role of inverted structures in financial crises.

A Form of World Bank *Correlated* Lending

Most multilateral financial institutions, like the World Bank, have severe limits on their ability to mismatch loans and funding. In order to minimize volatility and guard them from the risk of loss, the loans they make must be denominated in the same currencies in which they are funded, and any differences must be hedged in the currency swap market. Because nearly all of the funding raised by the World Bank and other multilateral institutions is raised in the major currency markets, where liquidity is deep enough to absorb their borrowing needs, this means that most of their loans are also denominated in the world's major currencies. But lending to LDCs in dollars, euros, or yen clearly increases the sensitivity of these countries to changes in international liquidity or currency value, and so constitutes *inverted* lending. When the local currency depreciates in real terms, usually during a period of poor economic conditions, the cost of servicing the World Band loan increases commensurately. When, on the other hand, the local currency is strengthening in relative terms, the cost of servicing the World Bank debt actually declines.

This is not the optimal way to assist in the development of poor countries. One solution for the World Bank and other multilateral lenders may be to reindex their loans to take into account the impact of local currency moves in the short term while maintaining the long-term currency value of the loan. How would this work? Instead of making a loan denominated in U.S. dollars for some period with a fixed coupon, for example, the World Bank could change the term of the loan to take into account real currency appreciation and depreciation, on the reasonable assumption that these currency changes reflect external conditions in a predictable way. The loan could be redenominated into local currency (although still payable in U.S. dollars) with the coupon being set as some margin over the average depreciation of the local currency over the past five or ten years, such that the expected coupon and principal payment is equal to what the original fixed-rate dollar coupon and principal payment would have been.

Because the coupon reflects average depreciation, the World Bank will earn as much in local currency terms on average as if it had lent in U.S. dollars. However, the timing of its payments is much easier

---

certain Brady bonds, like those of Mexico and Venezuela, were complex warrants that partially compensated for debt forgiveness by specifying additional debt payments in the case that oil revenues were to exceed some amount.

for the borrower to bear and actually forces the World Bank to act in a countercyclical way so as to reduce the volatility of foreign capital flows. During periods of unexpected weakness in the currency, when the country is facing a reduction in foreign capital inflows, the real value of the payments to the World Bank immediately decreases, and the greater the currency weakness, the greater the reduction in the real value of the debt servicing payments. During periods of greater-than-average currency strength, when, presumably, the borrowing country is doing well economically, its payments to the World Bank are higher in real terms.

The net effect for the borrower is obvious. Its payment obligations are directly indexed to the availability of foreign capital, so that the impact of changes in foreign capital flows is reduced. There isn't the moral hazard there might be in a "plain vanilla" loan in local currency because the borrowing country cannot use its ability to monetize its own currency to erode the value of its obligations. The only way to take advantage of the funding structure to lower the value of its obligation would be to have continuously accelerating depreciation. As soon as the currency's depreciation was less than it had been in the past five or ten years, its debt servicing costs would immediately begin to make up for the previous "low" debt servicing costs.

For the World Bank, there will be an increase in the volatility associated with its earnings, but on average, the amount of its earnings will stay fairly constant, and to the extent that it has a diversified pool of borrowers, the total earnings volatility will be low. What is more, countries that are on a path of sustained improvement and are pulling themselves out of LDC status will effectively subsidize countries whose economies are in a steep and sustained fall, thus automatically providing a small amount of debt forgiveness to countries that most require it.

Structures like these are fairly straightforward to design and easy to implement. Their impact, however, can be striking. They form a systematic, easily calculated way of allowing the multilateral lenders to make "equity-like" investments in LDC governments. These investments are equity-like because they involve some sharing of risks, with the World Bank benefiting from a country's development while losing out in the case of a country whose economy is in nearly permanent decline. This type of funding is the most basic type of *correlated* funding.

Types of Funding

Table 6.2 lists a variety of funding transactions that demonstrate different types of *correlated* and *inverted* funding. Although conditions and terms can vary, so that the amount of correlation or inversion can

Table 6.2. Inverted and correlated types of funding

Type of funding	"Normal" market volatility	Market breaks
Inverted		
Credit-sensitive structures (e.g., FRANs)	Credit spread component of coupon increases in falling markets and decreases in rising markets	Coupon can shoot up to extremely high levels.
Short-term dollar debt	Financing cost declines (increases) as credit spreads improve (deteriorate)	Cost shoots up as a function of currency weakness. Refinancing risk can become overwhelming
Putable external debt	Lowers borrowing cost at the expense of giving investors the benefit of interest rate increases	Borrower is forced to refinance.
Short-term local currency debt	In moderate volatility, costs decline (increase) as sovereign credibility improves (deteriorates)	Costs shoot up as real interest rates rise. Government is forced to trade refinancing risk with inflating money base.
Floating-rate local currency debt	In moderate volatility, costs decline (increase) as sovereign credibility improves (deteriorates)	Costs shoot up as real interest rates rise.
Long-term floating-rate dollar debt	Financing costs indexed to foreign interest rates	Cost shoots up as a function of currency weakness. Avoids refinancing risk.
Long-term fixed-rate dollar debt	Costs decline (increase) in real terms as currency strengthens (weakens)	Cost shoots up as a function of currency weakness. Avoids refinancing risk.
Correlated		
Callable external debt	Increases borrowing cost but gives the benefit of interest rate increases to borrower	Locks in long-term financing.
Inverse floaters	Coupons increase when index (e.g., LIBOR) declines, and vice versa	Depends on behavior of index.
Commodity-linked debt (direct link for exporters and inverted link for importers)	Costs decline (increase) as revenues decline (increase)	Although the dollar component of the debt increases linearly as a function of currency weakness, the commodity-linked portion softens the blow.
Fixed-rate local currency debt	In moderate volatility, costs decline (increase) as sovereign credibility deteriorates (improves)	Costs contract sharply as a function of currency weakness.
Foreign direct investment	Dividends depend on profitability	Dividend payments are interrupted.
Equity (for private sector borrowers only)	In moderate volatility, costs decline (increase) as sovereign credibility deteriorates (improves)	Costs contract sharply as a function of currency and market weakness.

also vary, in general I have listed the funding types in descending order such that the most stable types of funding are at the bottom of the table. Included in the table is foreign direct investment (FDI). Because this is usually in the form of equity and is generally not sensitive to market conditions, it can be among the safest types of financing available to an LDC, and it is usually eagerly sought by LDC policy-makers for this reason. I should point out, however, that Ricardo Hausmann, formerly the chief economist of the Inter-American Development Bank, has recently argued that high levels of FDI may represent a market failure for LDCs, since high levels of FDI are likely to occur when other forms of growth financing are not available. "The share of FDI in capital flows is not a measure of anything good happening in the economy."[18]

18. Quoted in Richard Lapper, "Foreign Direct Investment Predominance in Latin America is Bad Sign, Argues Senior Economist," *Financial Times*, March 23, 2000.

7

The Capital Structure Trap

The Impact of External Shocks

To return, for a moment, to the chapters on history and the *liquidity* model: in those chapters I argued that there are, broadly speaking, four stages to the long-term international lending financial cycle. First, some displacement causes a rapid liquidity expansion in the major global financial centers. Second, there is a sudden outpouring of capital flows to LDCs. Third, a second exogenous shock results in a rapid collapse of liquidity in the rich-country financial center. And fourth, the international loan crisis begins.

Not all shocks, however, involve a major long-term liquidity contraction. As I discussed in chapter 3 and at the end of chapter 5, it is necessary to distinguish between crises that come about after a period of sustained liquidity contraction and crises that are accompanied by short-term contractions that are really more in the nature of margin collapses. The former can lead to global debt crises, whereas the latter can be much less damaging if a country's capital structure does not force itself into default. The past few years have seen several shocks to the financial system in which the liquidity impact was very short term. In each case there may have been a temporary "flight to quality" and a collapse of margin lending, but both of these can, and did, revert quickly.

After the Asian crisis of late 1997, based on mistaken analogies with the 1980s, many analysts believed that the emerging markets had received a near-mortal blow. They expected that lending even to regions like Latin America would not recover for years. The firm for which I work, Bear Stearns, was virtually alone in predicting that the Latin American market would revive strongly in 1998 and, to use a phrase in my newsletter in November 1997, would be "bubble-like" by the end of the first quarter.

Our reasoning was straightforward. The Asian crisis had converted the large current account deficits of a number of Asian countries into even larger surpluses. In Table 5.1. I showed how the current account for the four most afflicted countries swung $124 billion from negative to positive. The obverse of these current account reversals was to be a huge increase in capital outflows from Asian countries into the United States, which would build up liquidity in the United States. Given the healthy state of United States risk appetite—the strong high-yield market at the time demonstrated this—it was just a question of time, in our opinion, before the Latin bond markets would boom. The Asian collapse, in other words, rather than being a consequence of a secular liquidity contraction, was actually enhancing a high-liquidity period.

In fact our reasoning turned out to be correct. The first quarter of 1998 was the biggest quarter in Latin American history for new bond issues, and the expected emerging market debt crisis failed to materialize at the time. This should not have been a surprise. Without a major liquidity contraction, there has never been a global debt crisis, and so the recent crises—as difficult as this may be to believe—actually occurred during an "optimal" time of abundant underlying global liquidity. Nonetheless their impacts were devastating in many cases.

Why do external shocks sometimes result in sharp but relatively short and containable market breaks and other times in financial and economic collapse? Princeton University economist Paul Krugman argues that the question arising from the recent financial crises that most needs to be answered is World Bank economist Guillermo Calvo's question: "Why was so large a punishment imposed for so small a crime?"[1] This question implies that there are mechanisms that transform minor policy mistakes into major economic disasters, and the trick is to figure out what that mechanism is. The literature is not always clear on this. Charles Kindleberger writes about the market distress that accompanies the realization at some point in the boom that credit positions are extended beyond some sustainable limit. A "slight premonitory movement" in the market occurs, but it isn't clear whether this will lead to chaos or will simply pass:

1. Paul Krugman, *The Return of Depression Economics* (W. W. Norton, 1999), p. 58.

"We have no crash at present, only a slight premonitory movement of the ground under our feet," wrote Lord Overstone to
his friend, G. W. Norman on 1 November 1845. From time to
time the stress abates. On other occasions it intensifies. More
and more speculators seek to get out of whatever was the object
of speculation, to reduce their distended liabilities, and to
switch into money; and more and more it becomes clear that
not everyone can do so at once. There is a rush, a panic, and a
crash.[2]

There has been no shortage of reasons proffered by analysts in an
attempt to explain the root causes of the crises. Morgan Stanley economist Stephen Roach refers to the two schools of thought regarding
the sources of the crises. The first school, in his words, "attributes this
unprecedented string of events to a flawed policy architecture, characterized by unsustainable budget deficits, misaligned exchange rates,
weak financial system underpinnings, excessive risk-taking, and political instability and corruption." The second school argues that "the
inexorable continuum of globalization may itself give rise to a steady
stream of strains and tensions that leave both borrowers and lenders
vulnerable to crisis."[3]

These explanations often have a strongly political flavor. One
group, the market liberalizers, focuses on corrupt policy-makers, in-
sufficiently hard currencies, weak fiscal discipline, crony capitalism,
official intervention in credit allocation, central planning, revulsion
to free trade, and other fundamental flaws in the underlying economy.
Another group, often broadly critical of the Washington Consensus
policies, prefers to blame market failures, conspiracies of politically
motivated speculators, herd behavior by twenty-eight-year-old bond
traders, "market psychology" factors, excessive "openness" to foreign
capital, et cetera.

In each case these many fundamental flaws in the underlying
economic structure—caused by, depending on your politics, either
too much or too little capitalism—were only exposed, presumably,
by the shock. But both sets of explanations miss the point. The problem
with the "market psychology" arguments—and their cousins the "self-
fulfilling speculative attack" explanations—is that they are circular
and explain very little. Panics occur, it seems, because they were
about to occur. The "fundamental flaws" argument, which is usually
the argument taken most seriously by analysts and policy-makers,

2. Charles Kindleberger, *A Financial History of Western Europe* (Oxford
University Press, 1993), p. 265.
3. Stephen S. Roach, "Learning to Live with Globalization," Testimony before the Committee on Banking and Financial Services of the U.S. House of
Representatives, May 20, 1999.

generally points out weaknesses in the political, financial, or economic structure of the affected countries—possibly real ones—and argues that specific reforms will protect the country from similar crises in the future. They provide, however, almost no explanation as to why shocks occurred when they did. Just as important, they do not explain why shocks did not occur during the Asian crisis in 1997 in countries like China, India, Taiwan, et cetera, which actually had many of the same fundamental problems as the countries that did succumb to the market collapses. Both sets of explanations implicitly assume that it is enough to point out some flaw in the system that existed prior to the collapse to explain the cause of the collapse, without specifying the mechanism that converted a general flaw into a collapse.

Transmitting Volatility

In spite of their solid grounding in what seems like common sense, these explanations fail to explain how a necessary adjustment becomes a financial calamity. They confuse the causes of disequilibrium with the process of adjustment—which I tried to separate in Figure 1.1. In chapter 1 I discussed the role of capital structure as a transmission mechanism for external shocks, and it seems to me that this is the most useful answer to the question of what determines whether an external shock becomes an irritant or a calamity. The virulence of the crisis is largely a factor of capital structure vulnerability. There have been attempts to propose this as the obvious place to look—for example in a recent article by Richard Brealy[4] and, perhaps less clearly, in several of Paul Krugman's articles.[5]

Other analysts have also pointed to the role of capital structure, although the point seems to be more controversial than it ought to be. For example, Michael Backman, in a book on the Asian crisis quoted approvingly by the *Economist* and the *Wall Street Journal*, among others, focuses largely on what he believes to be poor fundamentals as explanations for the crises. He argues that the causes of the crisis reflect "the dark side of business in Asia" and insists that it doesn't help "when the myth that Asia's collapse was *financial* or due merely to *speculators* continues to be perpetuated."[6] In a similar vein, former IMF head of global capital markets surveillance, David Folkerts-

4. Richard Brealy, "The Asian Crisis: Lessons for Crisis Management and Prevention," *International Finance* 2, no. 2 (July 1999): 249–72.

5. See, for example, Paul Krugman, "Balance Sheets, the Transfer Problem, and Financial Crises," Official Paul Krugman Website, January 1999. http://web.mit.edu/krugman/www/

6. Michael Backman, *Asian Eclipse: Exposing the Dark Side of Business in Asia* (John Wiley, 1999), p. 2.

Landau, calls the behavior of international financial markets "the least important source of instability." For him, the problem is policy failures and their destabilizing effects.[7]

But for some market participants and analysts, it is clear that the capital structure has very obviously played a role. In one of the best pieces on the Mexican Tequila Crisis, Guillermo Calvo, in analyzing the various proposed explanations for the contagion aspects of the crisis, points out that

> the "Tequila" effect is especially disconcerting because many affected countries had few direct links with Mexico, and had not patterned their policy regimes after Mexico's. Thus, in other words, it is hard to find "fundamentals" that could account for the "Tequila" effect.[8]

Earlier in the same piece Calvo argues that Mexico's crisis has made evident that balance-of-payments crises are not only provoked "by *flow* type disequilibria, like current account or fiscal deficits, but are also, and perhaps fundamentally, linked to financial vulnerabilities."[9] Others have made the same argument. Martin Werner, former deputy minister of finance of Mexico, argued in a class at Columbia University that Mexican authorities had mistakenly focused on flow disequilibria and not on stock disequilibria, when it was sharp adjustments in stock that precipitated the collapse of confidence. In his May 20, 1999, testimony before the House banking committee, Federal Reserve Bank Chairman Alan Greenspan made several references to maturity mismatches as a source of the Asian crises.[10] Former Treasury Secretary Robert Rubin made similar references in the policy speech he made at John Hopkins University a month later:

> One of the striking elements of the recent crises was the extent to which countries actually reached for short-term capital, and thereby greatly increased their vulnerability to crises down the road. The lesson of these experiences is that the greater protection provided by long-term borrowing is worth paying for.

He went on to discuss policies that would aim to encourage both a greater reliance on long-term borrowing and the development of

7. David Folkerts-Landau, "Testimony before a Hearing of the Committee on Banking and Financial Services," May 20, 1999.

8. Guillermo Calvo, "Capital Flows and Macroeconomic Management: Tequila Lessons," March 16, 1996, draft of a paper presented at the IMF-sponsored *Seminar on Implications of International Capital Flows*, Washington, D.C. December 11–15, 1995, p. 11.

9. Ibid., p. 1.

10. Statement made before the Committee on Banking and Financial Services, U.S. House of Representatives, May 20, 1999.

domestic debt markets. Finally, in one of the better short pieces on the topic, MIT economist Rudiger Dornbusch is fairly blunt. "Much of the discussion of what happened in Mexico, Russia, Brazil and Asia just cannot get itself to accept a simple proposition: the central reason for currency crises is deep mismanagement of national balance sheets, exchange rate policy and political responsibility."[11]

The Capital Structure Trap

Although analysts are often aware of the role of a country's financial structure in a crisis, we still lack a systematic model of sovereign crises. Why do some crises—Britain's abandonment of the European Exchange Rate Mechanism in 1992, Colombia's devaluation in late 1998, and Brazil's devaluation in 1999—quickly stabilize, while others degenerate? Although there have been a variety of attempted explanations, the most sophisticated explanation proposes that the cause of the recent crises lies primarily in the banking system.[12] According to this argument, countries with risky banking systems in which the amount of equity is insufficient to cover their credit risk or asset-liability mismatch are susceptible to financial crises. The transmission mechanism is primarily through the inability of the banking system to absorb shocks, and the process works in some ways through the feedback mechanism between the initial shock and the consequence of the shock.

In this case, as some exogenous shock works its way through the banking system, the breakdown of the banks has secondary effects on interest rates, liquidity, credit, et cetera that exacerbate the original shock. In order to protect a system from crises, bank capital requirements need to be beefed up and the possibility of an asset-liability mismatch reduced so that the banking system is protected from shocks. I do not disagree at all with this focus on the banking system and suspect that it is correct in seeing the mechanism here, largely because in most LDCs the banking system is the most important component of the national capital structure. But I would stress that it is not just the banking system but the entire capital structure—which involves a variety of ways in which assets and liabilities are indexed—where the exposure lies. The banking system approach is, in a sense, a subset of the capital structure framework.

11. Rudiger Dornbusch, "Private Market Responses to Financial Crises," *World Economic Laboratory Columns Archive* (October 1999): p. 1.

12. For example, an upcoming book by Columbia University professors David Beim and Charles Calomiris makes this argument, as I understand it from conversations with the authors.

It is always useful to turn on this subject to economist Hyman Minsky, whose "financial instability hypothesis" I discussed earlier. Minsky sees an economy as a system in which endogenous processes can generate "incoherent states." "Cycles and the crises," he says, "are not the results of shocks to the system or of policy errors. They are endogenous."[13] Minsky argues that crises are not caused because external events or bad policy choices force a revaluation of asset values but are instead determined inside the system. Like Minsky, I will argue that the capital structure of a country can be arranged in such a way that external shocks mechanically lead to these incoherent states. When the structure is lined up in this way, the country has stepped into what I will call a "capital structure trap," or a funding strategy that does two things:

1. It links financial or debt servicing costs to the economy in an *inverted* way.
2. More dramatically, it locks the borrower and its creditors into self-reinforcing behavior in which small changes, good or bad, can force players to behave in ways that exacerbate the changes.

In chapter 6 I distinguished between *inverted* and *correlated* types of funding. I pointed out that the former type of funding automatically acts to increase payments as external conditions deteriorate, while the latter does the opposite. The capital structure trap consists of an *inverted* liability structure in which an external shock can force both the borrower's revenue and its debt servicing expense to move sharply in an adverse direction. This occurs to such a degree that it forces a sharp increase in the probability of bankruptcy, which, by changing the behavior of investors, then forces the capital structure to move even more strongly in an adverse direction. This is what makes the trap different from an "ordinary" badly designed capital structure. A typical badly designed capital structure simply fails to take advantage of risk-reduction structures—in itself it does not add volatility. The capital structure trap, on the other hand, exists when the capital structure itself incorporates a feedback mechanism that causes the domestic impact of the external shock to feed on itself until the debt burden spirals out of control.

The capital structure trap is generally a sovereign or "large-system" problem, since for it to work the borrowing entity must be large enough to affect the volatility of financial inputs. Ford Motor Com-

---

13. Hyman P. Minsky, "The Financial Instability Hypothesis: A Clarification," in Martin Feldstein, *The Risk of Economic Crisis* (University of Chicago Press, 1991), p. 165.

pany, to take a random example, can put into place an "ordinary" unstable capital structure that wouldn't necessarily be self-reinforcing. It might, for example decide to convert all of its current debt into yen-denominated debt in order, perhaps, to take advantage of lower expected borrowing costs. But as inadvisable as such a strategy might be, it would most likely not consist of a capital structure trap. If Ford ran into a financing crisis, the behavior of the yen–dollar exchange rate would probably not itself be affected by the crisis and would not systematically worsen Ford's position. Of course if a Ford crisis caused investor nervousness about the U.S. economy and subsequently pushed the dollar lower against other major currencies, then there would be some self-reinforcing element in Ford's capital structure, but it would still probably not be a major factor.

The case is, however, different for a country. If a country borrows in a foreign currency, an unexpected shock to the currency can, by harming the country's ability to pay the external debt, put further pressure on the currency. Nonetheless there are ways in which even corporations put themselves into the trap. For example, a corporate borrower that faces a liquidity crisis may only obtain very short-term funding at such high rates that the debt servicing costs makes it even more unlikely that long-term investors get repaid. As each maturity rolls off, and default probabilities rise, the refinancing cost increases until it is unsustainable. At that point, the borrower faces a backward sloping supply curve and borrowers boycott all new loans. The process is self-reinforcing and continues until the initially small shock either forces the borrower into bankruptcy or is resolved by a large lender of last resort who provides sufficient liquidity before the borrower actually becomes insolvent.

The argument presented at the beginning of this section in which the cause of financial crises is a fragile banking system describes a classic capital structure trap. In this case, the external shock works its way through undercapitalized banks. As the shock increases the riskiness of the banking system, the banks are forced to react by reducing their loan exposure and trying to raise liquidity. Weaker banks and less creditworthy corporate customers are denied credit, or get credit only at very high rates, which increases their riskiness and puts pressure on all bank portfolios. As defaults begin to rise, already thin bank capital erodes and reinforces the tight liquidity in the system, and so on, until banks and corporations collapse among themselves. I will show this again when I discuss the Mexican example in the next part of this chapter.

What is important about the capital structure trap is that a financial collapse does not require panicked investors, irrational markets, Anglo-Saxon speculators, or even arrogant young bond traders. All it requires is a discrete body of rational investors with less than full information who react to uncertainty by increasing their required returns. In such a case, it is the self-reinforcing characteristic of the trap that forces the collapse, and it causes the collapse in a very mechanical way.

Watching the Trap Work

In chapter 6 I suggested that the conventional model of liquidity flows would normally encourage government officials committed to a series of "successful" policy reforms to retain confidence in the continuation of those capital inflows. Perhaps not surprisingly, during boom periods, LDCs have nearly always borrowed primarily in *inverted* structures, and given the influence of the sovereign borrower on financial volatility, these structures tend to be self-reinforcing. This kind of borrowing unwittingly forces them into the capital structure trap. At the extreme, this automatic self-reinforcing behavior can force a small shock to spiral out of control as market players indirectly act to increase the effect of the shock. Nearly every recent financial crisis has occurred because the affected country was caught in the capital structure trap.

Mexico and Indonesia can show concretely how the capital structure trap works. There were two self-reinforcing components to Mexico's trap. The first had to do with the indexation of local currency debt. After the 1994 devaluation, economic activity fell and domestic interest rates rose. Because nearly 100% of local borrowings were either short term or on a floating-rate basis, the increase in rates fed immediately into higher debt servicing costs. The immediate effect of declining revenues and increasing costs forced some corporations and individuals to default on their obligations as their reduced economic circumstances and ballooning interest rate coupons made them unable to pay their debt servicing costs.

This sudden increase in bad loans put pressure on the already precarious banking system and forced banks into a panic rush to liquefy their balance sheets. When everyone wants liquidity, however, the liquidity premium rises. The banks immediately raised their peso lending rates even higher as liquidity dried up. Of course this only increased the problems for the remaining corporate and individual borrowers. Because their loans were indexed to short-term interest rates, their costs shot up immediately before the effect of inflation could raise their revenues and asset values, pushing more of them to default. The self-reinforcing loop—high rates that caused consumer and corporate defaults that caused even higher rates—led ultimately to peso interest rates of well over 100%.

The second component that characterized Mexico's capital structure, short-term dollar-indexed borrowing, had a very similar sequence of events. In this case, however, the declining peso mainly increased the debt servicing costs of the federal government's Tesobonos exposure and thereby put pressure on the government's credibility. This, of course, increased the pressure on the peso and on local interest rates. When the two traps were combined, it was nearly inevitable that, following a devaluation, the crisis would spiral out of control.

Indonesia in 1997, with its large number of private corporations that had borrowed in U.S. dollars, provides another dramatic example of the trap. As I discussed in the previous chapter, borrowing dollars is a form of *inverted* borrowing, Indonesian corporations were able to take advantage of the booming economy and to reduce borrowing cost at the expense of assuming the currency risk. Following the relatively small initial currency break in July, which had actually stabilized by November, the formerly beneficial effect of the correlation caused the impact to reverse itself as the cost of dollar debt immediately increased when the Indonesian rupiah depreciated.

Because too many Indonesian corporations—many without dollar earnings—had borrowed in foreign currency and needed to hedge against further depreciation, some of the more leveraged ones were forced to buy dollars (sell rupiah) to prevent further currency losses that might have bankrupted them. In a market in which liquidity had suddenly dried up, this disorderly rush to buy dollars caused more rapid currency depreciation, which increased the debt burden for a larger group of dollar borrowers and placed a greater number of companies at risk of bankruptcy. This forced further hedging activity by these corporations, which, of course, caused further declines in the rupiah and larger debt losses affecting a wider group of borrowers. The process continued to feed on itself until eventually, under the expanding pressure, the currency broke beyond any rational level.

The important thing here is that although the rupiah crisis began in July and August, the real collapse of the rupiah began after November, when the effect of the previous devaluation began to be seen on corporate balance sheets. Contrary to popular beliefs, hedge funds were not actively shorting the rupiah to induce greater declines. On the contrary, there was a perception among them that the rupiah, like the Mexican peso in 1995, would quickly stabilize and then strengthen and—in combination with the high interest rates on rupiah bonds—would be very profitable for investors. After the initial break there is very good anecdotal evidence that the hedge funds were net buyers, not net sellers,[14] but the trap had already been sprung, and

14. I was in regular contact with three large "macro" funds, including the most famous of these, and our discussions about Asia generally centered on ways to gain protected access to *long* rupiah positions. There was very little interest in shorting the currency.

only a huge buyer of rupiah could have put a stop to the inexorable break in the currency.

Because both Mexico and Indonesia were caught in capital structure traps, the magnitude of the currency declines shocked even those analysts who prior to the crisis were most convinced that these countries' currencies had been overvalued. Whatever the "right" amount of depreciation would have been, analysts were nearly universally surprised by how much beyond any reasonable equilibrium level the currencies plunged. The most difficult question was why the currencies had not tended to some stable equilibrium—as they did, for example, in Brazil in 1999 and Thailand in 1984. The favorite "answers" were either to cite market irrationality or fundamental economic weaknesses, but of course these are just ways of not answering. The real answer lies in the way the market break forced players to act in ways that exacerbated the break. A self-reinforcing process has no stable equilibrium and will continue moving in one direction until a larger outside force causes it to unwind. Until defaults or massive bailout packages intervened, there was no way for the currencies to stop depreciating.

Selling the Breaking Asset

The trap almost always works the same way. Figure 7.1 shows the series of events that occurs following the external shock that forces the market collapse.

1. A fundamental disequilibrium that has been building up over time is suddenly forced to break. Usually this results in a sharp downward move in the currency. Generally in LDCs the disequilibrium shows up in the value of the currency and

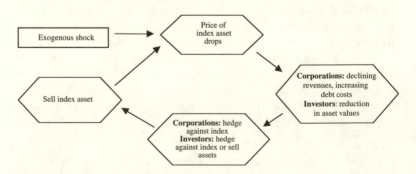

Figure 7.1. The capital structure trap

the adjustment takes the form of a currency break, but this is not necessary. It can also occur as a sudden rise in domestic interest rates, a refinancing boycott, a collapse in the value of collateral backing loans, a collapse in commodity prices, or any combination of these.

2. A significant portion of the country's external and domestic liabilities are indexed in an *inverted* way so that, as the market breaks, payment obligations immediately rise in real terms as a direct function of the break.

3. Although the break, since it occurs as a reversal of some previous disequilibrium, should benefit more domestic actors than it hurts, the size of the indexation immediately causes a tremendous run-up in default probabilities—which transforms the appetite of investors. Just as important, the effect of the break is widely diffused, so that there is no coordination in the response of actors (investors or borrowers).

4. In order to protect themselves from default, borrowers and investors are immediately forced to sell the "breaking" asset. In the case of dollar borrowers, this means buying dollars (selling pesos) to hedge the dollar liabilities. Local currency borrowers—who have mismatched their assets and liabilities because the local market consists only of short-term paper—must borrow ever-larger amounts (sell bonds) in order to pay principal and exploding interest bills. Their behavior is not a matter of psychology, panic, or herd mentality but rather a forced need to close out a losing "speculative" position.

5. The very act of closing out the position, of course, causes further price declines, which increases the number of actors that fall into the trap. The process is self-reinforcing until all actors are either fully hedged or in default. It is only then that the market stabilizes—perceptions of underlying value have very little to do with it.

Commentators like to discuss the herd psychology of a crisis, but what is impressive about the capital structure trap is how mechanical it is—improvements and deterioration in external conditions are automatically mirrored in the capital structure, and investors, traders, and borrowers are forced into extreme procyclical behavior. If "psychology" refers to behavior caused by the irrational response of traders and investors to perceived problems, there is almost nothing psychological about a capital structure trap.

The effect is the opposite when the borrower is funded in a *correlated* structure, such as with local currency fixed-rate debt. In this case the *real* cost of the debt will be automatically eroded by the inflation that accompanies the currency break. This kind of capital structure immediately acts to improve the borrower's financial position by *contracting* the debt overhang after a currency crisis. In Mexico's case, for example, had most internal debt been in the form of medium-term fixed-rate peso loans instead of floating-rate debt, Mexican borrowers would have immediately received partial relief after the devaluation as inflation eroded the debt burden. The worse the devaluation and subsequent inflation, the lighter the debt burden would have been. At the extreme, the debt burden would have been eliminated and the pressure on the borrowers removed altogether. At that point local exporters could begin to enjoy the effects of a weaker currency and corporate managers could return their attention to managing the operations of the companies.

This illustrates the main difference between the two types of capital structures. Following an adverse shock, the debt burden on *inverted* funding automatically expands and becomes part of the problem, and the more the market reacts to this problem the worse it becomes until the system breaks and the debt is "cleared," usually by means of massive defaults and debt restructuring. *Correlated* funding causes the debt burden to decline after a shock, and the worse the shock, the more rapid the decline. *Correlated* structures have an automatic tendency to arrive at a stable equilibrium, while *inverted* structures have an automatic tendency to increase instability in either direction and are fundamentally speculative whether the borrower intended it or not. It is this automatic tendency that makes the process of collapse seem so relentless. The debt structure reacts to the initial shock in such a way that the cost of the shock systematically expands at the same time that it is exacerbating the shock. The system is caught in a positive feedback loop that reinforces itself until some sort of breakdown occurs.[15]

Stepping into the Trap

LDCs generally place themselves in the capital structure trap for one of three reasons. During the boom periods in which they access large amounts of capital, levels of confidence concerning domestic policy reforms and the unstoppable nature of globalization are extremely high. Given the high confidence level, *inverted* structures seem like foolproof ways to lower financing costs over time. After all, if policymakers believe that borrowing conditions can only improve, why not

15. Incidentally, much of the debate about the dangers or usefulness of derivatives implicitly concerns the same issue. *Inverted* derivative instruments are by definition speculative and increase the buyer's volatility, while *correlated* derivative instruments are hedges. The instruments themselves are not intrinsically risky, but because they imply significant levels of leverage, both the hedging and speculative effects are magnified.

take on market risk, since it is likely to be only upside risk? Ironically, the trap is made worse when the economic policies are part of an international consensus on economic reforms, since policy-makers receive constant positive feedback about their policies. This encourages them even more in the belief that their policies will work over the medium term to keep the capital spigots open and, by reducing refinancing fears, it increases their willingness to take on risk. More important, international approval often comes with implicit or explicit bilateral or multilateral financial or political support that, as Columbia University professor Charles Calomiris has argued, may increase the risky behavior of both borrowers and lenders.[16]

The second reason LDCs place themselves in the capital structure trap usually occurs *after* the initial boom, when external conditions first start to become difficult. It may be that investors change the form of their lending in response to the greater risk perception, so that capital inflows are structured in a riskier way. I have already discussed in chapter 6 how models of imperfect information suggest that a typical investor response to excessive increases in credit risk and borrowing costs is to roll over debt with shorter tenors or to ration credit altogether. The desire of investors to manage their risks more carefully forces the borrower, paradoxically, into even riskier behavior. This happened most notably in the late 1970s, when some of the large commercial banks with heavy LDC exposure began to worry about the sheer size and manageability of LDC debt. Their response was partially to reduce their own lending—although usually by syndicating larger amounts of new loans to secondary banks, whose exposure mushroomed after 1978–79—and partially by shortening the maturity of new loans. The shorter maturities only had the effect, however, of increasing the refinancing requirement and, ironically, speeding up the day of reckoning.

But the borrower may also *willingly* engage in risky behavior for signaling purposes, and this is the third of the three reasons for walking into the trap. During periods of investor nervousness, borrowing countries may switch out of less risky forms of borrowing even when it is available and into riskier forms in order both to lower borrowing costs and, more explicitly, to signal confidence to investors by increasing the cost of a policy reversal. The process is nearly always misguided. The Mexican government, for example, stepped up the issuance in 1994 of dollar-linked Tesobonos to replace its normal domestic peso borrowings. This was done to reduce investor exposure to the currency while signaling Mexico's complete confidence in the

16. "The IMF's Imprudent Role as Lender of Last Resort," *Cato Journal* 17, no. 3 (Winter, 1998): 33–41.

integrity of the exchange policy—by radically increasing the cost to the country of devaluing the peso.[17] It worked partially, but in the wrong way—when the devaluation eventually came, the cost of the Tesobonos exposure nearly bankrupted the country.

Brazil did something similar in 1997–98. At that time investors were concerned about Brazil's high fiscal deficit and demanded high rates to compensate them for the risk of a currency break. The Central Bank responded by structuring its local currency borrowings on an overnight or floating-rate basis as a way of taking advantage of future expected declining borrowing costs—the inevitable consequence, they believed, of the effect on their credibility of their orthodox commitment to the currency. In fact things did not work out that smoothly. The short-term interest indexing of internal debt caused debt costs to increase immediately after every exogenous shock, and these shocks unfortunately were a regular feature of the global markets during 1997–98. This debt structure, by automatically running up the fiscal deficit, raised nervousness further, which further raised domestic interest rates, and so on toward the inevitable crisis. Instead of providing a breathing space, the floating-rate debt took on a life of its own as the feedback loop ensured increasing instability in the capital structure.

Inevitably the cycle of high fiscal deficits leading to currency pressure, leading, via the interest rate mechanism, to higher fiscal deficits, forced the currency collapse in January 1999. The irony is that during 1994–97, confidence in Brazil was so high that foreign investors would have gladly purchased three- to five-year fixed-rate local currency bonds at rates *below* Brazil's one-year rate. While bankers clamored to arrange such financings, the Central Bank rejected the possibility of locking in these rates because they believed them to be too high. It chose instead to assume the full interest rate risk on the grounds that its policies could only lead to one possible outcome: further rapid declines in interest rates. It also convinced itself, once conditions started deteriorating, that weakening investor interest could be overcome by increasing the country's credibility—and credibility could be increased by amplifying the damage that could be caused by breaking the currency.[18] I will discuss in the next chapter why Brazil, unlike Mexico, which had in some ways a similar structure, did not collapse altogether.

17. Timothy P. Kessler, *Global Capital and National Politics: Reforming Mexico's Financial System* (Praeger, 1999), p. 107.

18. Various conversations with Central Bank and finance ministry officials.

The Credibility Scheme

This strategy of increasing credibility by increasing the damage caused by a policy reversal is one of the terrible ironies of the process. In chapter 6 I discussed the relationship between credibility and volatility, and I argued that to the extent a country increases its expected volatility, and the costs of a mismatch, it loses credibility. Let me be a little more precise. There is a possible signaling effect in the capital structure. By designing a highly *inverted* capital structure, some officials believe that they are signaling to the market their complete confidence in their policies and their refusal to change these policies—if they do, their *inverted* capital structure will impose punishing costs. But credibility can exist in a sort of Laffer curve in which increasing the cost of monetary "misbehavior" will increase investors' confidence in government policies and, consequently, the government's credibility—but only up to a point. At some point, when the cost of misbehavior is high enough, credibility actually declines. Figure 7.2 shows why.

As the graph suggests, by increasing the cost of financial misbehavior, a process I am calling increased "monetary severity," there is simultaneously a decreasing probability that the government will willingly misbehave and a higher amount of damage to the country if it does so. For example, by indexing its borrowings to the dollar, as Mexico did in 1994 and Thailand did in 1996, policy-makers signal to investors that they are willing to increase the cost of an undesirable

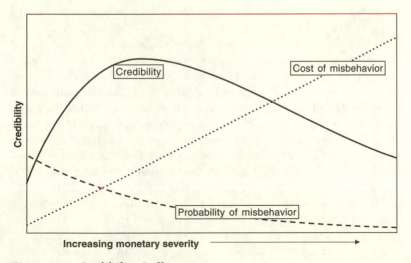

Figure 7.2. Credibility Laffer curve

policy shift in order to convince investors of their determination not to shift. The problem is that the cost to the country is also borne by the investor if it becomes high enough that the country is unable to meet its contractual payment obligations. This is what is meant by *financial distress*, and its effect is to reduce the value of outstanding obligations. At some point, the cost becomes so high that investors are unwilling to take on even a small probability of misbehavior. Add in a feedback loop in which investor reluctance acts to increase the probability of financial misbehavior (i.e., the country is "forced' to violate its monetary policy), and it is not at all surprising that at some point, investor perception of a country's credibility will decline as the cost of misbehavior increases.

In Brazil, the central bank president, Gustavo Franco, acted as if he believed that his monetary model could not fail and what he needed to do was prove to investors that Brazil was willing to self-destruct before it would give up the model. Although many bank economists applauded his actions, as evidenced by research reports, investors, not surprisingly, ultimately failed to see this as a good thing, and Brazil's credibility began declining rapidly. The most obvious place to look for evidence of declining credibility, the country's real interest rates, should have made it clear to Franco and even his most orthodox followers that the policy would probably not work, and as long as there was a reasonable probability of failure, the decision to impose a punishing monetary policy on the country should have, at the very least, been reexamined. In the end, of course, matters deteriorated quickly, exacerbated, as they always are, by unexpected external events, and the country was forced to devalue the currency. Even since the country has devalued and stabilized, the unstable short-term local debt structure, unfortunately, continues to be Brazil's biggest financial policy problem.

The problem is not a new one. Argentina fell into the same capital structure trap 110 years ago and followed the same misguided credibility-signaling strategy. The result was a nearly identical investor reaction that led ultimately to a sovereign financial crisis. In this case the Argentine banking system had been engaged during the 1880s in a rapid expansion of the money supply, which, after 1888, manifested itself in increasing gold withdrawals from the banking system. The government, believing that this simply reflected an extraordinary domestic economic expansion and trusting that in the long run foreign capital would keep gold levels high, defended the peso parity.

When previously enthusiastic British investors began expressing concern about political instability in Argentina in the late 1880s, the government tried to ensure confidence in the currency by converting its peso-denominated cedulas (mortgage bonds that were the largest component of foreign financing) into gold-backed cedulas. The government believed that if they increased the cost of devaluing to unacceptable levels, their credibility with British investors would soar. It didn't, and when the currency broke anyway in 1890, the suddenly expanding cost of the gold backing, combined with the panicked selling of pesos, forced the country into default, nearly precipitating the collapse of its chief banker, Baring Brothers, then England's most important private financial institution.[19] I discussed this episode in greater detail in chapters 4 and 5.

The Case of South Korea

Before concluding this chapter it is worth pointing out that the capital structure trap can often lead analysts to erroneous conclusions about the costs and values of certain economic policies because they confuse the destructive nature of the trap with fundamental weaknesses in the underlying economy. There is nothing like the spectacular crash of an economic entity to bring out criticism of its earlier strategies, whether or not the crash was caused by these strategies, and South Korea's shocking collapse in 1997 may be a case in point. On November 17, 1997, four and a half months after Thailand was forced to devalue the baht and three weeks after the Hong Kong stock index lost 10.4% in a single day, the Korean central bank, after weeks of fighting downward pressure on the currency, stopped defending the won. Within four days, amid much criticism at home for so humiliating a request, South Korea asked for IMF aid, and the president of the country, Kim Young Sam, went on television to apologize publicly for the disaster. In the following months the Korean stock market careened downward, the currency plunged, the rating agencies, who had already just revoked the country's AA ratings, set it off to "junk" status, and the country was forced into a humiliating $24 billion debt restructuring.

Analysts were and still are surprised by the sudden change in the country's fortunes. Before the crash Korea's fundamentals were actually fairly strong. The country had run a trade surplus as late as 1996, and its subsequent deficits were manageable. The current account deficit was under 4½% of GDP in 1996. Unlike Mexico, the case of Korea's domestic savings rate was very high, and again unlike Mexico, foreign capital inflows in Korea were more likely to fund investment than consumption.[20] It was even hard to argue that the won was overvalued—the IMF showed it as slightly undervalued relative to the

19. Roberto Cortes Conde, "The Origins of Banking in Argentina," in Richard Sylla, Richard Tilly, and Gabriel Tortella (eds.), *The State, the Financial System, and Economic Modernization* (Cambridge University Press, 1999), pp. 239–43.

20. Ha-joon Chang, "Korea: The Misunderstood Crisis," *World Development* 26, no. 8 (1998): 1555–61.

previous ten years.[21] The surprise over Korea's collapse is reinforced by the speed of the country's recovery. If the Korean economy was in such bad shape, after all, how was it able to turn around so quickly in the next two years? In February 2000, the Chase Bank wrote in a research report that "Looking at the numbers, it is still hard to explain how Korea's crash was triggered. Few of the normal warning signs were evident, but Korea tumbled from clear skies at 30,000 feet."[22]

The Chase research report focuses on weaknesses in the banking sector to explain the surprising fall, but this is only part of the story. South Korea's main problem, it turns out, was a classical capital structure mismatch in which both banks *and* corporations had participated. Although it may have had too much debt, the numbers did not seem particularly frightening—the Chase report points out that debt service was low and the balance of payments was not obviously weak. With only $160 billion of external debt—32% of GDP—it was hard to imagine that Korea could not handle the debt servicing. What was very troubling, however, was the way the existing debt was structured:

1. There was a huge maturity mismatch, with well over $100 billion of short-term debt that was used to fund long-term investments, whereas dollar reserves were miniscule (see table 7.1).
2. There was an even larger currency mismatch, with much of the debt in the form of "cheap" foreign currency while most of the funded assets were local assets and operations.

The Korean collapse was used as prima facie evidence that the Korean economy had been mismanaged, but this is an unnecessary assumption. Focusing on fundamental political and economic management may be useful in the long run, but it is less relevant as an explanation for the crisis—Korea's capital structure provides more than sufficient reason for the collapse. After all, although the Asian crisis spread to Taiwan, Hong Kong, China and India, none of these countries suffered the way Korea did, even though it is hard to propose that on average their underlying economies were that much better than Korea's. The differences in their respective capital structures, however, are striking—none of these countries had significant amounts of *inverted* debt. As evidence of the unstable capital structure, short-term external debt represented a very large fraction of total reserves (in evaluating liquidity risk, corporate analysts always offset

21. See Morris Goldstein, *The Asian Financial Crisis: Causes, Cures, and Systemic Implications* (Institute for International Economics, June 1998), p. 15.

22. Robin Hubbard, *International Fixed Income Research: Weekly Focus*, Chase Securities, February 11, 2000, p. 5.

Table 7.1. Selected economic indicators for South Korea

	1994	1995	1996	1997	1998
Real GDP growth	8.3%	8.9%	6.8%	5.0%	−5.8%
GDP deflator	7.7%	7.1%	3.9%	3.1%	5.3%
Unemployment	2.4%	2.0%	2.0%	2.6%	6.8%
Fiscal balance (% of GDP)	0.1%	0.3%	0.0%	−1.7%	−4.2%
Current account balance (% of GDP)	−1.0%	−1.7%	−4.4%	−1.7%	12.5%
Reserves (billions)	$21.5	$28.5	$29.4	$9.1	$48.5
External debt (billions)	$88.7	$119.7	$164.3	$158.1	$148.7
Change in exchange rate	2.7%	4.2%	−4.1%	−15.4%	−32.1%

Source: IMF

short-term debt with cash and marketable securities—equivalent to central bank reserves—held on the asset side of the balance sheet).

Short-term debt, however, only represented about 30% of Taiwan's reserves and even less for India and China—and in Taiwan and China's case the debt was more than covered by the enormous central bank reserves. The Philippines, which had only emerged from the LDC debt crisis of the 1980s, hadn't had the time to put into place the sort of *inverted* capital structure typical of its neighbors. Short-term debt, for example, represented 75% of reserves and about 19% of total debt, and the country emerged from the crisis relatively well, although poor economic fundamental have prevented any strong recovery.

Like its collapsing neighbors, South Korea had inadvertently placed itself in the capital structure trap in which an external shock could easily push investors and borrowers to act in a way that exacerbated the cost of the shock and increased its impact. The level of confidence in Korea was so high before the crisis that even if investors and the ministry of finance had been aware of the how unstable the capital structure was, they would probably not have been concerned. It was hard to imagine that any shock could have been strong enough to push the country over. But when the Asian economies started fall-

Table 7.2. Selected Asian debt ratios

	Short-term debt to international reserves	Short-term debt to total debt
Indonesia	160%	24%
Malaysia	60%	39%
South Korea	300%	67%
Thailand	110%	46%

Source: Author

ing so quickly and unexpectedly, investors quickly realized the country's debt structure vulnerability, and the Asian shock spread to Korea.

The enormous overhang of short-term debt made clear that refinancing risk—unimportant in good times—can become brutally perverse when creditors are forced to respond to it. Individual investors' refusal to turn over their debt before others had done so made it nearly impossible for South Korea, one of the richest and most successful countries in the world, to repay its debt according to its original contractual obligations. As investors waited to see how other investors would respond to Korea's maturity mismatch, the capital structure trap snapped shut amid the frantically self-reinforcing behavior of investors pulling lines. In addition, the desperate need of Korean corporate borrowers to buy dollars to hedge their ballooning (in real, local currency terms) foreign debt simply exacerbated the currency collapse. Korea's crisis did not begin to resolve itself until the capital structure mismatches were directly addressed—the country received a pledge of a $57 billion IMF package on December 3 and negotiated the restructuring of $24 billion in short-term bank loans on January 28.[23]

Since then, South Korea has rebuilt its balance sheet and is once again growing to recover its position as one of the twentieth century's great success stories. One of the results of the crisis, however, is nearly unanimous belief that Korea's brush with disaster was a consequence of an entrenched style of corruption and economic mismanagement. Korea's problems, as foreign and Korean experts insisted, were caused by the combination of crony capitalism, lack of transparency, strong-arm central planning, closed domestic markets, an overly regulated business environment, and the public allocation of credit. In the words of a 1999 article in *the Economist*,

> [Korea] has acknowledged its faults with remarkable candor. It has not tried to blame foreigners for its troubles, nor has it hid behind tariff barriers or currency controls. Instead, it has pledged to abandon the economic system that took it from poverty to prosperity in a generation.[24]

There may or may not be serious deficiencies in the functioning of the Korean economy,[25] but they were not the cause of the 1997–98

23. Details come from Callum Henderson, *Asia Falling: Making Sense of the Asian Crisis and Its Aftermath* (McGraw-Hill, 1998), pp. 285–309.

24. Quoted in a circulated draft of Robert Wade, "Wheels within Wheels: Rethinking the Asian Crisis and the Asian Model," to be published in Nelson Polsby (ed.), *Annual Review of Political Science 2000*, Annual reviews, 2000.

25. I personally doubt that the country was nearly as poorly managed as South Korea's critics insist, and in fact would argue that whatever strategy of management accounts for the amazing growth spurt Korea has enjoyed needs

Korean disaster except indirectly in that they may have contributed to excess leverage. First, the same system has largely been in place since the 1950s, and rather than a regular victim of financial collapse, Korea has actually managed during this time to achieve a rate of growth and prosperity that is probably unprecedented. Second, Korea's problems developed when its high current account deficit in the 1990s, which forced it to take on foreign capital, was financed with an inherently unstable structure. The Bank of Korea, in particular, had been using its reserves to help domestic banks roll over their foreign borrowings, so that prior to the crisis the country had foreign reserves of around $6 billion but at least $100 billion of short-term foreign debt.[26]

In such a condition, Korea was inordinately susceptible to an ordinary "bank run," and when the run started in Thailand, it was the unstable capital structure that brought the country to its knees. It is easy to posit what would have happened had Korea actually built a *correlated* capital structure and taken in all of its foreign capital inflows in the 1990s in the form of long-term dollar loans, fixed-rate won bonds, and equity. In such a case there would have been no Korean crisis, just an economic slowdown reflecting temporarily weak export markets. And it should not be surprising that the Korean economy turned around so quickly. When a profitable and solvent bank encounters a bank run, the run may be enough to bring the bank to its knees. But if the bank is rescued by a liquidity package, there is no reason why it should not quickly recover profitability. Like such a bank, Korea quickly recovered, even though the global economy on which Korea depends for exports was substantially weaker than it had been.

to be enshrined in our ideas about development policy. For some well-argued nonconsensus views, see Bruce Cummings, *Korea's Place in the Sun: A Modern History* (W. W. Norton, 1997), and Robert Wade, *Governing the Market: Economic Theory and the Role of Government in East Asian Industrialization* (Princeton University Press, 1990).

26. J. A. Kregel, "East Asia Is Not Mexico: The Difference between Balance of Payments Crises and Debt Deflation," *WoPEc Working Paper Archive*, working paper no. 235, May 1998, p. 15.

8

Toward a Theory of Sovereign Capital Structure Management

The Lack of a Framework

The concept of *correlated* funding is an old one and, the history of financial crises notwithstanding, has been a tool long used by authorities to reduce the costs of risk. In Babylon three thousand years ago, it was used to protect borrowers from being forced to make excessive payments during periods of low revenues. Paragraph 48 of Hammurabi's code, for example, lists a rule that limits the obligations of a debtor—who was most likely to be a farmer—according to weather conditions. "When a storm prostrates the grain, or the harvest fail, or the grain does not grow for lack of water," it commands, "in that year he need not give his creditor any grain, he washes his debt tablet in water and pays no rent for the year."[1] According to the code, in other words, the obligations of a debtor are reduced under conditions in which his revenue is likely to be very low—his debt payment is correlated to his earnings. This same sort of *correlated* payment structure is also a basic tool for corporate and banking specialists who want to limit earnings volatility, increase asset value, and reduce for a corporation the probability of financial distress.

In earlier chapters I argued that financial distress is extremely costly for sovereign borrowers because of its disruption of capital inflows and policy-making. These high costs suggest that it is to the

1. Quoted in Nicholas Dunbar, *Inventing Money: The Story of Long-Term Capital Management and the Legends Behind It* (John Wiley, 2000), p. 23.

146

long-term benefit of LDCs that volatility be managed and reduced so that the costs of periodic financial crises are minimized. But, in spite of the existence of liability management groups at some ministries of finance, there has been little useful work done so far to manage the national capital structures at most LDCs. Part of the reason for this is that to date the analysis of the role of capital structure has been fractured. Policy-makers, bankers, and economists have usually recognized the importance of capital structure instability—including aspects of the capital structure trap—*after* a crisis has occurred, but they have failed so far to develop an analytical framework.

For example, following the Mexican crisis of 1994, analysts immediately understood the problems of excessive amounts of short-term government borrowings indexed to the dollar, although that did not prevent South Korea, Indonesia, or Brazil from allowing short-term dollar borrowing to mushroom over the next few years. The Indonesian crisis of 1997 made obvious to everyone how dangerous it is when noncooperating local corporations have simultaneously to hedge large amounts of dollar debt. Brazil showed the feedback system that tied together floating-rate internal debt, interest rate levels, the fiscal deficit, and investor confidence. It also showed why issuing external debt with embedded put options might lower financing costs, but at an unacceptable increase in risk. South Korea, with its short-term dollar debt amounting to many times total reserves, made clear the self-fulfilling nature of refinancing risk. In each case, borrowers and lenders had constructed very unstable capital structures with self-reinforcing tendencies. And in each case a small, adverse shock quickly spiraled (or threatened to, in the case of Brazil) as the capital structure trap forced the system into destructive behavior. In retrospect, the structural flaws in each case became obvious.

But before the shock there was no commonly accepted and widely known framework within which to understand how the shock would be transmitted. Brazil is a particularly interesting case precisely because its economy did not break down the way Mexico's did following the devaluation in January 1999, despite widespread fears that it would. During a conference at Columbia University in October 1998, I argued, as I had since the summer before, that given the country's overvalued currency and unstable capital structure, a Brazilian devaluation was inevitable, and that if the country devalued immediately before reserves ran out, it would stabilize quickly at a relatively low cost to the economy. Although the argument was somewhat controversial, it was based on the small net amount of short-term dollar debt owed by Brazilian corporations, most of whom had already hedged their exposure in the domestic markets by mid-1998. Since the only important entity that owed net dollars was the government (along with certain public sector entities), as long as there was a sufficiently high level of reserves to make dollar-linked payments as they came due, there would not be a forced run on the currency.

Furthermore, precisely because Brazilian corporations had used it to hedge their dollar obligations, unlike in Mexico in 1994, much of the dollar-indexed debt issued by the government (known as "NTN-Ds") was owned not by foreigners but by Brazilians. For these reasons it seemed clear that the benefits of devaluation—a more competitive export sector and, most important, the removal of currency pressure on high local interest rates—would not be overwhelmed by a market collapse. There was no "mechanical" component of a currency devaluation that placed the country in the capital structure trap. Brazil's big risk was not that corporations would destroy the currency in their rush to hedge short dollar positions, or that foreigners would rush to convert NTN-Ds into dollars, but rather that the country's huge floating-rate federal debt burden would spiral upward if rates stayed high. But rates were high—above 40% when inflation was in the low single digits—precisely because the Central Bank needed to defend the unsustainable exchange rate. If rates continued at these levels, the currency would collapse anyway, whereas if they devalued while Brazil still had substantial reserves, the market would initially react badly, but it would soon stabilize, and real rates would decline.

In fact, as we now know, the short-term impact of the Brazilian devaluation turned out to be far less damaging than even the most optimistic forecasts at the time. The Brazilian capital structure was extremely unstable because of the floating-rate local currency debt, but the instability would be transmitted through the fiscal deficit, and not the currency. For this reason the likelihood of currency chaos was a much smaller problem than the feedback relationship between local rates and the fiscal deficit. This continues to be Brazil's greatest risk and may still force the country into a crisis if some external or internal event were suddenly to force interest rates to climb sharply before the stock of federal debt is reduced.

Capital Structure Management

For all its potential importance, capital structure management has not been a fundamental part of the banking and debt management strategy at the sovereign level, at least among LDCs. In fact, as I have discussed, LDCs usually unwittingly design capital structures that amplify volatility. Good times, which tend to be reinforced by the typically *inverted* capital structure of most LDCs, *seem* more robust and permanent than they actually are, but when a country is affected by some external shock, the result can be devastating. One policy change that must emerge from these crises is a reorientation in the financial strategy of LDCs in which the analysis and design of stability in the capital structure plays a central role in planning. Maintaining stability in the sovereign capital structure would, in this case, become the main defense against the possibility of financial crises.

To my knowledge there has been little systematic work done by LDCs—or by bankers and academics—on modeling the components of a national capital structure to understand the way external shocks can be neutralized. I am not sure why this is so, but I would hazard a number of guesses:

- Finance and central bank policy-making at the national level is generally managed by economists, and they tend professionally to have a limited understanding of the importance of volatility shifts and of "trading" or finance risks. Economists think more about expected outcomes than about the range of expectations and the impact that the probability distribution can have on expectations. For this reason there may be confusion beyond the most basic level about the importance of capital structure and its impact on market stability. Risk management, liquidity, and price gapping is better understood by financial market specialists, who tend to be very aware of volatility and probability distributions.
- Several LDCs have set up "liability management" groups within the finance ministry or the central bank. These have generally not been policy-making bodies, however, and their concepts of liability management are usually insufficient. They generally focus on debt exchanges, the fixed-floating and currency mix of external debt or of reserves, etcetera, and when it is not irrelevant, their approach often leads to a mistaken focus.

  For example, a number of countries are concerned with the optimal mix of fixed-rate and floating-rate external debt—perhaps because the efficient fixed-floating frontier is a common analytical tool in corporate finance. But for a country highly sensitive to changes in the cost of foreign capital, floating-rate debt has little value. On the contrary, it makes a great deal of sense to borrow on an inverse-floating basis, but few if any LDCs do so.[2] Of course the advice of liability management spe-

2. Inverse floaters are bonds whose coupons decline as interest rates rise, and vice versa. In a rising interest rate environment, in other words, the cost of servicing the debt declines. Because of their heavy dependence on foreign capital, LDCs usually suffer when foreign interest rates rise—particularly if the rise is accompanied by a reduction in general liquidity. In such a case, taking on the obligation to pay more on floating-rate debt seems risky. At the very least, a borrower should lock in rates as much as possible. A more active strategy would involve its swapping its debt into inverse floaters.

cialists at most international investment banks tends to focus on the same issues, since they are unlikely to have thought systematically about the differences between sovereigns— whose capital structures are very complex and not limited simply to external debt—and corporations.

- Risk management almost by definition requires a neutral outlook. In other words, the best design of a capital structure implicitly assumes no predictable or systematic direction in the movement of credit spreads, currency exchange rates, commodity prices, volatility, risk and liquidity premiums, etcetera beyond what is already implicit in market prices. Such a design also assumes that even where there is a long-term trend, the path is unlikely to be smooth but instead will incorporate several reversals and setbacks.

  But LDC policy managers—often, it is true, encouraged by eager bankers and journalists—have an overly confident attachment to their most optimistic expectations and implicitly incorporate their predictions into their capital structures. These expectations always assume that the local economy will continue to improve, that foreign investor behavior will respond to fundamental changes (hence to improvement), that credit spreads on external debt must decline, as must local interest rates and currency volatility—in short, all the variables that seem to demonstrate their policy successes. Even if they turn out to be right in the long run, because they implicitly assume away the probability that the path toward their expected outcome is likely to be very jagged, they ignore the possibility of temporary reversals. As a consequence, and not surprisingly, the structures they favor are, almost by definition, *inverted* structures.

- There also may be an element of gaming, or even of moral hazard. In poor countries, the need for improvement is so great, and the success of reforming governments may be so dependent on rapid economic and social improvement, that it may make sense for policy-makers to gamble heavily so as to "double up" any of the benefits of their policies in the short term.

Whatever the reason, LDCs must address the issue directly. An important first step would be to develop the analytical framework within which to measure capital structure stability and to incorporate it into the basic financial strategy of an LDC at the ministerial level. This requires a "portfolio" approach to liability management, in which both sides of the balance sheet are included in the equation. The second step would be to create a function or group at the national level whose role would be to monitor the country's susceptibility to financial instability and help design a more stable structure.

Setting up the Indexation Table

So what would the group do? This can only be answered on a case-by-case basis since there is a wide range of sensitivities that affect different LDCs differently, but there are some basic steps that can be taken. The first step is to identify and isolate the risks implicit in the way in which the country generates wealth and growth. Those risks that can be hedged with financial contracts should be hedged, while the remaining risks should be managed strategically. These risks can be evaluated by examining the "asset" side of the country's balance sheet, and I list some of the relevant "asset-side" issues here.

- How do oil prices affect the country? Is it a net exporter or a net importer, and are the associated capital flows an important source or use of foreign capital? In the case where it is a net importer of oil, is oil production nonetheless an important part of the federal budget, as in Mexico?
- What about other commodities—is the country heavily dependent on one or more commodities for export earnings?
- How do capital inflows affect the value of the currency? Is it materially undervalued or overvalued on a purchasing power parity basis?
- To what extent are the prices of consumer goods indexed to the U.S. dollar? What about real estate prices? Local interest rates? Insurance rates and payoffs?
- What is the relationship between foreign investment and local economic growth? Is domestic investment currently dependent on foreign savings? Net numbers are not very useful here—if domestic savings rates are high, net capital inflows may be low. But if a significant portion of those domestic savings is invested overseas, the gross component of foreign savings in domestic investment will be high.

Of course this is only a partial list—the number of additional issues to be considered is very large; but these issues can be fairly obvious for specialists who have learned to think about assets, businesses, and earnings in terms of indexation.[3] The next step is to consider the national liability structure, not just at the federal level, and not just in terms of external debt. State, municipal, corporate, consumer, and

---

3. I use the word "indexation" to refer to payments that are calculated not in nominal amounts but in relation to some other variable. For example, a floating-rate note is an indexed note in which each coupon is set according to some short-term index, such as LIBOR. An inflation-indexed bond is one in which the fixed coupon is multiplied by some principal amount that rises with inflation. Any series of payments can be indexed—to the price of oil, for example, or to the price of a stock.

mortgage-related debt and payment indexation must also be considered. The structure of the banking system is key, as is the relative importance of banking, capital markets, and retail investment in financing borrowers. Once again, it is important to examine every component of the liability structure in terms of a table of indexation. Any way in which the country has exposure to market risks should be listed. Issues include:

- Where are the major systemic mismatches between liabilities and assets? This includes mismatching in timing (e.g., lending short against long-term repayment schedules), in currency (e.g., lending dollars to a domestic retailer), and revenue indexation (e.g., lending on a floating-rate basis to a construction company, who typically earns less from the construction business when rates are high).
- Are there implicit or explicit options embedded in debt? Who loses from increases in volatility?
- Are there other types of indexation? Are salaries, mortgages, utility services, etcetera indexed to the dollar, inflation, or anything else?
- How do corporations invest their excess cash? (Although this may seem like as asset issue, it gives a sense of the net exposure a company may have.)
- What is the gross dollar (or any other foreign currency) position of the country? How is that divided among the sovereign sector, the state sector, and the private sector? Net numbers are no good—it is not obvious, for example, that private sector dollars or dollar assets held offshore or even domestically are available to repay sovereign debt.
- What is the dollar position of the banking system? Once again, net numbers are not very useful. If local banks have borrowed dollars overseas and are lending on a dollar-indexed basis to local corporations, it may seem as if they have no currency exposure. But if those corporations do not automatically earn enough income indexed to dollars to liquidate the loans fully as they come due, all that has happened is that the currency risk has been hidden in credit risk, and the banking sector is vulnerable to sharp increases in currency volatility. Conceptually it is as if the bank had sold an out-of-the-money option on the currency, and this option can suddenly become very expensive exposure if the currency suddenly devalues.
- Does the local currency debt market permit duration matching at the corporate level? In other words, is there an active, liquid, medium-term or long-term fixed-rate market in local currency? Can corporations fund investments with long-term borrowings whose repayments are predictable and correlated with the investments?

- Are there systematic reasons that encourage mismatching? An example of such is the withholding tax system. Many countries require that borrowers pay withholding tax on the coupon component of their debt, or do so indirectly by requiring that a portion of the proceeds of the debt be lent interest-free to the central bank. The problem is that direct or indirect withholding taxes penalize borrowers who borrow in currencies with high nominal rates, since a greater portion of the net present value of the payments consists of interest rather than principle.[4] Since local currency debt tends to have higher nominal rates than dollar debt, the withholding tax effectively incentivizes local borrowers to switch out of local currency borrowing and into dollar borrowing, which is riskier.

Once these questions have been answered, it becomes possible to set up a sort of indexation chart in which all indexation mismatches flow through the national "equity" account.[5] As the account is stress-tested by assuming sudden changes in commodity prices, changes in the cost of financing, periods in which no refinancing occurs at all, political events, etcetera, it is possible to determine where the country's sensitivities lie. To the extent that there are significant mismatches in the way that the country—or parts of the country—are indexed, these become the teeth of the capital structure trap.

The government can then begin to unwind the trap either by using tax and regulatory incentives to switch the indexation of the liability structure or by designing its own debt structure to counteract the mismatch. This is not to argue that the government should control and manage both the private sector component and the public sector component of the national capital structure. On the contrary, the private sector should be encouraged to develop its own funding strategy that

4. For those who are interested, this is easy to prove. Assume that a borrower chooses to borrow a given amount in either a high-interest-rate or a low-interest-rate currency. The NPV of any loan is by definition the sum of the NPV of the principle payment and the NPV of the coupon payments. Since the principle payment in the low-interest-rate currency loan is discounted at a lower rate than the principle payment in the high-interest-rate currency loan, it must have a higher NPV. But since the NPVs of the two borrowings are by definition equal, the NPV of the low-interest-rate currency coupon payments must be lower than the NPV of the high-interest-rate coupons. The withholding tax is a fixed percentage of the coupon payments, so that the NPV of the tax payments is higher for the high-interest-rate currency loan. Of course, although withholding tax comes out of the payments received by the lender, the borrower actually pays the withholding tax because lenders require higher coupons to compensate for the tax.

5. Obviously there is no "equity" in a national balance sheet. I am using the term simply to refer to the residual after assets and liabilities are netted.

fits its risk needs. But there is an overarching role for the national government. First, it should eliminate distortions, such as the withholding tax, that create incentives for private sector borrowers to borrow in a risky way. Second, it should design its own borrowing program so as to counteract the risks that are imbedded in the national capital structure (risks that include the private sector capital structure).

Recognizing Indexation Mismatches

It is important to note that mismatches can occur in a variety of unexpected ways that only become obvious within the capital structure framework. I will discuss two examples current at the time of this writing: Argentina and Brazil. In the case of Argentina the main financing problem lies simply in the sheer volume of external debt, which amounts to well over 50% of GDP. In and of itself this is not a good number, but when we combine it with Argentina's monetary system, the level of external debt becomes even more serious because of the sensitivity of the country's monetary base to capital flows. Argentina has effectively doubled up its exposure to changes in foreign currency flows both through its external debt, about which it has little control, and its monetary base, about which it has no control thanks to its currency board. Its debt level is so high that simply servicing the debt—even assuming no further trade deficit that also needs to be financed—will ensure that external debt-to-GDP ratio will continue to grow unless GDP can power forward at 6–9% growth rates in the face of high financing costs.

During 1999 and 2000 the government claimed—with the agreement of most Wall Street analysts—that it could resolve its debt problem by improving its fiscal account, turning it from a significant deficit to a significant surplus. The theory here is that if it is able to run a fiscal surplus, it will generate more pesos than it spends. It can then use these surplus pesos to buy dollars from the private sector to pay down its external debt. In this way there will be a net reduction in the external debt. But viewing Argentina from a national capital structure framework makes evident the arithmetical problem. Argentina—the country, not the government—as a whole needs a certain amount of dollars every year simply to continue servicing its trade deficit and its external debt, over 80% of which is sovereign. Until the end of 2000, the sovereign government was raising in the international debt markets nearly all the necessary dollars both for itself—to pay interest on its debt—and for the private sector (it effectively supplies the private sector with dollars through the fiscal deficit).

But here is where the constraint exists. Even if the Argentine government *were* able to run a fiscal surplus, the country as a whole would continue to need to raise increasing amounts of dollars to service the current account. All a fiscal surplus would do is to shift onto the private sector the burden of raising dollars to meet the country's huge refinancing need. For international bankers, however, there is a real question as to whether this is at all possible—in fact most bankers are fairly pessimistic about the ability of the private sector to replace the sovereign in raising dollars. If the private sector cannot do so, it means that the "fiscal surplus" solution to managing the sovereign debt burden—even ignoring the political constraints—may be unrealistic and constrained by the limited ability of the private sector to raise dollars internationally. A fiscal surplus will not help except to the extent that it shifts default risk away from the sovereign and onto the private sector. Fiscal surpluses are good for credibility, but only trade surpluses will pay down the foreign currency debt. The capital structure framework demonstrates the need for a much more radical approach to the debt-servicing problem than the current one.

For a second example of capital structure mismatching I will return to Brazil's local currency federal debt. Although this may not be obvious at first, one of the main "assets" against which federal local currency borrowing is indexed is credibility in the ability of the government to reduce the federal fiscal deficit—and investor sentiment is highly sensitive to this credibility. The mismatch occurs because the debt is mostly either short-term or indexed to floating rates. This creates a spiraling effect in the fiscal deficit that can work wonders in some circumstances or wreak havoc in others. When investors become optimistic about the government's handling of the fiscal deficit, interest rates immediately decline. Since debt servicing costs currently account for more than 100% of the deficit, as they decline the deficit immediately improves, and along with this improvement, investors lower their projections for future fiscal deficits. As these projections decline, optimism about the eventual elimination of the deficit increases, further lowering interest rates, and so on. In these cases Brazil is caught up in a virtuous cycle of declining fiscal deficits and declining interest rates.[6]

The problem is when some external shock reverses the process. This forces interest rates higher, which immediately shows up as a higher deficit, which reduces credibility in the government, which

6. As a general rule, countries that enjoy "virtuous cycles" tied to their capital structures are at a very high risk of a rapid turnaround in conditions. A "virtuous cycle" often exploits the same sort of mechanism that can become a "vicious cycle."

forces rates even higher, and so on. When Russia collapsed in late 1998, causing rates in all LDC markets to rise, it was the expanding Brazilian federal deficit that frightened investors and pushed the country to the edge of disaster, although this was not obvious at first. The then-president of the Central Bank, in disassociating himself from the causes of the crisis, insisted at the time that Brazil had not made any serious policy mistakes. The Russian crisis, he argued, was a sort of act of God, and there was nothing Brazil could have reasonably done either to predict it or to protect itself from it.

This only shows that he misunderstood the role of the national capital structure. It was already obvious to many that the structure of Brazil's local debt market was so unstable that any external shock threatened to push it over the edge. Indeed, I had been writing about it since June 1997, when I published an article in *Gazeta Mercantil*[7], as had Celso Pinto, Brazil's most prominent economic journalist. With real interest rates already so high, and with no gap between a change in base rates and a change in interest payments[8], it didn't require much to push the debt-servicing burden to unsustainable levels. The Russian crisis did just that, but in an election year it shouldn't have been surprising that some negative shock might occur. The policy mistake made by the Central Bank was not in failing to predict the Russian crisis but in allowing such an unstable structure to put Brazil at the mercy of external shocks.

Instead of encouraging the development of a medium-term fixed-rate market for its debt so that interest rate risk could be passed on to investors, preferably foreign investors, the Central Bank actually tried to slow down its development. The bank did this for two reasons. First, it was concerned that the development of a long-term currency market, which at that time was eagerly demanded by foreign investors hoping to lock in the possibility of profit as the economy improved, would reduce it's ability to control the currency. The fear was that longer term local currency debt held by foreign investors would trade freely among those investors without central bank interference. If investors could readily short the instrument among themselves, they could set negative pricing signals for the rest of the market that were

7. *Gazeta Mercantil* is one of Brazil's leading business and finance newspapers. Michael Pettis and Ricardo Fleury Lacerda, "A Divida Externa e a Crise Financeira," *Gazeta Mercantil*, June 19, 1997.

8. The main risk-management advantage of long-term fixed-rate borrowings is that changes in base interest rates are "shared" between borrowers and lenders. If rates unexpectedly rise, in other words, the full burden is borne by the lender until the original loan is repriced, in which case it becomes the borrower's risk. If the repricing takes place daily, the full risk is borne by the borrower.

beyond the government's control.[9] Second, the bank believed that in-terest rates were too high and insisted that the development of the market had to wait until they were much lower. As an aside, at the time when there was most demand for medium-term local-currency paper from Brazil (in the second half of 1997) one-year rates were in the 20–21% range, and bankers had proposed issuing three-year to five-year paper at 17–18%. Rates soon increased to well over 40–50% a year later and, thanks only coincidentally to the Russian crisis, Bra-zil was forced to devalue the currency.

Neutrality of Outlook

The example of Brazil leads us into an important measure in deter-mining the success of a national liability management effort, and this is the market neutrality of the managers. When the liability managers and the designers of the economic system are the same group of peo-ple, the setup implicitly requires a sort of cognitive dissonance on their part. They must design an economic system in which they have great confidence while at the same time creating insurance through the capital structure that is implicitly a bet against the success of their design. It requires a great deal of pragmatism for a policy-maker to be comfortable with a *correlated* capital structure at the same time that he is forging a new economic structure for his country. On the one hand the financial managers who are planning to reform a country's economy and move it forward must be great optimists to take on their task. On the other hand the debt managers must be pessimists who see danger and volatility lurking everywhere. Rather than trust to the objectivity and pragmatism of practitioners, it is much safer to keep these functions separate, or perhaps even to bring in outside advisers to perform the analytical function of evaluating the risks imbedded in the capital structure and to recommend structural changes.

There is an important reason for requiring a fundamentally pessi-mistic outlook, and that is the weak and unpredictable relationship between changes in an LDC's underlying economic health and move-ments in the components of the borrowing cost. It may seem intui-tively obvious that borrowing costs and credit spreads respond to the creditworthiness of the borrower, since changes in the probability of default or in recovery rates affect the value of debt. But it does not necessarily follow that changes in the borrower's condition are suffi-cient to determine changes in credit spreads. It is easy to confuse the

9. Conversation with Celso Pinto, following his interview with Gustavo Franco, president of the Central Bank of Brazil.

two points. When policy-makers are absolutely convinced that they are taking the right steps in improving the creditworthiness of the sovereign borrower, they become equally convinced that the sovereign credit spread is going to decline over time. Given the generic and almost automatic confidence LDC policy-makers seem to have in the long-term improvement in the country's economic conditions, this leads to a natural tendency to want to keep debt maturities short so that sovereign borrowers can take advantage of declining credit spreads as they refinance their maturities.

But this is a mistaken policy. I have already argued that LDCs are inordinately sensitive to changes in external conditions because of their reliance on capital inflows and commodity prices. This implies that internal factors are much less important in determining changes in credit spreads than unpredictable external factors are. Since that is the case, any sovereign borrowing strategy that does not implicitly assume a fairly neutral position about the direction of credit spreads can involve a significant increase in volatility—and hence in the probability of distress. To avoid this, a borrowing strategy should make no assumptions about future credit spreads other than that on average they will probably look like current spreads and that they are likely to vary in either direction. The assumption that credit spreads are unpredictable must be fundamental to the liability management strategy—hence the need for pessimism. Even when there are rumors that a country is about to be upgraded, for example, the probability will already be discounted in current prices, and, as Mexico in 1993 demonstrated (most bankers expected Mexico to be upgraded to investment grade before the end of 1994), such confidence is often misplaced. No matter how determined the policy-makers are to do things right, there will still be far more uncertainty in future credit spreads than they think. A country's borrowing strategy should never imbed credit-spread assumptions in the debt structure.

This, by the way, is not just an LDC problem. Even among U.S. corporations, for example, credit spreads seem to be only partially affected by internal, company-specific considerations, with most of the explanation for change lying with external factors. In a very interesting recent study on the determinants of credit-spread changes in U.S. corporate bonds, the authors of the study attempt to determine how changes in internal company-specific factors (default probabilities, recovery rates, etcetera) affect change in the borrower's credit spreads. The relationship, they find, is weak. In the conclusion to their study they write:

Our results show that the factors suggested by traditional models of default risk explain at most 25% of the variation in credit spreads as measured by the adjusted R^2. Furthermore, an analysis of the residuals shows that they are highly correlated, and a principal component analysis reveals a single factor, equally weighted across all bonds, explains more than 70% of the remaining variation. . . . In contrast to the predictions of structural models of default, aggregate factors appear much more important than firm-specific factors for credit-spread changes.[10]

If this is true for U.S. corporations, it cannot be surprising that it is even truer of LDCs, whose lower ratings and greater sensitivity to external conditions make them more susceptible to market risks. And if 75% or more of credit-spread changes are explainable by non-country-specific factors, even if the policy-makers have discovered and will execute the right strategy, the probability that credit spreads will not decline is still very high. A sovereign liability management strategy that imbeds predictions of future interest rates or credit spreads in the national capital structure (an *inverted* structure) will add volatility to the national economy.

Risk Management and Cost Reduction

There is another important but poorly recognized point about managing the national capital structure, and that has to do with the country's ability to manage its financing costs. For many officials responsible for determining the borrowing strategy of a country, one of the most important concerns is minimizing the country's overall borrowing cost. Although this may sound like an obvious point, in fact minimizing borrowing costs in the long run is not at all just a matter of choosing maturities, currencies, and timing so as to minimize the expected borrowing cost of any particular transaction.

The overall borrowing cost for public and private sector borrowers in an LDC is determined primarily by the medium-term perception investors have of risk. The greater the probability a country will restructure or default on its debt, the more expensive will be its borrowing cost. The quickest way to bring down borrowing costs, therefore, is to reduce the probability of some sort of systemic crisis that can push the country into default. This can best be done by structuring a country's borrowing in a *correlated* way, which directly reduces financial distress costs by reducing the probability of bankruptcy. If sovereign borrowers, for example, were to limit their borrowing largely to medium-term and long-term fixed-rate bonds de-

10. Pierre Collin-Dufresne, Robert S. Goldstein, and J. Spencer Martin, "The Determinants of Credit Spread Changes," *Working Paper Series 99–15* (Columbus, Ohio: Charles A. Dice Center for Research in Financial Economics, 1999), pp. 18–19.

nominated in their own currency, at first glance it may seem that financing costs would be high compared to borrowing in dollars. Real interest rates in local currency, after all, are generally higher than they are in dollars.

But real interest rates are often high precisely because of the currency risks that LDCs with large dollar borrowings take. As Mexico and Asia showed dramatically, LDCs with large mismatches run the risk of sharp and uncontrolled currency devaluations, and local currency investors, not unnaturally, demand high risk premiums to protect them from catastrophic devaluations. As a sovereign switches its borrowing structure from very risky dollar debt to a low-risk fixed-rate local-currency debt, it is very likely that the real cost of borrowing will decline dramatically.

Perhaps just as important, sovereign borrowers with large dollar debts are generally given low credit ratings, since their ability to service this debt is limited. These sovereign credit ratings act as a constraint on the credit ratings of local corporate borrowers. If a country is rated BB, for example, this means that the rating agencies believe its bond obligations are risky enough to be considered highly speculative. Because a sovereign default would almost certainly involve a general expropriation of foreign currency by the government, no corporate borrower domiciled in that country, no matter how strong its balance sheet, will be able to obtain a credit rating higher than BB. This of course raises the borrowing cost for all local borrowers. Since a sovereign credit rating reflects the perceived ability of a country to repay its debt, the easiest way for a country to raise the rating on its external debt is to reduce the amount of its external debt.

Credit Asymmetry in *Correlated* Structures

Aside from the impact on reducing the probability of financial distress, it turns out that an appropriate debt management strategy can have another more technical impact on reducing borrowing costs. One of the less obvious consequences of *correlated* debt structures is a credit asymmetry that works to the benefit of both borrowers and lenders. This asymmetry exists because the real value of the borrower's obligations varies directly with its implicit creditworthiness. When there is an improvement in the external conditions for the borrower, the real value of the borrower's obligations is higher. When conditions deteriorate, the obverse happens.

How does this work in practice? Let us assume that a country, which we will call Poyais, is heavily dependent on oil exports as its major source of revenue. Obviously if oil prices increase, the country's credit improves, and if oil prices decline, the country's credit deteriorates. What would happen if Poyais were to issue a bond whose coupons were correlated to oil prices? First, as I have already discussed, it would reduce volatility in its capital structure by linking debt servicing costs to oil export revenues, and this would lower the impact of oil price changes on its economy. But there is a second impact that benefits both Poyais and its investors.

In order to show the effect of this impact, let us assume that oil prices are currently $20 a barrel. Let us further assume, for simplicity's sake, that there is a 33% chance that oil prices rise to $25 and remain there, and a 33% chance that they fall to $15 and remain there. I should point out that if these unrealistic assumptions are relaxed, the mathematics of credit asymmetry will not change but the calculation will be more complex. For my purposes I will assume that we are structuring a $100 million bond issue for Poyais as a seven-year bond whose coupon is $8 million if oil prices decline to $15, $10 million if they remain at $20, and $12 million if they rise to $25. This is a variation on the airline bond example of chapter 6, and it represents a type of *correlated* financing.

Because the market recognizes that the Poyaisian credit is sensitive to oil prices, its required yield to take on Poyaisian risk must also reflect the levels of oil prices. Specifically, at current levels, or $20 a barrel, it would require a 10.00% yield for a seven-year Poyaisian obligation. If oil prices were to rise to $25, the market would discount seven-year Poyaisian risk at 8.23%. Finally at $15 a barrel for oil, the market would require a 12.00% yield on a seven-year Poyaisian bond.

What is the present value to investors of the *correlated* bond versus a "straight" or "plain vanilla" bond with the traditional fixed coupon? We know that if Poyais were to issue a seven-year $100 million plain vanilla bond with a fixed coupon of $10 million, since oil prices are at $20 a barrel its bond would be discounted at 10.00% and the present value of the bond would be $100 million. Our *correlated* structure is more complicated. There are three possible outcomes, each with a 33% probability. These outcomes and their equivalent present values can be listed as shown in the table below.

The expected net present value of the three outcomes (which we get by adding the three values and dividing by three) is $100.40 mil-

	Price of oil	Coupon	Required yield	Net present value
Outcome 1	$15	$ 8 million	12.00%	$ 81.74
Outcome 2	$20	$10 million	10.00%	$100.00
Outcome 3	$25	$12 million	8.23%	$119.46

lion. At that price, the expected yield on the bond is 9.92%, or eight basis points less than the country's "straight" borrowing cost of 10%. This means that by issuing a *correlated* bond with the same expected payments as the "straight" bond, Poyais not only improves its capital structure but can in theory also raise money at a lower cost. Of course if investors actually want a "straight" bond, they can buy the Poyaisian *correlated* bond and simultaneously enter into an oil hedge in which they pay away part of the coupon if oil prices rise and receive extra income if oil prices decline. Their credit mix is still better than a "straight" bond issue because the obligation shifts away from Poyais and toward the hedge counterparty whenever Poyais's credit deteriorates. Although it may not be immediately obvious, the borrower can take advantage of this to lower borrowing cost: immediately, as investment bankers learn to create structured products that disaggregate and individually price the risks; and over the long term, as the country's sensitivity to shocks declines.

This is not a special case. All forms of *correlated* financing have this quality—the payment structure is tilted so that the obligor owes more when it is a better credit risk and less when it is worse. If Poyais were a major oil *importer*, it would achieve the same benefits by reversing the structure described here and raising the coupon when prices declined, and vice versa, and the creditworthiness of the bond would improve in the same way as in this example. And we don't need commodity price sensitivity to take advantage of this asymmetry. If a country were adversely affected by increases in dollar interest rates, as most LDCs are, by borrowing on an inverse-floater basis it could also take advantage of the credit asymmetry.

Credit Asymmetry in *Inverted* Structures

There is a corollary to this. *Inverted* capital structures also implicitly reflect credit asymmetry, but in a way that harms both borrower and investor. This is true of all *inverted* structures. In March 1998, Argentina pioneered a new type of transaction—called a Floating-Rate Adjustable Note (FRAN)—that emphasized liability inversion. There had been a great deal of market instability and price volatility among Latin American bonds, and investors were fed up the continual price swings in their bond portfolios. At the same time the Republic of Argentina needed to raise dollars but, because the market was depressed, was uncomfortable locking in the required credit spreads. An Argentine banker at Morgan Stanley, Diego Ferro, came up with a very clever solution for both problems. He designed a U.S.-dollar-denominated seven-year bond issue whose coupon was set equal to the yield on another "benchmark" Argentine bond issue. If the market for the Argentine benchmark bond had strengthened during a coupon period (and, consequently, it's yield declined), the next coupon would be reduced, whereas if it had weakened, it would be increased.

This structure was a variation of what is called a "credit sensitive note." These notes, often used by U.S. high-yield borrowers who are expecting an improvement in their operations, typically have coupons that are indexed to their credit rating—if the rating, usually by S & P or Moody's, improves, the coupon is reduced, and vice versa. The FRAN structure reworked this basic concept to bring it closer to market measures of risk and better serve the market's needs. Investors liked the structure because the coupon always rose and fell to match the required yield, so that the bond should in principle always trade at par and its volatility would be extremely low. The Argentine government liked it because it was certain that the Argentine credit could only improve and, as it did, its borrowing cost would fall along with the coupon. By indexing its coupon on a seven-year bond to its future borrowing costs, it was as if the Argentines could raise medium-term money today while taking advantage of future credit spread improvements. The government launched the issue in March 1998, and it was hugely successful, raising $1 billion. Within months several other sovereign and public sector borrowers in Latin America had copied the structure.

Toward the end of 1998, however, when markets began falling after the Russian crisis, the various FRAN structures began to perform very badly in the secondary market. This partly reflected their low liquidity, but it also reflected the realization by investors that they were taking on huge credit asymmetry. Whenever the risk of financial distress seemed particularly high—as it was to do several times in the next two years—no one wanted to own the bond at anything close to par, even though the coupon was in theory high enough to justify the risk. Consequently, it always traded at a significant discount.

The reasoning of these reluctant investors was straightforward. If conditions deteriorated so much that the borrower defaulted, the FRAN was no better than any other Republic of Argentina bond. But if the Argentine credit recovered and its bonds traded up, the coupon on the FRAN would immediately decline, unlike the coupon on "plain vanilla" Argentine bonds, so that the investor would lose much of the upside benefit. The present value of the various potential outcomes turned out to be lower than the present value of a straight bond with the same range of outcome distributions—in exactly the opposite way that I calculated for the Poyaisian oil-indexed bond. Even though they were designed to trade at par, they could only do so within "normal" volatility: the market had stumbled onto credit asymmetry.

It was not just investors who were hurt by these structures. The problem for FRAN-type borrowers was also potentially ugly, as they saw their interest costs soar at precisely the wrong time—whenever the market was in such bad shape that borrowers were effectively cut off from borrowing. Technically, the probability of financial distress was much higher for FRAN-style borrowers. It was fortunate that there were too few of these bonds outstanding to seriously affect total external debt servicing costs. After a brief flurry of issuance in 1998, the structure has found disfavor and will probably not be used again, although I suspect that many overly optimistic sovereign borrowers will continue demanding highly *inverted* structures whenever overall borrowing conditions are less than optimal.

Preparing for Payment Difficulties

I have argued earlier in this book that there is overwhelming evidence that international payment difficulties are not simply caused by policy mismanagement on the part of the borrower but can reflect overwhelming external shifts. This means that with the best will in the world a country that is heavily dependent on foreign capital flows may experience periods in which repayment can be interrupted.

One aspect of the liability management portfolio or capital structure framework, which may be controversial, is an explicit recognition on the part of LDC borrowers of the need to resolve future debt crises (and this is controversial precisely because it means acknowledging the *likelihood* of future crises). It requires that, as part of the sovereign financing strategy, there be explicit strategies to deal with external shocks and their effects on interrupting capital inflows. It also requires a way of limiting the "gapping" effect of a sovereign crisis, by which I mean the discontinuous nature of a sovereign default—when all external debt simultaneously becomes unpayable. Because gapping risk is extremely difficult to hedge and can create tremendous inefficiencies for the borrower, investors are forced into procyclical behavior whenever there is a crisis.

The strategy to reduce gapping risk may include setting different levels of seniority for debt repayment, contingency and liquidity facilities, etcetera. This allows the borrower to discriminate in making payments so that debt restructurings can be done selectively while still maintaining some access to the markets. But a strategy to reduce sovereign gapping may also mean simply that the sovereign refrain altogether from or severely limit its borrowing in foreign currencies. Instead, it would allow and require that corporate borrowers take the lead in raising external debt, since corporate defaults during a crisis tend to be continuous (i.e., no gapping) and can be resolved on a case-by-case basis. The effect of this focus on resolving possible debt crises should be to reduce the financial distress costs of a sovereign default, which have historically tended to be extremely high.

Sovereign defaults have often taken years, even decades, to resolve. During this time investors could not accurately evaluate repayment prospects since they depended on the bargaining positions of all relevant players. Furthermore, because there were few mechanisms by which investors and borrowers could agree on even reasonable modifications, the process was always antagonistic and confused. There are two important consequences of this confusion: first, during a period of payment interruptions, bonds trade at lower prices than they might otherwise have done, and second, the market arrives at a clearing price much more slowly. The period following a sovereign default is nearly always brutally difficult for both the bondholders and the borrower. Part of a sovereign liability management strategy must be to recognize the possibility of payment difficulties and to design strategies to lower the cost of financial distress and to speed up the recovery. I will discuss this in more detail in chapter 9.

Should Sovereigns Borrow in Foreign Currency?

The discussion of acknowledging the probability of payment difficulties for LDCs brings up an important issue. In an article published in late 1999, *Latin Finance* argued that credit rating agencies were judging Latin American sovereign risk too negatively because of their earlier mistakes in Asia and Russia—where the rating agencies were severely criticized for having misjudged the borrowers before the crises. Moody's Investors Service's reduction of Argentina's rating in October 1999 was cited as a prime example of this overcompensation. The chief Latin American economist for the Spanish bank Banco Bilbao Vizcaya was even quoted in the article as saying: "There has been a deliberate attempt to do the region down. The rating agencies are backward-looking with their methodology, so that Latin countries' history of credit default has led to an anti-Latin bias in comparison with the rest of the world."[11] What is surprising in this statement is the suggestion that a "backward-looking" methodology is somehow inappropriate for analyzing sovereign credit. In fact the best indicator of whether a country will default in the future has always been the number of times it has defaulted in the past. Given the track record of sovereign defaults, not only it is reasonable to assume continued vulnerability among LDCs, but it would be irresponsible to pretend anything else.

This leads us to the obvious question that arises from the discussion about sovereign debt restructuring. Is the sovereign borrower the most appropriate conduit for foreign investment into an LDC? The

11. "Controversial Calls: Basel Proposals Would Affect Ratings," *Latin Finance*, November 1999, p. 16.

question is really three indirect ones. First, is the importance of protecting sovereign creditworthiness "different" from protecting the creditworthiness of other borrowers in the country? Second, is the risk of default high enough that the sovereign credit can be threatened? And third, even if it is, are the long-term costs of occasional sovereign defaults lower than the long-term benefits of foreign investment being channeled through the sovereign (e.g., lower costs of capital, better coordination of investment flows, etcetera.)?

Max Winkler pointed out in his famous 1933 study on foreign bond defaults that the only guarantee that a sovereign won't default on its external obligations is if it *has* no external obligations.[12] In general, LDCs import a huge amount of volatility because of their immature local financial markets, their sensitivity to commodity prices, and their dependence on foreign capital inflows. Because of this imported volatility, the history of LDC suggests that there is a high probability that there will be wide-ranging regional defaults during the next global liquidity contraction. This is a fairly persistent emerging market problem. As I discussed in chapter 5, even the United States in the nineteenth century suffered mightily from these periods of global financial crisis, with large-scale defaults by U.S. states, banks, railroads, and other entities on obligations owed to British, Dutch, and French investors. Since the U.S. government never borrowed in foreign currency, however, it saved itself from the humiliation of defaulting along with the other U.S. entities that weren't so lucky.

Does the lack of sovereign defaults (as opposed to corporate defaults) matter? The history of emerging markets suggests that the volume of capital inflows is one of the main determinants of economic growth. The LDC debt crisis of the 1980s amply demonstrated that after a debt crisis, without the rapid return of foreign capital, emerging market countries have never been able to recover sufficiently quickly to regain the growth path. This has important policy implications. Since debt crises are probably inevitable, and, as I will argue in the next chapter, since LDCs should focus on getting capital to return to the country as quickly as possible following a crisis, markets must be permitted to clear. As distasteful as it may seem, risk-loving "vulture" investors, or short-term speculators, have a very important role in the recovery process because, by buying cheap, risky assets during the most chaotic part of the collapse, they often act as the initial stabilizers. This means that these types of investors need to be encouraged to jump into the market quickly. Once prices have stabilized and investor confidence has returned, capital inflows from "higher quality" investors will cause the economy to start up and the investment process to recover.

12. Max Winkler, *Foreign Bonds, an Autopsy: A Study of Defaults and Repudiations of Government Obligations* (Roland Swain, 1933).

But when markets are artificially propped up, or banks are permitted to hide the losses on their assets, these investors will refuse to participate in the market because there is no way to judge value and no way to understand the underlying demand/supply dynamics of the market. The LDC debt crisis of the 1980s was probably more severe and long-lasting than it needed to be because, for so many years, international banks were able to camouflage the value of their loans and to deny the market-clearing mechanism. Without clear price signals, high-yield investors, flush as they were with cash in the 1980s, refused to buy deep-discount loans even when countries with perfect interest-servicing records (such as Mexico and Chile) had loans yielding 20% and more. After several years of permanently declining loan values, few investors dared to step in. I discussed in chapter 7, using an options framework, why investors will not invest in a company experiencing financial distress.

This is why protecting the sovereign credit is so important. Although defaults in general may not be avoidable for the region, a sovereign default has radically different consequences from private sector default. Private sector defaults may be extremely difficult for the economy in the short term, but ultimately they are manageable, even when generalized. When large numbers of corporate, municipal, and even state borrowers default, the economy can suffer greatly in the beginning. But after the initial panic, the market will eventually stabilize as asset prices fall to levels below which speculative risk-hungry investors can plan profitable short-term plays as they begin to rechannel foreign capital into the country. Sovereign defaults, on the other hand, are difficult to manage because there are no institutions for orderly workouts and there is a huge uncertainty about the process. Furthermore, during a sovereign default, the availability of foreign currency is almost always controlled and restricted by the national government, so that even speculative investors with the appetite to buy risky assets stay away—no matter how "cheap" assets are—since there is no obvious exit strategy. This makes it difficult for the market to arrive at a credible clearing price without undergoing a long, protracted, grinding process of liquidation.

The only way to protect the sovereign credit in even the most adverse of circumstances must involve severe restrictions on the total amount of sovereign external debt. Furthermore, since the sovereign implicitly guarantees the obligations of the domestic banking system and other institutions that are too big or too important to fail, it should also restrict the foreign currency borrowings of these institutions. These institutions, whose debts are likely to be assumed by the sovereign in case of default, should be considered part of the sovereign umbrella, and their credit should be protected. It is worth adding that net caps on foreign currency borrowings by banks are less useful than gross caps, since net caps can hide a huge amount of real currency risk that may seem to be hedged. When a Thai bank borrows dollars, for example, and lends dollars to a Thai retailer, it may show no dollar exposure on a net basis. Nonetheless, the retailer's currency mismatch will almost ensure that, in the case of a crisis, it will be unable to access dollars and will be forced to default on or restructure the loan. As a result, the bank will find itself in a short dollar position. If the crisis is severe enough and enough banks are short dollars, the systemic risk can put currency pressure on the sovereign.

A major difference between countries that progressed from emerging market to developed country status and those that didn't is the speed with which they recovered from crises. Countries that were successful, like the United States or Japan, seemed to get over the periodic financial crises and return to rapid growth much more quickly than the ones that haven't been successful. There are many reasons for this, but one thing that is striking, perhaps not surprisingly, is the relative absence of sovereign defaults among the successful countries. As much as we would like to think, however, that the creditworthiness of a sovereign borrower during a financial crisis reflects its superior management skills or honesty, the truth is probably less exciting. Historically, sovereigns with little external debt continued to service their debt on schedule during crises while sovereigns with a great deal of external debt were forced to default or to restructure. If this is true, then Max Winkler was right—and sovereigns that have borrowed heavily in foreign currency will always be at risk of a sovereign default.

The Local Currency Market

If sovereigns limit their borrowings in foreign currency, they are dependent on local currency markets to meet their funding needs. I have already made several references to the role of fixed-rate local currency markets in managing volatility, and the main point is worth repeating: fixed-rate local currency debt is a highly *correlated* type of funding—the closest thing to equity-like funding for sovereign borrowers. In fact the development and active use of a fixed-rate local currency market for funding government and corporate financing needs is probably the *single most important step* an LDC can take in reducing its sensitivity to external shocks.

There are two reasons for this. First, longer term debt directly reduces refinancing risk. Second, and more important, because inflation in low-credibility countries generally surges after a currency crisis, the cost of fixed-rate debt, instead of shooting up to unmanageable levels, actually declines in real terms during the crisis, thus providing some relief for producers and automatically improving their leverage ratios. The real reduction in debt servicing reduces pressure on the economy during a currency crisis instead of reinforcing it.

In good times it is easy to figure out why sovereign and corporate borrowers have been reluctant to use this market for borrowing—real interest rates in local currency tend to be higher than real interest rates in dollars, and in good market conditions, the local currency tends to appreciate in real terms. If borrowers begin to assume that local currency appreciation is inevitable, the cost of local currency debt is expected to be much higher than the cost of dollar debt. Notice, however, that the high relative cost of local debt occurs partly because of strength in the local currency—and since assets for the most part are also denominated in local currency, the borrower is still getting most of the benefit of currency appreciation. Local currency borrowing only means that the borrower shares a part of the total benefits with his investors.

If this type of funding is relatively expensive in improving conditions, the value for borrowers must arise when conditions deteriorate, and of course it does. If deterioration in the underlying economy is accompanied by a weakening of the currency or an increase in nominal interest rates, which for an LDC is almost always the case, the inevitable deterioration in the borrower's assets is hedged by the local currency debt. The local currency debt, although it forces a sharing with investors of the benefits of relative improvement in the currency, also forces a sharing of losses, and the worse the underlying the condition, the greater the portion of the burden that is forced onto investors. This acts as an automatic stabilization mechanism.

The real importance of this market is in crisis mitigation. When all or most borrowers are dollar borrowers, their efforts to hedge their short dollar position in a period of declining rates forces them all to act to reinforce whatever pressure there is in the currency. As I showed in the case of Indonesia in November and December 1997, when corporations are forced to react to weakness in the currency, their stampede to hedge can destroy the currency. As the currency weakens further, there is a widening of the circle of corporations for whom short dollar positions threaten to wipe out their capital. They then must also hedge, putting more pressure on the currency, which widens the circle further. But for fixed-rate local currency borrowers, the effect of the crisis is the opposite. Since large devaluations are generally associated with increases in inflation, the worse the devaluation, the more quickly the debt burden erodes. These borrowers find themselves in an improving financial position precisely as the overall economy degenerates, and this permits them to act as automatic stabilizers for the overall economy. Instead of reinforcing the crisis as dollar borrowers do, they counteract it.

Most Latin American governments, however, have not taken advantage of market opportunities to extend the yield curve. During stable times many governments were convinced that a continuation of their policies would lead to lower inflation and lower interest rates. They believed that by borrowing long term they were locking in excessively high borrowing costs. During less stable times, on the other hand, government finance officials refused to borrow long term, or they borrowed only on a dollar-indexed basis, because they wanted to signal to the market their confidence in their own improving condition. Doubling up the risk was seen as a way of encouraging confidence. But both beliefs are misguided. Capital structures are a crucial transmission mechanism for external shocks, and a high-risk premium is the cost of safety. Because investors know this, local interest rates will decline largely as a consequence of improving credibility. Ironically, a short-term capital structure can often signal the reverse of what government officials intend and can increase the very risk premium that is judged to be too high—choosing a risky term structure is not the right way to signal a credible policy mix. I showed this when I discussed the credibility Laffer curve in chapter 7.

The Mexican Local Currency Market

Governments have been slow to understand this, and few LDC markets have made the effort to develop this sort of funding. As a result, with limited exceptions, most sovereign, public sector and private sector borrowers have been forced to rely on much more volatile types of capital structure. Mexico, for example, has been talking for years about extending the duration of its peso borrowings beyond one year. Until recently it had only issued bills with maturities ranging from 28 days to 364 days, and except for a brief experiment with two-year notes in 1995, it kept postponing any longer dated issue. The Mexican government finally, on January 25, 2000, successfully auctioned three-year fixed-rate bonds for the first time. On May 23 of the same year, it auctioned the first five-year fixed-rate bonds. According to the government, it had waited so long because peso volatility and lack of investor confidence had prevented it from doing so earlier.[13]

Of course it is probably unnecessary to point out that, in retrospect, Mexico's ability to predict peso interest rates was very poor—yet in spite of the overwhelming evidence it seems nearly impossible to convince government authorities of the possibility of their own interest rates ever rising. Nonetheless, there are two questions now for Mexico

13. In fact, there had been earlier periods of tremendous investor demand for longer dated peso instruments, for example during much of 1993 and early 1994, but the government had refused to satisfy this demand on the grounds that rates were still declining and the government would be better off by waiting. In that case, of course, it turned out to be wrong.

now. (1) Will Mexico begin to think of a long-term market peso as an important risk management tool that is most needed precisely when volatility is high and confidence is low (i.e., issue even when conditions are clearly not optimal)? (2) Will the Mexican finance authorities be able to resist the temptation to use peso bond issuance as a speculative tool with which to gamble on peso interest rates (i.e., will they issue regularly regardless of whether or not the finance ministry agrees with the market's interest rate expectations)? If the answer to both questions is affirmative, we may see develop over the next five years an active, liquid market that stretches out to ten years or more. To the extent that long-term fixed-rate peso funding becomes an important part of the way in which Mexican entities fund themselves, both domestically and externally, the damage caused by the inevitable next external shock should be much lower.

Mexico has always had a short-term and floating-rate peso market, and it is important to make a sharp distinction between a short-term or floating-rate market and a medium- or long-term fixed-rate market. One of the functions of a capital market is to spread risk and return to both savers and users of capital. This benefits savers by permitting them to participate in the growth of the economy and, more critically, protects users from the huge swings in expectations typical of these markets. When local banking and capital markets only accommodate short-term borrowing, this forces users of capital to assume all the risk—refinancing risk as well as interest rate risk. When the market is under stress, say after a currency break for example, floating-rate debt forces the borrower to confront higher borrowing costs at the same time that he is facing pressure on his operating side. Given the huge volatility in real rates typical of LDCs, this is not a minor point. During the Asian and Latin American crises of the past five years, it was not uncommon to see real rates shoot up to 40% or more. This obviously has a procyclical effect on local borrowers, since it forces them to cut back sharply every time the economy contracts. Because of the huge increases in domestic interest rates, some bankers have argued that the self-reinforcing way that floating-rate local currency debt transmits external shocks is even worse for a country in crisis than that transmission caused by dollar debt.

In table 6.2 we listed a few different types of funding and compared the impact of different external conditions on the funding type. As the table shows, local-currency fixed-rate debt has the quality that the debt burden tends to decline most rapidly in a market crisis, thus providing relief in linear proportion to the extent of the crisis. This acts as an automatic stabilizer by contracting the borrower's debt servicing burden as conditions deteriorate. This list is not exhaustive, of course, but it indicates how capital structure should be viewed and how the indexation between the revenue or asset side of the national capital structure is linked to the debt-servicing and liability side.

9

Debt Restructurings within a Corporate Finance Framework

The Debt Restructuring Process

There is a long and extensive history of sovereign debt restructurings that stretches back hundreds of years and that is particularly rich in the nineteenth and twentieth centuries.[1] The process typically ranged from one or two years, in many cases, to the approximately sixty years that it took Mexico to resolve the issues related to its London market bond offerings of the 1820s. Before that particular process was completed, Mexico and its creditors experimented with interest capitalization, debt for equity swaps, collateralized lending, debt forgiveness, open market purchases, and the full panoply of restructuring techniques still used today. One hundred years after that restructuring was finally completed, Mexico was again involved in a sovereign debt restructuring, although this time the debt that was being restructured was in the form of bank loans. The process was shorter this time, but it was nonetheless complex. During the 1980s, and before the agreement on the final "Brady" solution had been reached, the United Mexican States, along with fifty-one other public sector borrowers and the central bank, had signed eighty-nine separate agreements with over nine hundred different commercial banks and other creditors involv-

---

1. I have found particularly useful Vinod Aggarwal, *Debt Games: Strategic Interaction in International Debt Rescheduling* (Cambridge University Press, 1996), which is an attempt to develop a game theory model for sovereign debt restructurings. See also Edwin Borchard, *State Insolvency and Foreign Bondholders* (Yale University Press, 1951).

ing nearly $60 billion of debt. Fifty-four of those agreements were amended at least once, with all the necessary parties agreeing to the amendments. As part of the various agreements, Mexico and its creditor banks agreed on new loans for interest payments (interest capitalization), debt-equity swaps, debt-for-debt swaps, currency agreements, debt repurchases, and collateralized bond agreements. This doesn't include the billions of dollars of private sector debt that was also restructured.[2]

During both of these periods Mexico found it very difficult to raise capital in the international markets. In this chapter I will attempt briefly to consider the sovereign default process, which I will also interchangeably refer to as the restructuring process, as part of the corporate finance framework. The purpose of the chapter is to outline some of the issues in debt restructuring that incorporate liability management insights and that specify the goals of the restructuring exercise. A debt restructuring, after all, is simply a type of debt management exercise, and a capital structure framework that seeks to minimize volatility and price gapping while maximizing "value" to the borrower is applicable to this part of the debt management continuum.

There are, of course, differences between debt restructuring and "ordinary" debt management. There are also several factors that constrain and control the sovereign restructuring process. Our finance framework will need to incorporate these constraints. A partial list of the relevant differences between ordinary debt management and debt restructuring includes the following.

1. Factors that constrain the ability of the borrower to achieve its strategy:

   • *Changes in volatility assumptions.* Distressed debt changes the volatility assumptions of both creditors and obligors. Because they are implicitly short put options, creditors generally hate to see increases in volatility, but if the debt is sufficiently impaired, it effectively becomes a long synthetic call option.[3] In such cases creditors may seek in-

---

2. Alfred Mudge, "Country Debt Restructure: Continuing Legal Concerns," in *Prospect for International Lending and Rescheduling* (Matthew, Bender 1988), pp. 18–16.

3. This is explained more formally in Michael Pettis and Jared Gross, "Delta, Kappa, and the Equity-like Features of Speculative-Grade Debt," in Michael Pettis (ed.), *The New Dynamics of Emerging Markets Investment: Managing Sub-Investment-grade Sovereign Risk* (Euromoney Publications PLC, 1997), pp. 37–50. A revised version of this appears as an appendix to this book.

creases in volatility in a way that may not benefit the borrower.

- *No new investment.* I discussed in chapter 6 the implicit tax that creditors of restructuring countries impose on new investment. When this is combined with the high uncertainty associated with financial distress and the restrictions on capital outflows that restructuring countries typically impose, it is not surprising that new investors shun restructuring countries, even when in principle there are profitable investment opportunities.

- *Legal framework governing loans.* Any restructuring solution must conform not only to the legal framework under which the loans are governed but also to the legal framework of other jurisdictions that may affect the process. For example, if Ecuador has substantial assets in the United States, in the case of default it can be subject to investor pressure under U.S. law.

- *Enforceability.* Are all investors forced to accept a negotiated solution? Can "rogue" investors disrupt the process? Can the borrower subsequently change the terms of the contract?

- *Homogeneity of lenders.* The more similar or the fewer the lenders, the more likely it is that their objectives can be articulated and an agreement reached that meets their needs. As the number of types of lenders gets larger, the number of conflicting objectives expands exponentially, and the likelihood of a solution that satisfies all creditors contracts. However, in such a case the great variety of goals among creditors may allow the borrower to play creditors off against each other in order to arrive at a better outcome.

- *Political stability of borrower.* Low capital inflows (or capital flight) are generally accompanied by a weak local economic performance. In these circumstances the government will have usually lost a great deal of credibility and may find it hard to develop a consensus. Furthermore, disaffected elites may use wounded national pride to oppose any agreement with creditors. The debt restructuring process is always messy, and an opposition party can easily use the process to attack the government. Can the government truly negotiate, and can its agreement be relied on?

- *International economic conditions.* A stable global economy may be more conducive to arriving at a solution than a distressed one, although a borrower can game the process and play off players in periods of distress or political conflict. Changes in commodity prices and global liquidity conditions can change export earning and refinancing projections.

- *Precedents.* A restructuring that is seen as a precedent for other, larger debt restructurings may be much more difficult to resolve peacefully because there are implicitly a much larger number of players interested in the outcome.

2. Factors that should determine the goals and strategies of the restructuring process:

- *Return to the market*. The most important end result of a debt restructuring should be the most rapid return to the financial markets. Without capital inflows, LDCs almost never grow.
- *Manageable debt servicing*. The result of the restructuring process should be a permanently manageable level of debt servicing for the borrower. The debt servicing formula must be able to accommodate changes in external and internal conditions, such as increases or declines in commodity prices, unexpected changes in GDP growth, etcetera.

I list the constraints first because most debt restructurings over the past few years implicitly begin with the constraints and seem almost to place less emphasis on the strategic objectives of the restructuring. There is a "strategy" of course, but it usually is simply to get the greatest possible amount of debt reduction up front, while taking into consideration some other largely tactical points: Should eurobonds be included in a restructuring of Brady bonds? Is it fair to haircut Brady debt further, given that it already has provided debt forgiveness? What about official debt? And so on. Most of the work consists of maneuvering through the constraints—particularly the legal constraints.

But to approach sovereign debt restructurings this way is a mistake. The corporate finance framework provides a fairly clear strategy that focuses on two issues: (1) How do we maximize the amount of value to be distributed to creditors and to the borrower? (2) How do we distribute the proceeds? These two questions are not independent of one another, and the answer to both must consider the process over time and as external conditions change. In chapter 6 I discussed the goals of a company's treasurer or CFO and argued that a sovereign entity must think within the same framework. This applies also to the restructuring process, whose goal must be to return to the sovereign borrower as quickly as possible the four capital structure objectives that I discussed at the beginning of chapter 6: flexibility, stability, the minimizing of volatility, and the exploiting of relative value. This permits the most rapid return to the market and allows the government to concentrate on more important policy issues when the restructuring is completed. The way future cashflows and debt servicing costs are indexed has a major impact on all these goals and thus on the creation of value for investors and for the borrower.

The Restructuring Process in the 1980s

It is worth taking a brief look at the U.S. bankruptcy procedures to gain insights into the sovereign restructuring process. The bankruptcy process as it applies to U.S. corporations is relevant because it is an explicit attempt to address the costs associated with the disruption of debt servicing. An optimal bankruptcy process is not so much a liquidation proposal as it is an attempt to maximize the value of the assets by reducing the costs of bankruptcy and maintaining, if appropriate, the operational value of the entity. Most of the bankruptcy process can be described as occurring in three steps. The first step is to create breathing room for the borrower by automatically stopping debt servicing requirements. This involves acknowledging the need to restructure and preventing the disruptive effects of individual creditors seeking unilaterally to protect their claims.

The second step permits the borrower to raise short-term liquidity for its immediate "operating" needs by granting seniority status to new debt raised after the restructuring process has begun. The terms of the agreement permit the borrower to make loan repayments on this senior debt even while repayment obligations on older debt is being renegotiated. The objective, of course, is to facilitate the ability of the borrower to continue raising money for the necessary operations that ultimately maximize the value of the borrower. Finally, the third step consists of the actual restructuring and reorganization of the obligations. The restructuring doesn't require unanimous approval from the creditors—more than 50% of the creditors representing more than two-thirds of the claims is sufficient to effect a restructuring. The U.S. bankruptcy process restricts the claims of lenders and permits differences in seniority status precisely in order to maximize the total value of the payments that will be delivered to lenders.

I have discussed in the first three chapters the relationship between capital flows to LDCs and growth. It is almost axiomatic within the *liquidity* model framework that without a recurrence of capital inflows, LDCs achieve minimal growth at best. Latin America, during the Lost Decade of the 1980s, is a dramatic and disheartening piece of evidence, and during the entire restructuring process, both creditors and obligors agreed that the resumption of voluntary financing was one of the key objectives of both sides of the negotiating table. But from a corporate finance framework it seemed as if the debt restructurings of the 1980s were almost designed to prevent capital from ever returning.

There were three points, in particular, that hurt the process and prevented the optimal resolution of the crisis. First, the major affected players never recognized the full extent of the problem. In every case the restructuring process involved short-term postponements of principal repayments, so that within a few years everyone had to return to the negotiating table. Debt restructuring became a permanent condition, and because it is an unpredictable process characterized by bluffing, grandstanding, and political shifts in both the creditor and obligor countries, there was a permanently high level of uncertainty attached to each of the restructuring country economies. Such high levels of uncertainty require, at the very least, very high discount rates on investments.

Second, the repayment schedules were rigid. There was insufficient focus on finding equity-like sharing provisions that helped eliminate the volatility impact of excessive debt. For borrowers that meant there were limited incentives to increase export earnings if rigid debt servicing schedules absorbed any increase, and any change in earnings, net of debt payments, was associated with a far greater level of volatility than is already standard for LDC economies. Third, and most important, there was a permanent debt overhang for the entire decade that has still not been completely resolved. I have already shown that with a debt overhang, potential new investors have no incentive to invest. If the amount of debt owed is greater than the country can pay, any foreign investor had to accept that if his investment increased the country's debt servicing capacity, that increase would be shared among all investors. Even if a $100 million outlay resulted in $200 million of additional value, most of that additional value went to increase the value of the existing debt and only a small portion returned to the investor.

Debt Forgiveness and Volatility

The first of these issues was only resolved after nearly a decade of negotiations when banks had built up sufficient reserves to acknowledge the long-term nature of the problem and to permit partial debt forgiveness. The second two issues were only partially addressed, the former with Value Recovery Rights[4], and the latter with partial debt forgiveness (which was reduced by the need to borrow money to purchase collateral). The basic debt forgiveness argument from the creditors' point of view can be summarized in figure 9.1. This graph simply points out that when a country has excessive external debt, its creditworthiness will respond to changes in the amount of debt outstanding. Since the creditworthiness of the borrower affects the rate

---

4. Value Recovery Rights was the name given to certain warrants attached to the Par and Discount component of Brady bonds of certain countries—most important, Mexico and Venezuela. These warrants allowed investors, based on a complex and unwieldy formula, to benefit from higher oil prices.

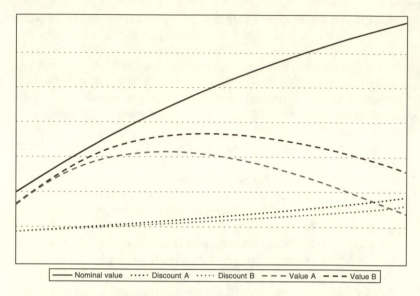

Figure 9.1. Relationship between value and nominal amount of debt

at which future payments should be discounted, the actual present value of the country's obligations are not likely to be a linear function of the nominal amount of the contractual obligations.

The result is a sort of Laffer curve in which the present value of a country's debt (shown in the graph as "Value A" and "Value B") may be at a maximum at some level substantially below the highest possible nominal obligation. It is possible, in other words, to increase the value of the debt by reducing the nominal amount of contractual payments—debt forgiveness.

There are some important points to be made about this well-known relationship. The most important is that the shapes of the value curves are very sensitive to the discount rate. If the discount rate does not decline rapidly with the amount of debt forgiveness, then the curve will peak at the right side of the graph. Debt forgiveness, in this case, will not benefit the creditor, and he will be likely to resist it. When the sovereign borrower is relatively solvent (for example, when it is experiencing a liquidity problem and not a problem of too great a debt burden), reductions in the amount of outstanding debt will have little impact on improving its overall ability to pay and hence will not affect the discount rate. In such a case, of course, it is hard to argue for debt forgiveness—what the borrower needs may simply be an extension of current maturities.

When a sovereign borrower has a genuine difficulty in servicing the debt—in other words when the debt burden significantly impairs its creditworthiness—debt forgiveness may have tremendous benefits for both the borrower and the creditor. This is because the discount rate will become very sensitive to the change in the amount of obligations. Notice in the graph, however, that there are two market value lines, each associated with a different discount rate. These show, obviously enough, that if there were some way to shift the discount rate lower, for any given nominal amount of debt, the market value of the debt will be significantly higher. Changes in the appropriate discount rate are as important in determining value as shifts in the nominal amount of debt.

The option framework that I have discussed in chapter 6 (and in the appendix to this book) sets out how the process works. It is axiomatic within this framework that the present value of any nominal amount of debt is equal to its value discounted at a risk-free rate less the value of the implicit put option imbedded in the debt. By reducing the value of this implicit option, the bondholder will benefit by an increase in the value of the debt. How can we reduce the value of this option? One way is to reduce the volatility of the underlying "asset," and I have already discussed ways of doing so—by correlating debt-servicing payments with revenues. Volatility reduces the very large "time value" component of the option associated with low-quality debt.

In figures 9.2 and 9.3 we make a related point. In each graph, the upper line represents earnings, which are used to make debt payments. The lower line represents debt payments—they are fixed in

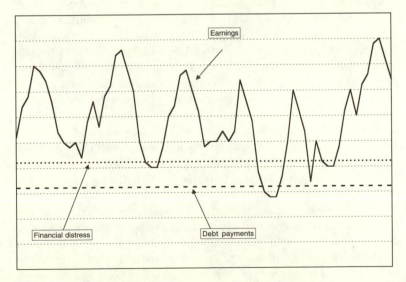

Figure 9.2. The impact of linear payments on distress

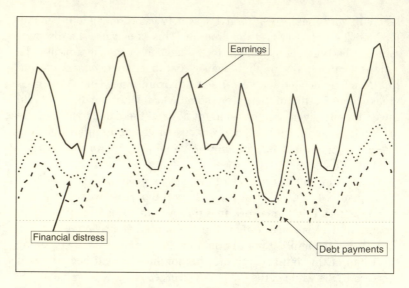

Figure 9.3. The impact of correlated payments on distress

figure 9.2 and vary partly in line with earnings in figure 9.3, and they sum to the same amount in either graph. Finally, the middle line represents the borderline below which if earnings fall, the borrower can be said to be in financial distress. Figure 9.3 shows the effect over time of a restructuring that involves payments uncorrelated to the borrower's future revenues.

As these revenues vary over time, there are three suboptimal results. First, during good times there is no additional benefit to lenders and no incentive to the borrower to speed up the repayment. As a consequence, neither side is able to take advantage of the credit asymmetry I discussed in chapter 8. Second, the residual revenue to the borrower after debt servicing (the upper line less the lower line) is even more volatile than the already risky gross revenues, with all the social and economic costs associated with greater volatility. Third, and perhaps most important, during unexpected periods in which the revenues of the borrower decline beyond some level, the likelihood of the borrower approaching new periods of financial distress are high. This is shown occurring four times during the period indicated by the graphs.

These periods of financial distress, of course, place additional burdens on both borrowers and lenders. For the borrower, financial distress is associated with 1) an extension of its exclusion from capital markets and 2) new uncertainty associated with the possibility that it will be forced to restructure its obligations. For the lender, it means that the value of its assets declines with no symmetrical and commensurate increase during the "good" periods. It has locked in much of the downside of an "equity-like" instrument while giving up much of the upside.[5] Perhaps most damaging, if the distress becomes severe enough, the lender may be forced into a new restructuring that further reduces the amount of the obligation. This has occurred regularly during sovereign restructurings in the 1980s, the 1930s, and several times in the 19th century, and will probably occur again with Ecuador later in this decade.[6] In figure 9.2. although the sum of debt servicing payments are identical to those in figure 9.3, because of the way they are indexed there is no point at which the borrower is in financial distress. These problems are limited or even eliminated as the payment obligations are indexed correctly to revenues.

Basic Restructuring Rules

Because each restructuring country has fairly unique characteristics, it is difficult to propose a restructuring framework except in the most general terms. As in any debt management process, the process must begin with a recognition of what the expected debt burden is that a country can reasonably support and what the country's indexation matrix looks like. Beyond this the experiences of the 1980s, as well as the long difficult restructurings of the 1930s and the nineteenth century, suggest some basic rules for restructuring countries.

1. In spite of the natural desire to postpone addressing a difficult issue, the debtor should force a rapid recognition of the crisis. It is much better to have a brutal, short crisis than to let it linger on for many years. It is also self-deluding to ignore the price of debt in the secondary market as an indication of distress. Once debt trades at a steep discount in the secondary market, the relationship of investors to the borrower changes. In practice this means that obligors and investors must be forced into agreeing on a realistic program immediately, although because of the heterogeneity of the lending group and the conflicting goals of some of the lenders, the burden of imposing discipline must inevitably fall on the sovereign obligor.
2. The process should be kept reasonably fair. There will always be the temptation during difficult periods for the bor-

---

5. Remember that as the quality of the debt declines, its delta (or sensitivity to underlying conditions) increases, and as the quality improves, the delta declines. See the appendix to this book.

6. In August and September 2000, the Republic of Ecuador agreed with its creditors to a restructuring of its external debt (including its Brady bonds, which were already the consequence of a previous restructuring of bank debt a few years earlier). The agreement involved a "forgiveness" of 40% of the face value of the debt.

rower to impose or threaten to impose a drastic solution on investors. Since the ultimate goal must be to regain access to the international capital markets, however, any solution must be consistent with this goal. This doesn't mean, though, that borrowers have to take the warnings of investors too seriously. Investors *always* threaten that any changing of the contractual terms will permanently cut off the borrower from foreign capital, whereas adherence to the terms will speed recovery. History, however, does not bear this out at all. During periods of global financial distress, no country in difficulty gets capital access, no matter how eagerly it has played by the restructuring rules. During periods of liquidity expansion, when capital begins flowing to LDCs, investors do not seem to differentiate among borrower countries on the basis of their restructuring behavior as much as they do on the basis of the current ability to justify growth optimism. A country that manages to resolve its debt problems permanently is given a lot of leeway—as long as it has not made itself a pariah, it will regain access along with everybody else.

3. There must be a once-and-for-all solution to the debt overhang. It is important to distinguish carefully between a solvency crisis and a liquidity crisis. A country that is in crisis simply because it mismanaged its maturity schedule—like South Korea in 1997 or perhaps Mexico in 1994—will solve its debt problem by extending maturities. It should extend them as far out as possible and stagger the maturities so as to protect itself from a repeat occurrence. If the crisis is caused, however, by a real inability to carry the debt repayment burden, the debt must be partially forgiven. Nothing is as debilitating as a repeated sequence of debt crises. In order to make large-scale debt forgiveness palatable, creditor countries can offer investors equity-like payments in which they benefit heavily in case of a significant economic upturn. The good feeling this will leave with investors during economic upturns will speed up the return to the capital markets once the creditor country is beginning to grow again.

4. The restructuring should create structures that line up the interests of the creditor country, existing investors, and, most important, new investors. Significant debt forgiveness up front that comes with large upside participation and other equity-like kickers can help accomplish this objective. In this case, both the creditors and the borrower benefit if the value of the "kicker" rises dramatically. These kickers, however, should be substantial. The limited payments associated with the Value Recovery Rights incorporated in some Brady bonds were always too small to be of great value to investors and, consequently, did not have a significant impact on reducing the fixed component of the borrowers' repayment schedules.

5. In line with the preceding, the borrower should choose instruments that allow it to share risks with investors. The restructuring agreement should be explicitly designed as a
highly *correlated* debt structure. This accomplishes three objectives. It reduces the volatility of the borrower's revenues,
net of debt servicing costs, allowing it greater flexibility and
certainty in planning. It reduces the probability that because
of unexpected circumstances the restructuring agreement
will have to be renegotiated in the future. And because of the
positive credit asymmetry, it increases the value of the restructuring package for the investor.

Even though it has become a commonplace observation, it is still
worth repeating that any future restructuring is unlikely to resemble
the restructurings of the 1980s because of the radically different nature of the lending instruments and the creditor group. The 1980s debt
was in the form of bank loans (the obligor is known or easily discovered) owed for the most part to members of the banking community
in G7 and other rich countries. Lee Buchheit, who advised on many
of the restructurings, describes the differences in this way.

Public bondholders are not regulated entities like banks. They
are less susceptible to government pressure. They cannot be expected to agonize over the geopolitical consequences of their
actions in the same way as the international banking community, and, bluntly put, there are thousands upon thousands of
them out there who could potentially cause trouble. If debt
problems were to recur in some of the developing counties,
it is not at all clear that negotiated solutions could be pur-
sued without the threat of harassing litigation by some creditors.[7]

Imbedding Restructuring Provisions into New Debt

There is a great deal of useful work on corporate debt restructurings
that explicitly uses a corporate finance framework for restructuring
strategies that maximize value for debtholders and equityholders.
Thomas Jackson describes the bankruptcy process as "a system designed to mirror the agreement one would expect the creditors to form
among themselves were they able to negotiate such an agreement from
an *ex ante* position."[8] Jackson is talking about a bankruptcy process,

7. Lee C. Buchheit, "Cross-Border Lending: What's Different This Time?"
Northwestern Journal of International Law and Business 16, no. 44 (1995): 53–
54.

which is of course different from the sovereign restructuring process, but the goals of the creditors are in principle the same.

However, these goals are much more difficult to realize in a sovereign restructuring. Typically, whenever sovereign borrowers have trouble repaying bond issues, their only real options are either to pay on schedule or to default. Renegotiating bond terms is a difficult option because international markets lack an orderly workout procedure, and any material change in bond terms usually requires unanimous investor consent, even though it is nearly impossible to identify all bond investors. Without a bankruptcy court that can impose a solution on all parties, the conflict over sovereign bond defaults usually runs on until the process has exhausted both borrowers and investors.

For this reason troubled sovereigns rarely tamper with bonds except as a last resort. Bank debt, on the other hand, can be more easily renegotiated. During the debt crisis of the 1980s, when the amount of outstanding bonds was about 5% of total debt, the potential cashflow savings from defaulting on bonds was probably too small to justify the costs, and so sovereigns continued to service them even when they interrupted bank loan payments.

But over the past few years, particularly since the beginning of the Asian crisis, there has been a renewed focus on restructuring provisions for bonds. Official and academic sources have made many proposals about easing bond restructurings by inserting provisions into new sovereign bond indentures. These provisions might include, for example, requiring a smaller majority to approve changes in terms, making restructuring mechanisms enforceable, or assigning different levels of seniority to debt as it is issued. The goal is to introduce some flexibility on a voluntary basis. These suggestions have been controversial, and a growing group of investors oppose them on the grounds that they will increase excessively the likelihood of payment interruptions.

These concerns are ultimately misguided. Investors naturally want the cost of defaulting to be very high in order to deter sovereigns from tampering with their bond terms. This gives bondholders implicit seniority over banks, whose loans are easier to restructure. But in the case that a sovereign is forced to renegotiate anyway, the costs of financial distress must be included in the investor calculus. Some investors believe it is nonetheless worth preserving high bankruptcy costs in order to maintain the seniority of bonds. It is true that these high costs may make interruptions less likely, but the likelihood of

8. Thomas H. Jackson, "Bankruptcy, Nonbankruptcy Entitlements, and the Creditors' Bargain," in Richard A. Posner (ed.), *Corporate Bankruptcy: Economic and Legal Perspectives* (Cambridge University Press, 1996), p. 40.

default is also partially a function of the savings associated with de-faulting. These savings climb steeply as the total amount of bond debt climbs.

If we were still living in a world in which most private lending to sovereigns was comprised of bank loans, as in the 1970s and 1980s, we might reasonably expect that the savings to sovereign borrowers of defaulting on bonds would not be enough to justify the additional cost. In this case the implicit seniority of bonds would remain intact. But today, as much as 80–85% of international borrowing is in the form of bonds. The world we live in resembles earlier periods of in-ternational financing, when countries borrowed largely in the capital markets, not from banks. In those days payment difficulties always affected bonds because, like today, they formed the bulk of the pay-ment obligations. During the debt crises of the 1930s or the 1870s, for example, almost all the defaulted external debt consisted of interna-tional bonds. The current large amount of bond financing means that the implicit seniority of bonds has already been largely eroded.

The Cost-of-Default Tradeoff

Figure 9.4 shows the by-now-familiar Laffer curve relationship be-tween the cost of defaulting and the value to investors. The graph shows how, not surprisingly, the probability of default declines as the cost of default to the borrower increases. This increasing cost, how-ever, is also borne by the lender in the case of a default, since a bor-

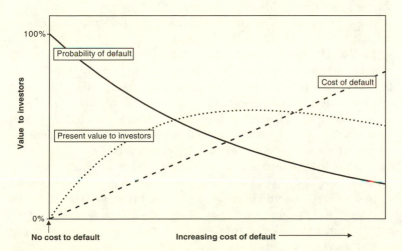

Figure 9.4. Cost of default Laffer curve

rower that already has difficulty in paying its debt must necessarily reduce its payments as its ability to pay declines further. If it is high enough, at some point the cost to investors can become so large that even at low probabilities, the expected value to the investor may be too high.

There is little question that the cost of defaulting should always be high so as to prevent too easy a recourse to defaulting. However, as the graph indicates, there is also a level beyond which it is excessive and uneconomic, particularly for investors. In the United States the reasonably orderly process of corporate bankruptcy has the economic rationale of benefiting both borrowers and lenders by reducing the likelihood that bankruptcy costs exceed the optimum level. With sovereign bonds, the high bankruptcy costs may force the residual value of a defaulted sovereign bond to be much lower than it should be. In fact, as I have discussed elsewhere, excessively high bankruptcy costs may be part of the reason sovereign bonds typically trade at higher yields than similarly rated U.S. corporate bonds.

An orderly bankruptcy process benefits borrowers because it allows them to arrive reasonably quickly at a workable solution to what may otherwise be an intractable problem. It benefits lenders because it can speed up the borrower's recovery and permits an accommodation in which the value of the security can be maximized. No one would argue that corporate bankruptcy procedures have scared off investors from buying U.S. corporate bonds, and a sovereign procedure should not scare off sovereign bond investors either. On the contrary, a small increase in a sovereign's flexibility in dealing with unpredictable external shocks will help investors maximize the residual value of repayments. Sovereign bond issues should include provisions that improve the likelihood of a reasonable accommodation if a sovereign is forced to interrupt payments. For investors this can only be beneficial.

Realistically speaking, of course, it is unlikely that countries will rush to include restructuring provisions in their new bond offerings because of the negative signaling effect that it may have. Borrowers may fear that to include restructuring provisions may indicate to lenders their lack of confidence in their own ability to pay. Lenders, who generally hate novelty in loan terms, may be concerned that they are on the wrong side of the cost-of-default curve. It is not clear to me how to resolve the problem, except perhaps after a default event has occurred. Certainly the ability to minimize the cost of future restructurings should be a provision in any restructuring agreement. In the next and final chapter of this book I will discuss some of the implications of the capital structure approach to sovereign debt management for the international financial community. This may be the forum in which to discuss the possibility of a multilateral agreement to insert "slack" into future sovereign borrowings.

PART IV
CONCLUSION

Because lending to and foreign investment in LDCs are driven by external factors, and because national capital structures are so unstable, the next few years will continue to see major disruptions in emerging markets. The chaos of 1994–99 came about largely because of short-term margin collapses and not because of major liquidity contractions. There is reason to believe that the next three to five years will continue to see good global liquidity conditions, thanks partly to the effect of the euro and partly to the possibility that Japan's erratic monetary policy may bring about inflation during the decade. But the next real liquidity contraction may be even more damaging to LDCs than the recent financial crises.

10

Conclusion

The New Financial Architecture

The Money Doctors

The story by now is well known in academic lore. A famous academic, one of the world's leading proponents of deregulation and free markets, is invited to come to Chile following a period of difficult economic conditions and political conflict. He and his follower propose a series of measures to open up the economy, which include reducing banking restrictions, freeing up the allocation of credit, eliminating trade tariffs, and deregulating the local economy. The heart of the reform proposals is a program to strengthen and maintain the value of the currency, both domestically and internationally, by locking in its foreign exchange value. It also liberates the banking system and permits banks to engage freely in a number of activities that had been, until then, proscribed. "According to the theoretic premise on which his economic concept was inspired," reports an account of the reforms by the Central Bank of Chile, "the financial system tended automatically towards equilibrium." Consequently it should be permitted to migrate freely toward its stable equilibrium.

After the changes have been implemented, it seems that the reforms are a huge success. Under the guidance of the foreign experts and their domestic allies, the structure and framework of the economy is wholly transformed. Soon large amounts of foreign capital pour into the country, and Chile undergoes an economic boom and becomes a model for the region. Foreign economists laud the reforms and predict that Chile is on its way to becoming on par with the wealthy economies of Europe and North America. Bankers in New York and London

189

hail the local financial authorities and assure the press that as long as these liberalizing policies are continued foreign investors will be eager to continue funding the infrastructure and consumption needs of Chile. Other LDCs begin to look favorably at the policies designed by the foreign experts and implemented by Chile, and soon the Chilean policies are widely copied in the region.

This story may sound like it might have happened twenty-five years ago, when Milton Friedman's "Chicago boys" transformed Chile in the 1970s and 1980s with their heavy dose of what Latin Americans now call neoliberal economic policies. But in fact the story is much older than that. The foreign expert who so beguiled the Chileans was the French academic Jean Gustave Courcelle-Seneuil, one of Europe's high priests of free market capitalism and the person invited to Chile in 1855 to become the government's official economic adviser. His reform program began with the 1860 Law of the Banks, which he wrote, and subsequently he and his zealous followers deregulated the economy, slashed tariffs, and opened up the mining sector to foreign investment. Such was their zeal that they even later privatized the nitrate mines acquired from Peru in the 1882 War of the Pacific. They were also able to help Chile get firmly onto the gold standard.[1]

At first, the reforms seemed to work. For a while the Chilean economy boomed as the country participated in the global prosperity of the 1860s. The initial success, however, did not last. The financial crisis that spread through Europe, the United States, and Latin America in late 1873 was as devastating for Chile as it was for its neighbors. As world commodity prices fell, the Chilean economy collapsed, the banking sector was decimated, and Chile nearly defaulted on its foreign debt. Many historians have fairly or unfairly blamed Chile's problems on the free market policies promoted by Courcelle-Seneuil. They argue that the changes in the banking laws led to the destruction of the currency and the abandonment of convertibility in 1878; that the 1864 tariff reduction caused the subsequent failure of domestic industry; and that privatization resulted in a concentration of ownership among a very small group of Chileans and foreigners.

Whatever the causes of the subsequent crisis, the story illustrates two common themes that are part of the lending-induced economic growth that LDCs generally enjoy during periods of capital inflow. First, no matter how different the economic regimes, when a group of LDCs receive huge foreign capital inflows, there is always the assumption that capital flows are *responding* to a set of economic reforms or policy changes, when in fact it may simply be that they are

1. Although I've used a variety of sources, including the Banco Central de Chile website, the best single one is Albert O. Hirschman, "Inflation in Chile," in Paul W. Drake (ed.), *Money Doctors, Foreign Debts, and Economic Reforms in Latin America from the 1890s to the Present* (SR Books, 1994), pp. 133–36.

causing them. Political and economic reform is a fairly consistent need of most LDCs, and governments, particularly new governments, always promise change. It may be that these reforming governments find it easier to implement their policies when huge capital inflows stabilize the currency, encourage domestic growth, and provide the resources necessary to satisfy elites that might otherwise oppose the reforms. What is less clear is that the market is actually *rewarding* these reform policies and that a certain amount of caution is justified in considering the relationship between a particular set of policies and the subsequent capital flow–generated growth. After all, Chile did receive huge capital inflows during the period following the free-market reforms of the 1850s and 1860s, but so did Russia, the Ottoman Empire, Egypt, Colombia, Tunisia, Spain, Austria-Hungary, Peru, Romania, and the Confederate States of America. It is hard to argue that these countries followed a common set of economic policies that were all equally rewarded by foreign investors. And it is not at all clear that if Courcelle-Seneuil had never been invited to Chile the capital inflows would have been any different.

Second, there is a long tradition among LDCs of experimentation with liberal and even *laissez-faire* economic policies, and during periods of capital inflow local policy-makers seem inordinately susceptible to the advice of foreign experts promoting these policies. The popularity of these experts, called "money doctors" in earlier times, seems to exist independently of how unsuccessful their advice has been in previous debt cycles. Chile is a particularly intriguing example of a country enamored of money doctors and foreign economic expertise. It has survived nearly identical baskets of reform proposals, not just in the 1860s and the 1970s but also in the 1920s, when the country invited and received a visit from the most famous money doctor of all, Edwin Kemmerer. In his visit to Chile, Kemmerer received public adulation and wildly supportive street demonstrations. The country eagerly followed his recommendations, among other things enacting the Monetary Law of 1925, which eliminated all restrictions on the import or export of gold, permitted free coinage, and put Chile on the gold standard. In the end, however, Chile performed no differently during the subsequent global liquidity contraction from any of the countries that had been too poor to retain Kemmerer's services. In fact it took only seven years before the country was forced off the gold standard and into default, after a costly and painful attempt to hang on.

The Corporate Finance of Currency Regimes

It is not just Chile that suffers from money doctors. Edwin Kemmerer himself advised a large number of countries in Latin America, Asia, and Eastern Europe, as did other experts. In 1905, partly following the advice of money doctor Charles Conant, Mexico, one of the leading silver-producing countries in the world, converted to the gold-exchange standard.[2] Because the current gold-silver exchange rate implied an overvaluation of the peso, the silver peso had to be forced to begin circulating at a level above its then intrinsic value. In order to accomplish this, Mexico's finance minister at the time, Jose Limantour, shrunk the money supply sharply in order to deflate prices and force the peso to a higher value that could then be pegged to gold.[3] Most historians attribute the subsequent fall of President Porfirio Diaz, which started the period of the Mexican revolution, to economic distress and failed promises on democracy. It is not at all implausible, however, that at least part of the reason for the Mexican revolution was an excessively hard monetary policy that led to deflation and a great deal of suffering among the middle class, farmers, and industrial workers. The money shortage that followed Limantour's harsh monetary policies, which was exacerbated by an unexpected rise in silver prices, was probably a major contributor to the economic distress of the last years of the Porfirio regime. As an aside, it is perhaps not surprising that after the beginning of the revolution in 1910, Mexico rejected gold-backed currencies in favor of inflationary and inconvertible money.

In spite of the advice of money doctors, the relationship between hard and stable money and rapid economic development is perhaps not as clear as it ought to be, even though among most economists the importance of sound money is often an article of faith. Economic historians, however, have been much less certain. The problem arises in part because periods of rapid economic growth were not always periods of sound banking and stable money. Bank historian Raymond de Roover makes the point explicitly when he surmises, in discussing the early economic experiences of the United States, that "perhaps one could say that reckless banking, while causing many losses to creditors, speeded up the economic development of the United States, while sound banking may have retarded the economic development of Canada."[4]

I am not enough of an economist to enter into the debate between hard money and flexible monetary policy, but there are important cor-

2. The United States only a few years earlier had gone through its own political gold-related turmoil culminating in William Jennings Bryan's famous "cross of gold" speech at the Democratic National Convention of 1896.

3. Emily S. Rosenberg, *Financial Missionaries to the World: The Politics and Culture of Dollar Diplomacy, 1900–1930* (Harvard University Press, 1999), p. 21.

4. Julius Kirshner (ed.), *Business, Banking, and Economic Thought in Late Medieval and Early Modern Europe: Selected Studies of Raymond de Roover* (University of Chicago Press, 1974), p. 236.

porate finance implications of a foreign currency regime that must be considered as part of the policy debate. In the 1890s and 1910s English bankers began saying, in reference to Bank of England monetary policy, that "7% brings gold from the moon." High interest rates and tight monetary policy in the major financial centers, in other words, can suck in money from almost anywhere. The problem for LDCs is that long before high rates start diminishing the gold reserves of the moon, they will severely contract foreign currency supply in any low-credibility country in which the ability of the central bank to draw foreign currency with high interest rates is limited.

Monetary policy in the United States, Europe, and Japan can have a multiple effect on monetary conditions in the world's smaller economies, and their economic structures and banking systems may be too frail or rigid to adjust quickly. There is a hierarchy of markets from the center to the peripheral markets, and changes in the center can be amplified as they move through the system to the periphery. This is how liquidity expansions in the financial centers can become asset booms in the smaller countries on the periphery, and how contractions can create crises. This relationship is not limited to rich countries and LDCs but can even occur within a country. In the U.S. bond markets, for example, traders in the high-yield markets keep a close eye on changes in the U.S. Treasury and high-grade markets in order to determine the overall direction of their own markets, which can be heavily influenced by changes in risk and liquidity premiums.

The currency regime can be seen as one of the mechanisms that links up the markets. Very tightly linked currency regimes, like dollarization and currency boards, act like the gold standard to force a tight link between local conditions and changes in the monetary policies of the rich-country financial centers. Small changes at the center can have drastic effects on the periphery. When the Bank of England in the nineteenth century raised interest rates in order to reverse gold outflows, which it did many times, the impact of the contraction tended to be greatest on the peripheral countries, which were often explosively and messily forced off the gold standard. In all likelihood, dollarized countries or countries with rigid currency boards will likewise be forced either into very sharp contractions, or will be forced off dollars altogether, should the U.S. Federal Reserve Bank decide to contract the money supply in the United States.

Of course to the extent that their capital structures are designed to punish any deviation from the fixed exchange rate, the pressure to devalue may actually be greater because of the effect of the credibility Laffer curve I discussed in chapter 7. As I have argued repeatedly in this book, capital structure is a sort of volatility machine. It represents the relationship between the borrower and external market risks, and it determines the way market volatility is transmitted into the local economy. For low-credibility countries, liability management must be about reducing volatility and preserving the integrity of economic policies. The country's overall capital structure should be designed primarily to pass volatility onto investors. This is particularly true for countries that hope to maintain fixed-rate currency regimes. Whatever their other fundamental benefits, these currency regimes necessarily increase a country's sensitivity to external shocks in the short term because of the automatic link between domestic interest rates and capital flows. It is not surprising, consequently, that countries with very aggressive, risky capital structures have been so spectacularly unable to maintain fixed-rate regimes. This is unlikely to change, but the proper response is not necessarily to float the currency but rather to fix the capital structure. Fixed or floating, the volatility machine must be used to *defend* credibility.

The Role of Analysts

Perhaps one problem faced by the market is that, unlike equity analysis in the United States, sovereign analysis has typically been unable to focus on or understand the relationship between capital structure and the risk of financial distress. As a consequence there has not been a clear system of rewards and punishments for countries that design *correlated* or *inverted* structures. Analysts failed, for example, to understand how very unstable the capital structures of Mexico, Thailand, Indonesia, and South Korea were. These structures at first presented investors and local borrowers with "virtuous cycles" of growth and declining financing costs. But the mechanism that creates virtuous cycles is the same mechanism that creates vicious cycles. For this reason analysts may have at first underestimated the probability of crisis.

This showed up as a failure to project the possibility of a very wide range or distribution of potential outcomes, as well as a misunderstanding of the process that created crises. After the Mexican and Asian crises, most analysts then assumed that all devaluations were catastrophic. In the case of Brazil, the failure to evaluate the country's capital structure prevented them from seeing that, as a (very) few analysts had argued since early 1998, the cost of not devaluing was far greater than the cost of devaluing would be. Whereas the focus should have been on the feedback mechanism between the internal debt and fiscal credibility, analysts instead obsessed over the likelihood of maintaining the *Plano Real,* which determined the currency policy.

This ignoring of capital structure does not occur in the U.S. corporate market, at least to the same extent. The analysts who cover a U.S. company, for example, are certainly interested in the underlying fundamentals that will shape the development of the U.S. market, in a way analogous to sovereign analysts. They will also focus on specific management policies that will determine the company's marketing position vis-à-vis its competitors, just as sovereign analysts will evaluate the economic, social, and political policies of an LDC. But the analysis will not stop there. Equity analysts will also examine the company's capital structure and judge its appropriateness. If a domestic U.S. retail company, for example, were one day to decide that because of low yen interest rates it would convert most of its funding into yen-denominated commercial paper, analysts would explode in wrath. The huge uncorrelated risks that management was taking—currency risk and refinancing risk—would significantly increase the likelihood of financial distress, and the company's stock price would be hammered while its borrowing costs would soar. Eventually, management would be forced out and, if bankruptcy hadn't yet occurred, the company would have to redesign its capital structure to match up risks in a more prudent way.

If Mexico or Korea, on the other hand, chooses an equivalently risky financing strategy, the warnings are merely perfunctory, and in some cases the strategy is even welcomed because it is expected to lower overall financing costs. The relationships between expected cost, risk, and financial distress are forgotten.

The converse is also true. If a very risky, unhedged airline makes a major move to hedge certain operating risks, such as the price of oil, the price of its debt and equity will immediately respond to the decrease in the probability of financial distress. But if India were to enter into a major hedging program to tie the cost of its external debt inversely to oil prices (India, like an airline company, implicitly runs a "short" position in oil), the immediate effect on the price of its debt in the secondary market would probably be minimal. Analysts and investors would not see the effect on financial distress.

This is probably because the effect of capital structure on the likelihood of distress is simply not part of the toolbox of sovereign analysts, most of whom are economists and have a very limited finance theory background. For them, the capital structure is a "nominal" issue and not part of the "real" issues driving economic growth. This prejudice, by the way, is not completely mistaken. Except under conditions of financial distress, the growth of the "asset side" of the economy—its ability to generate wealth—is largely independent of capital structure which, for the most part, is really concerned with the way the returns on investment are distributed to the providers of capitals (and with bridging the gap between domestic savings and domestic investment, in the case of foreign capital flows). However, as I have tried to show in this book, there are two aspects of capital structure that are crucial. The first aspect is the effect of the perception of distress on the cost of capital. And the second is the effect of capital structure on the *probability* of financial distress. Even the best economic policies in the world are unlikely to provide much long-term benefit if they are subject to brutal swings and regular crises.

The Reality Check

Let's start with a grim reality check: It turns out that financial crises are the rule and not the exception. According to the International Monetary Fund, over the 1975 to1997 period, there were 158 exchange rate crises and 54 banking crises in a representative sample of 22 industrial countries and 31 developing nations. Moreover, for this sample, there were 32 recorded instances when a country was judged to be suffering from the combined impacts of both currency and banking crises. By definition, crises are not predictable events. If they were, policy-makers would move preemptively to nip the next crisis in the bud. Rest assured, there will be another financial crisis in the not-so-distant future. The current outbreak of financial market euphoria makes that possibility seem remote. But the record of history begs to differ. The time to begin thinking about the next crisis is now.[5]

Throughout this book I have argued that the financial crises facing LDCs come roughly in two shapes. The first and more debilitating comes about when there is a major long-term contraction of liquidity in the rich-country financial centers along with a sharp reduction in commodity prices. During this period, most capital flows to LDCs are cut off or significantly reduced, and there is little that can be done by the LDC borrower except protect its credit and wait out the period until liquidity flows become normal again. If the borrower finds itself in the position that it has large maturities coming due—either because of a maturity mismatch or a sharply *inverted* capital structure—it may face payment difficulties.

The second type of financial crisis takes place *during* a period of normal or excess liquidity and occurs as an unexpected temporary shock to the system. The shock can occur for a variety of reasons— the assassination of a presidential candidate, a market crisis in another part of the world that causes a "flight to safety," a sudden disturbance in the rich-country markets that results in a temporary collapse of margin, etcetera. Depending on how the shock is transmitted into the LDC economy, it may result in a temporary slowdown in

5. Stephen S. Roach, "Learning to Live with Globalization," Testimony before the Committee on Banking and Financial Services of the U.S. House of Representatives, May 20, 1999.

growth and investment or it may cause a market collapse. As the preceding quotation from Steven Roach points out, these shocks are a fairly common occurrence.

There are two important characteristics of these types of financial crises that must be addressed by financial policy-makers. First, both types of financial crisis can cause market and policy volatility that will significantly undermine the long-term growth prospects of LDC borrowers. Second, the factors that set off either type of crisis are largely exogenous and almost always unpredictable—although long-term shifts in global liquidity are less so. This has two important implications that will affect the finance policy of an LDC. First, there is very little any individual country can do to reduce the likely occurrence of shocks, since these are not locally controllable phenomena—they largely represent adjustments to global disequilibria. And second, because of their disruptive effects on the local economy, the national capital structure must be designed explicitly to minimize the effect of these shocks. Together these imply that policy-makers must assume that shocks will occur randomly and that the country's national capital structure will be able to absorb these shocks by passing off both upside profits and downside costs to investors. The volatility machine imbedded in a country's capital structure, after all, transforms movements in market prices into the real economy in a very predictable way. It is a fairly straightforward process to consider different types of domestic and external funding and determine their correlation with the underlying economy.

Credibility is about managing volatility—a country with low credibility is one that is perceived to be either unwilling or unable to maintain the integrity of fiscal, monetary, or exchange-rate policies in the face of shocks. Because the policies of LDCs already suffer from low credibility, and because an unstable national balance sheet is the most common cause of financial collapse, sharp increases in volatility can threaten the viability of the fiscal and monetary regime. This combination of high volatility and low credibility requires a very disciplined approach to a national liability management strategy. Financial instability carries an enormous cost. Even if we are able to figure out what exactly are the appropriate development policies a country should follow, the history of most LDCs is also the history of repeated failed attempts to develop and follow through a series of policies aimed at arriving at economic growth. But it is rare that any government can maintain the integrity of its economic policies over the long run when faced with periodic market collapses.

The history of the two different types of financial crises may provide an important warning about the crises of 1994–99 and what our future expectations should be. Because the past fifteen years have been a period of expanding global liquidity, the recent financial crises were structurally different from the sovereign crises that began in 1929–31 and 1981–83, both of which occurred during major international liquidity contractions. As long as global liquidity was expanding, there was little chance that these crises would lead to the grinding series of global defaults that we had seen in the past. There has never been a global debt crisis that wasn't preceded by a global liquidity contraction.

Unfortunately, however, the relatively rapid recovery of the markets following the recent crises may be leading us to conclude that the world must be in structurally better shape than it was, for example, in 1981. This is a serious mistake. The main relevant lesson of the recent past is not that LDCs are better able to handle crises; it is rather that they were nearly overwhelmed in spite of the optimal liquidity conditions of the past several years. Among U.S. economists there is a raging debate about the amount of liquidity in the system and the relationship between excess liquidity and domestic asset prices. It is not clear how the debate will resolve itself; it does seem pretty clear, however that if the United States were to see a sudden increase in inflation, it would quickly apply the monetary brakes. Although LDC borrowers may still have a few more years of relatively easy credit in which to get fiscal and monetary conditions in order, the sustainability of high global liquidity is not infinite. If history is any guide, the easy credit *will* eventually reverse itself. When that happens, the growing debt burden may become unmanageable, and there should be little doubt that the number of defaults will increase sharply (see figure 10.1).

To this end LDC finance ministries and central banks should think of themselves as national asset-liability committees whose primary goal is not so much to raise "cheap" funding as to minimize the volatility implicit in the national capital structures. But most government officials responsible for finance policy get their strategy exactly backward. Alan Greenspan has made much the same criticism recently, although he did not take the insight far enough.

> For too long, many emerging market economies have managed their external liabilities so as to minimize their current borrowing cost. This short-sighted approach ignores the insurance imbedded in long-term debt, insurance that is almost always well worth the price.[6]

It is this misunderstanding of the role of liability management, rather than crony capitalism, bad banks, or any of the other culprits usually

6. Statement made before the Committee on Banking and Financial Services, U.S. House of Representatives, May 20, 1999.

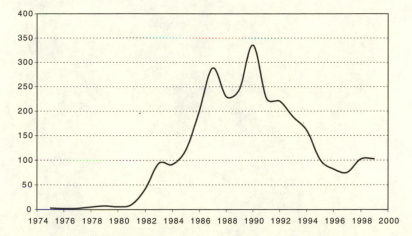

Figure 10.1. Total sovereign debt defaults (in US$ billions)

blamed for the crises, that explains the speed and surprise with which markets have collapsed.

Although the title of this chapter refers to "the new financial architecture," I have not yet said anything about the topic, because it is not clear to me that the optimal reform of the global financial system involves the system itself. Although there is undoubtedly room to improve the financial architecture—the structure of private sector and multilateral financial institutions, the relationship between official and private creditors in case of financial distress, crisis management mechanisms, and so on—the recent financial crises were not a consequence of the malfunctioning of the international system. They had to do with poor liability management at the local level. The problem with the current architecture is not that global financial markets are too volatile or free capital flows too dangerous but that sovereign capital structures are not usually designed with this volatility in mind. Here is where the World Bank, the IMF, or other multilateral agencies can play a useful role. Rather than act as an economic doctor dispensing potentially harmful medicine after a crisis, the IMF should evaluate sovereign risk management and make sure that LDC members build stable capital structures whose primary objective is to dissipate unexpected shocks. In the end, an optimal capital structure is not enough to ensure that an economically backward country will develop rapidly. The wrong capital structure, however, will guarantee that, no matter what the policy mix, its economy will break before it can achieve its goals.

Appendix

The Option Characteristics of Sovereign Debt

Traders and investors in emerging markets often refer to the "equity-like" characteristics of certain types of sovereign debt.[1] By this they typically mean that that the prices of these various debt instruments can have the high returns and the range of volatilities typically associated with equity. Furthermore, like equity, this type of debt can show great sensitivity to changes in the market's perception of the "value" of the country.[2]

Some investors even take it a step further and compare very highly discounted sovereign debt—debt trading at prices equal to or below 20% of the nominal value of the debt—to a "call option" on the obligor country. The market price of the debt is effectively treated as if it were the "premium" on the option. This suggestion is at first surprising. Most traders know that the payoff structure of a risky bond can look very similar to that of a written put option. They know that a bond holder has many of the same characteristics as an owner of a bond with no default risk who is also short a put option on the assets of the company. If that is the case, the position of a bond holder, like

1. This appendix is adapted from Michael Pettis and Jared Gross, "Delta, Kappa, and the Equity-like Features of Speculative-Grade Debt," in Michael Pettis (ed.), *The New Dynamics of Emerging Markets Investment: Managing Sub-Investment-Grade Sovereign Risk* (Euromoney Publications PLC, 1997), pp. 37–50.
2. For one of the better analytical pieces on the subject, see Gary Evans and Jose Cerritelli, "The Brady Bond and Loan Sector: Smells Like Equity, Walks Like Equity and Talks Like Equity," Baring Securities, *Emerging Markets Debt Research*, November 1994.

that of any unhedged option writer, should always improve by a re-duction in volatility and should always deteriorate by an increase in volatility. In fact, it is one of the commonplaces of corporate finance that lenders do not like volatility.

Yet holders of very deep discount debt often actually *do* seem to welcome volatility. In that case, they are not acting like investors who are *short* unhedged put options but rather like ones who are *long* the options. Since equity has some of the characteristics of call options, including their responses to changes in volatility, these positions in highly discounted debt seem clearly to be in some way *equity-like*.

Before going further I should clarify what it means for an asset to be "equity-like." There is an implicit assumption that normally *equity* reflects most of the changes in expectations concerning an issuer's future earnings, and that debt is far less sensitive to such changes. An equity position in a company is assumed to give the investor all of the upside or downside associated with changes in the asset value or earning power of the company. Debt, on the other hand, is assumed to be largely unaffected by these changes. By calling certain emerging market debt *equity-like*, traders and investors seem to be suggesting an inversion in the relationships.

Although it is not clear that comments made by traders and inves-tors about the *equity* characteristics of debt have always been intended literally, it turns out that the intuition expressed by these market play-ers may in some cases be literally true and in others very close to it. This is because debt does have a very direct relationship to underlying value, and this relationship varies depending on the credit quality of the issuer: when the credit quality of the issuer is very low, the rela-tionship becomes very high, as I will show. In order to show why this is so, and to measure and quantify that relationship, I will borrow from option theory the concept of "delta," which measures the sen-sitivity of the value of an option to changes in the price of the un-derlying asset.

Specifically, the delta of an option is the mathematical ratio be-tween a nominal change in the value of the option and the nominal change in the market price of the underlying asset. The premium on an option with a delta of 0.50, for example, will change by 50 cents (in the same direction) when the market value of the nominal amount of the assets underlying the option moves by $1.00. Every option has an associated delta that can be calculated fairly precisely if the ex-pected volatility of the underlying asset can be estimated, and the change in "wealth" of an investor who owns the option will mirror that of an investor who owns the delta percentage of the underlying asset.

In this appendix I will try to develop a framework that expresses the value of debt and equity positions as a function of the portfolio delta. I will use this framework to understand and analyze how and why the "normal" characteristics of debt and equity can merge and even invert themselves when the value of the debt is low. Furthermore, by extending the option analysis of low-quality sovereign debt, we can extend our understanding of the risks of low-quality debt and the relevant hedging techniques. As an aside, this analysis applies not just to emerging markets debt but rather to all low-quality or highly volatile debt.

Equity Is a Call Option, but Debt Is Two Put Options

Most market players understand what it means to describe equity as having most of the characteristics of a call option on the asset value of a company. Equity holders receive all the "upside" of the value of the company once the company's debt is paid off, and their downside is limited to the value of their equity investment—which is a fraction of the market value of the company's assets.

As a consequence, equity holders have an exposure to changes in the value of a company's underlying assets that is similar to that of investors who are long call options on those assets, and the price sensitivity of that exposure looks very much like the option's delta. Furthermore, the greater the "intrinsic value" of the equity (i.e., the lower the debt-to-assets ratio), the more directly the change in the value of the underlying assets is reflected in a change in the value of the equity. Similarly, both the equity and the call options should have the same sensitivity to changes in the volatility of the assets' value— the lower the intrinsic value of the option, the more they will benefit from an increase in volatility.

Within the same framework, on the other hand, bond holders are typically thought of as being long a bond with zero default risk and short a put option on the assets of the company. The strike price of this put option, expressed as a percentage of the underlying assets, is equal to the total debt divided by the asset value of the company (I will refer to this strike price hereafter as the *par* value). I should add that since there can be different types of debt with different levels of seniority, the strike price is actually equal to the sum of all debt of *equal or greater* seniority, divided by total assets.

It turns out that bond holders also effectively have a *long* position in a *second* put option. This put option is struck at a price equal to all debt that is senior to that owned by the bond holders divided by the asset value of the company. (If there is no debt that is more senior, the strike price is effectively *zero*, and hereafter I will refer to this strike price as *zero* whether or not there is more senior debt.)

The existence of the long position of put options struck at *zero* is an important but not always obvious point. It reflects the limitation of liabilities—to the current market value of the underlying asset—of a put option that is implicitly extended as part of a loan (unlike the exposure of writers of call options, who have unlimited liability). Although this limitation of liabilities may seem an obvious point, what is less obvious, but extremely important for an investor in heavily discounted debt, is the effect this limitation has on the "normal" attributes of an option.

I will discuss this effect later, but first, to illustrate the *existence* of this second put option, consider a company whose balance sheet is as shown in the diagram below. The company is assumed to have assets of $100. Its capital structure consists of $10 of senior debt, $70 of junior debt, and $20 of net worth.

We can compare the payoff structure of an investor in the junior debt of the company with that of an investor who is short a put option on the company's assets struck at $80. In both cases, if upon the debt's maturity the assets of the company are worth more than $80, the investors suffer no losses—the bondholder can be fully paid out of the value of the assets, and the option seller sees the option expire unexercised. If, on the other hand, the assets have a market value greater than $10 and less than $80 at expiration, both investors suffer losses exactly equal to the difference between $80 and the market value of the assets. The bond holder loses because he receives less that the $80 owed to him, and the option seller loses because he must pay the intrinsic value of the option.

So far their payoffs are identical. It is when the value of the assets declines to below $10 that their payoffs diverge. While the holder of the junior debt has his loss capped at his investment of $70, the writer of the put option can have his loss increase to beyond this number. In order to continue being able to compare the payoff structure for the bond holder to that of an investor in options, we need to add something to the latter's portfolio.

Assets	Liabilities
Total assets $100	Senior debt $10 Junior debt $70
	Equity
	Net worth $20

To make the payoff for the junior bond holder mirror an option position, we must include in that position a long put option struck at $10 (which I will refer to as the put option struck at *zero*). By doing this, the investor with the option portfolio will earn profits on his second, long, option exactly equal to the additional losses beyond $10 that he suffers on his first, short, option. Only in this way can the junior bond holder's position be disaggregated into a bond with zero default risk and an option portfolio. (The analysis does not change if there is no debt with greater seniority. In that case the option writer's losses are still capped by the par amount of the relevant debt.)

This combination of options reflects an important property of debt, namely, that a debt holder cannot lose more than the value of his loan, even if the value of the underlying assets declines to *below* the level beyond which the bond is worthless. The existence of the second put option, struck at *zero*, is what in effect limits the loss.

Bond Payoff Structure

Figures A.1–4 show the payoff structure of a bond wholly in option terms. In the graphs, for simplicity's sake, it is assumed that debt consists of zero-coupon notes—this permits us to ignore the complication of coupon payments. The existence of coupons would require that we treat the debt as a much larger number of options with a greater range of expiration dates.[3] Simplifying the graphs by treating the debt as zero-coupon bonds does not change the analysis at all.

Figure A.1 lists the traditional payoff structure for the short put option implied in any corporate bond. This is nothing more than the payoff curve for a put option that can be found in any basic option textbook. As the graph implies, the bond holder will get at maturity the face value of the bond minus the option payoff if the value of the company's assets is less than the face value of the debt (i.e., the "option" expires in the money). As I have already discussed, the losses to the option writer, or bond holder, are actually capped at the face value of the bond. This requires that the bond holder have implicitly "purchased" a second put option on the company's assets—"struck" at a level past which any losses on the short put will be countered by profits on the second, long, option. The payoff on this long put option is described in figure A.2.

---

3. Each coupon would have to be treated as a separate way-out-of-the-money put option and its value subtracted from the overall value of the default-free bond.

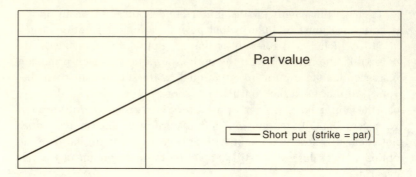

Figure A.1. Short put position

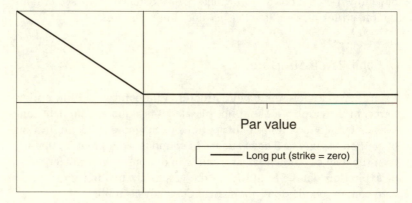

Figure A.2. Long put position

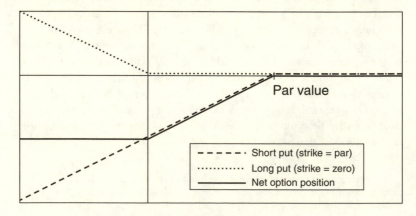

Figure A.3. Option combination

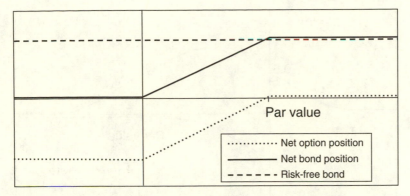

Figure A.4. Net bond holder position

Figure A.3 combines both options and shows the net payoff on the implicit option portfolio at the bond's maturity. The net payoff to the bondholder is as follows: (1) Where the value of the assets exceeds the bond's par value (both puts are out-of-the-money), the payoff is simply the par value of the bond. (2) Where the value of the assets is below the bond's par value but greater than *zero*, the short put option (at par) is "exercised" in-the-money, and the bond holder receives the par value of the bond less losses on the option. (3) Where the net value of the assets is below *zero*, the payoff on the long option cancels any further losses on the short option, and the bond holder loses the full value of the bond but nothing more. Figure A. 4 combines the net option position with the par payment of the zero-default-risk bond. As we can see, it represents exactly the payoff for a bond holder according to the creditworthiness of the borrower.

What Is the Bondholder's Delta?

So far all this is fairly straightforward. Where it becomes more interesting is when we use the equivalent option portfolio implied in a bond to measure the bond holder's range of deltas as the credit quality of the borrower changes.

Since a bond holder effectively has two separate option positions, and every option has a specific delta, we can express the bond holder's sensitivity to changes in the value of the underlying assets as the net of the two separate delta positions. Figure A.5 describes this sensitivity at every point along the credit spectrum. The two dotted lines show the deltas for the two separate options, while the solid line combines the two to show the net delta position.

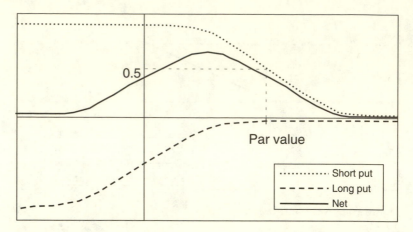

Figure A.5. Bond delta as a function of a borrower's creditworthi-ness

A delta curve has a regular and predictable relationship to the ratio between the strike price and the market value of the underlying asset.[4] The general rule is that options that are very far out of the money have deltas that approach *zero*, since at that point small changes in the value of the underlying asset have little effect on the value of the option. Conversely, when options are very far in the money, small changes in the value of the underlying asset are very closely matched by changes in the value of the option. The delta, in other words, approaches *one*. Finally, when an option is at the money, its delta is approximately 0.50, which means that small changes in the value of the underlying will cause changes in the value of the option in a ratio equal to approximately 50%.

In Figure A.5, the upper dotted line indicates the delta of the *short* put option. Since the option is struck at par, when the value of the assets is *equal* to par, the option is at-the-money. At that point the position's delta is approximately 0.50, and the bond holder gains (loses) in value 50 cents for every $1.00 increase (reduction) in the value of the assets.

At levels where the asset value significantly exceeds par, the option is far out-of-the-money, the bond holder is unconcerned about an "exercise" of the option against him, and his sensitivity to changes in the value of the underlying assets is very low. In other words, as the graph shows, his delta approaches *zero*. If the value of the assets is significantly below par, the option is in-the-money, and the bond holder's

4. A delta of *one* represents a perfect one-for-one relationship between a change in the price of the underlying and the change in the price of the option.

sensitivity to price changes increases. At that level his delta approaches *one*.

The delta of the long put option struck at zero is the mirror image of the short put option, except that it has shifted to the left enough so that when the asset value is *zero* (and the option is at-the-money), the delta is approximately −0.50. This is represented by the lower dotted line. The solid line in the middle is simply the sum of the two delta positions, and it represents graphically the net sensitivity of the bond holder to changes in the value of the obligor's assets.

Figure A.6 we once again describes the net delta position of the bond holder, but here we include as well the delta of the equity holder, whose position resembles that of an owner of a long call option struck at the debt's par value. An equity holder's payoff looks very much like that of an owner of a call option on the underlying assets when the option has a strike price equal to the amount of outstanding debt, or par. When the asset value is approximately equal to par, therefore, the value of the equity will change at roughly 50% of the rate of change of the underlying debt. In other words, it will have a delta of about 0.50.

Figure A.6 shows that at high levels of creditworthiness, the equity holder's delta approaches *one*, and at very low levels, it approaches *zero*. In this graph it is clear that just below the point of insolvency, or par, the two deltas meet at approximately 0.50. It is at this point, theoretically, that small changes in the value of the issuer's assets should have the same dollar effect on the value of the debt as on the value of the equity. Furthermore, to the left of this point a bond holder's delta position increases for a while before declining again,

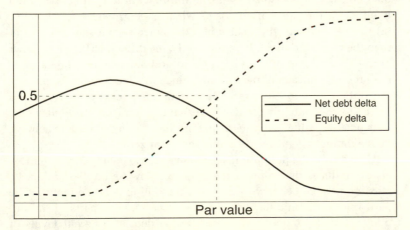

Figure A.6. Debt and equity deltas as a function of creditworthiness

whereas an equity holder's delta position continues to decline. Beyond this point a bond holder has a higher delta than the equity holders.

Perhaps this is what is meant when we say that low-quality debt can have *equity-like characteristics*: the debt has a relatively high delta that can in fact approach or exceed the delta of the equity. Since we typically think of equity as a security whose value is highly sensitive to the earning power of the issuer, when the relationship is inverted and it is the debt whose value is more highly sensitive, that debt becomes *equity-like*.

To go a little further, the delta lines suggest that a bond holder in a company that has a negative net worth can be as sensitive to changes in the value of the issuer's assets as an equity holder in a relatively creditworthy company. As an aside, I should note that this analysis suggests that a bond holder is most sensitive to changes in the value of the assets not when the assets are nearly worthless but rather when the value of assets is roughly midway between par value and *zero*. This is because at this point the delta of his long put position begins to have a noticeable effect on his net position delta.

What Is the Value of Debt?

The net delta of a debt instrument quantifies the rate at which the value of debt changes with respect to the value of the underlying asset. Obviously, we can use this net delta to determine the actual value of the debt as a function of the value of the borrower's assets. In Figure A.7, I have done just that. In the graph, the two dotted lines show the value of each of the implicit options relative to the implicit value of the debt, which is also shown. The implicit value is of course equal to either (1) the value of the assets when the borrower is insolvent or (2) the par value of the debt when the borrower's assets are greater than the borrower's debt. In other words, the difference between either of the option lines and the implicit value line is simply the value of the premium of each of the options. Since the bond holder is long the put option at *zero*, the associated premium is always positive and increases the value of the debt over and beyond the implicit value. This positive value increases as the implicit value declines, to achieve its maximum when it is at-the-money, or at *zero*.

Conversely, the put option at par—which the debt holder is short—always reduces the value of the debt to below its implicit value. Its maximum value occurs at par, when the option is at-the-money. The hard line in the middle sums up the three separate parts of the implicit portfolio to show the value of the debt at different levels of creditworthiness. As the graph clearly shows, and not surprisingly,

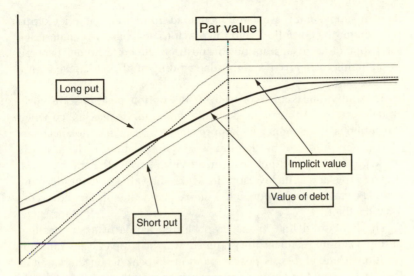

Figure A.7. Components of debt value

the value of a borrower's debt varies with the value of the underlying assets, but its rate of change is always lower (its delta is always less than one). Furthermore, the delta is highest (and the rate of change of the debt's value most closely approximates the rate of change of the value of the assets—the 45° line) somewhere halfway between par and *zero*.

The Bond Holder's Appetite for Volatility

Because we are able to describe debt holders as effectively having portfolios of option positions, we can take the further step of examining their appetites for volatility. The sensitivity of the value of an option to changes in the volatility of the underlying assets can be fairly simply described in terms of the option's kappa (or vega, as it is also known). Positions with positive kappas are positions whose value increases when volatility increases, and the higher the kappa the greater the sensitivity. Positions with negative kappas, conversely, improve in value when the volatility of the underlying assets declines. Long option positions have positive kappas, whether or not the option is a put or a call, because, other things being equal, the value of the option will increase with an increase in volatility. For obvious reasons, short option positions have negative kappas.

If an investor is both long and short options at different strike prices, his kappa can be positive, negative, or both. Each position has its own kappa, and these can be summed up to arrive at a net kappa position for the portfolio. From the previous analysis, we can describe the kappa of each separate option position the bond holder has and by summing them arrive at an understanding of his net kappa. Figure A.8 does this.

The individual kappas of each of the option positions are fairly straightforward. As a rule the kappa of an option is maximized when the option is at-the-money and approaches *zero* as the option becomes increasingly in-or out-of-the-money. The dotted line in the graph is the kappa for the short put position struck at par. As the graph shows, it is negative and at its lowest point when the value of the underlying asset is equal to par. It approaches *zero* as the value of the underlying asset declines.

The light solid line in the graph is the kappa of a simple long option position. Again, as the graph shows, the kappa for the long put position struck at *zero* is positive and at its peak when the value of the asset is equal to *zero*. It approaches *zero* as the value of the underlying asset increases.

Finally, the *net* kappa position—represented by the thick solid line—is simply the sum of the long and short kappa positions. The combination of options produces a net kappa curve shaped like a reversed *S* between *zero* and par. It approaches its highest (positive) point when the value of the underlying assets reaches *zero* and its lowest (negative) point when the value of the underlying assets is equal to par.

The shape of the curve has several interesting implications. In the first place, debt obligations of a creditworthy issuer have a negative

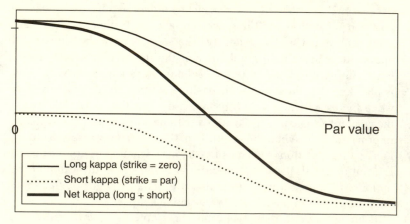

Figure A.8. Net kappa as a function of creditworthiness

kappa. This has the unsurprising implication that creditors of a solvent issuer do not like increases in volatility. However, the kappa becomes less negative as creditworthiness declines, and it is positive over a fairly large portion of the area within which the borrower is technically insolvent. At its limit, when the debt is nearly "worthless," the kappa is strongly positive. This suggests that it is not at all unreasonable for holders of certain types of severely impaired debt to welcome volatility. Under certain conditions, in other words, debt holders share with option holders an appetite for volatility.

Is Deeply Discounted Debt a Call Option on the Country?

We can take the analysis of a debt holder's appetite for volatility a little further. I mentioned earlier that some investors have described very deeply discounted debt as effectively a call option on the country. Although this may seem surprising at first, it turns out to be a fairly accurate description: in fact, deeply discounted debt can indeed look very much like a *synthetic* call option.

A synthetic call option is a long position in the underlying asset and a long position in a put option on the same asset. I have shown that the delta of the short put option (struck at par) implicitly included in a bond holder's position has a delta that approaches *one* as the value of the underlying assets declines and as the option goes increasingly in-the-money. We also know that the delta of any asset relative to itself is by definition *one*.

This is simply another way of saying that the delta of an option that is very highly in-the-money will approximate the delta of the underlying asset. In other words, both an investor in the underlying asset and the writer of a deeply in-the-money put option on that asset will have sensitivities to changes in the value of the underlying asset that are nearly identical. The option writer's position will mimic that of an investor who is long the underlying asset.

Consequently, if the debt is nearly "worthless," the debt holder will be short a highly in-the-money put option—whose changes in value mimics that of the underlying assets—and he will be long an out-of-the-money put option. Since a synthetic call option consists of the long put and the long position in the underlying, his net position will look very much like a synthetic call option struck at *zero*. Conceptually, this may be an easier way to see why it is possible for debt holders under certain conditions to welcome volatility and, further, to see why a holder of very low-priced debt does indeed act as if he owned a call option on the country. In a sense he *does* own a synthetic call option created by the two put option positions that he implicitly assumes when he owns the debt.

Applying the Framework to Sovereign Debt

Unlike with a company, it is difficult to measure the value of a country's "underlying assets," since there is no agreement as to what is an appropriate index. Numerous proxies have been used—export ratios, domestic stock market indices, and even commodity prices (in the case of countries that are heavily reliant on one or more primary commodities to generate export earnings).

In spite of this difficulty, however, there are at least five issues that the conceptual framework presented in this discussion may help clarify for traders and investors in their analysis of low-credit-quality sovereign debt:

1. *Under certain conditions the market value of external debt may be more sensitive to the "underlying" value of an uncreditworthy borrower than other "equity-type" indicators.* There are cases—countries whose credit is impaired—in which the price sensitivity of the debt is high enough that its delta can approach or exceed 0.50. Investors who hold the debt, therefore, must be able to assume the sort of volatility that would more usually be considered typical of equity investors. In addition, they have the same range of potential total returns that equity investors typically do.

2. *In the case of very highly discounted debt, debt holders are effectively long a call option on the underlying value of the borrower.* The important conceptual difference between highly discounted debt and equity is that the debt is an in-the-money option and equity is an out-of-the-money option. In other words, debt will have a higher kappa as well as a higher delta (i.e., its value will be more sensitive to changes in the underlying value than will equity). This, of course, will change as the underlying assets increase in value.

3. *An increase in the volatility associated with repayment prospects is not always negative for debt prices.* Under certain conditions, debt holders of uncreditworthy borrowers can see the value of their holdings improve by increases in volatility, unlike debt holders of creditworthy borrowers who are always helped by *reductions* in volatility. These are borrowers whose credit is so impaired that the kappa effect of the long put option struck at *zero* begins to outweigh the short put option struck at par.

4. *There is a "correct" option value for any country's debt, no matter how creditworthy or uncreditworthy that country is.* This valuation will depend primarily on the volatility of fu-

ture expected earnings (measured in the currency in which the debt is denominated) and can be used to evaluate the relative worth of debt and equity on the same underlying asset. However, to the extent that an investor seeks either to arbitrage relative value imbalances between the market value and the theoretical value of a country's debt or to hedge positions in that country's debt, it is important to develop some proxy whose value changes in some predictable way in relation to the country's "underlying value." One possibility is that some proxy for the country's equity markets—such as a broad-based equity index—could also serve as a proxy for the underlying assets. For commodity exporting countries, an alternative may be to consider the present value of future expected commodity exports as a proxy for the underlying value and to use the actual commodities as the hedge.

5. *If an investor can determine or construct a proxy for the "underlying value" of a country, in principle he can hedge debt positions or arbitrage pricing mismatches.* This is perhaps the most important issue suggested by the framework described in this appendix. Of course, since any proxy will be very rough, the investor will always be subject to enormous basis risk, although the latter can be at least partially diversified away. However, particularly during panics when markets perceive creditworthiness of sovereign borrowers to have weakened considerably, it makes a great deal of sense for investors to identify liquid and marketable proxies whose values are expected to be highly correlated with some measure of the country's underlying value to foreign investors. They should then take delta positions that are negatively correlated with the net delta of the borrower's debt.

6. *When the delta of debt is high, investors will not invest in local projects even if the return is very high.* This is because any increase in value is shared between debt and equity investors as a function of their relative deltas (which always sum to unity). For example, if a borrower is on the verge of bankruptcy (both deltas are close to 0.50), assume that an investor has the ability to invest $100 for an immediate increase in NPV of $150. Although in itself this would be a good investment, the rewards will be shared equally so that debt holders will see their value increase by $75 and equity holders will see their value increase by $75. Unless both debt and equity holders jointly invest, the $100 investor will take a $25 loss.

Conclusion

When a trader refers to the equity-like characteristics of certain types of debt, whether he realizes it or not he is implicitly saying that the debt has a high delta and its value is very sensitive to the sorts of conditions that we typically associate with equity—that is, expected earnings and the expected volatility of those earnings. In this appendix I have tried to work out the assumptions explicitly and to describe the conceptual framework within which the comparison between debt and equity is meaningful.

Further discussions of what serves as a proxy for the "underlying value" of a country are beyond the scope of this discussion, but it is reasonable to assume that this theoretical underlying value is indexed in some way to expected external earnings. If this is the case, the sensitivity of the market value of a borrower's external debt should have a specific and predictable relationship to the underlying value of that country's expected external earnings, and that relationship can best be described in terms of the delta of the debt. To the extent that these relationships can be quantified, investors are in a better position to manage their exposures and control the risks that are necessarily implicit in price discontinuities by developing partial hedges that reduce their net delta positions.

Bibliography

This bibliography is divided into five broad categories to make it more user-friendly. Obviously many of the citations can fit into more than one category, but I have tried to list it within the most appropriate category.

Economic and Financial History

Adelman, Irma, and Erinc Yeldan. "Is This the End of Economic Development?" *Structural Change and Economic Dynamics* 11 (2000): 95–109.

Andreau, Jean. *Banking and Business in the Roman World*. Cambridge University Press, 1999.

Bacha, Edmar, and Carlos Diaz Alejandro. *International Financial Intermediation: A Long and Tropical View*. Princeton Studies in International Finance no. 147, May 1982.

Bagehot, Walter. *Lombard Street: A Description of the Money Market*. 1873; reprint, John Wiley, 1999.

Borchard, Edwin. *State Insolvency and Foreign Bondholders*. Yale University Press, 1951.

Bordo, Michael D., Barry Eichengreen, and Douglas A. Irwin. "Is Globalization Today Really Different than Globalization a Hundred Years Ago?" National Bureau of Economic Research, working paper 7195, June 1999.

Brown, Brendan. *The Flight of International Capital*. Routledge, 1987.

Bulmer-Thomas, Victor. *The Economic History of Latin America since Independence*. Cambridge University Press, 1994.

Capie, Forrest, and Geoffrey Woods (eds.). *Debt Deflation in Theory and History.* MacMillan, 1997.

Chown, John F. *A History of Money from AD 800.* Routledge, 1994.

Cortes Conde, Roberto. "The Origins of Banking in Argentina." In Richard Sylla, Richard Tilly, and Gabriel Tortella (eds.), *The State, the Financial System, and Economic Modernization.* Cambridge University Press, 1999.

Cotterell, Arthur. *East Asia from Chinese Predominance to the Rise of the Pacific Rim.* Oxford University Press, 1993.

Cottrell, P. L., and Lucy Newton. "Banking Liberalization in England and Wales 1826–1844." In Richard Sylla, Richard Tilly, and Gabriel Tortella (eds.), *The State, the Financial System, and Economic Modernization.* Cambridge University Press, 1999.

Cummings, Bruce. *Korea's Place in the Sun: A Modern History.* W. W. Norton, 1997.

Dawson, Frank Griffith. *The First Latin American Debt Crisis: The City of London and the 1822–25 Bubble.* Yale University Press, 1990.

Drake, Paul W. (ed.). *Money Doctors, Foreign Debts, and Economic Reforms in Latin America from the 1890s to the Present.* SR Books, 1994.

Eichengreen, Barry. *Golden Fetters: The Gold Standard and the Great Depression, 1919–1939.* Oxford University Press, 1992.

Eichengreen, Barry. "The Baring Crisis in a Mexican Mirror." *International Political Science Review* 20, no. 3 (July 1999).

Eichengreen, Barry, and Richard Grossman. "Debt Deflation and Financial Instability: Two Historical Perspectives." In Forrest Capie and Geoffrey Woods (eds.), *Debt Deflation in Theory and History.* MacMillan, 1997.

Eichengreen, Barry, and Peter Lindert. *The International Debt Crisis in Historical Perspective.* MIT Press, 1989.

Engels, Friedrich. *Socialism: Utopian and Scientific.* In Lewis F. Feuer (ed.), *Marx and Engels.* Anchor Books, 1959.

Ferguson, Niall. *The House of Rothschild: Money's Prophets 1798–1848.* Penguin Books, 1999.

Ferguson, Niall. *The House of Rothschild: The World's Banker 1849–1999.* Viking, 1999.

Fernandez-Ansola, Juan Jose, and Thomas Laursen. "Historical Development with Bond Financing to Developing Countries." *IMF Working Paper* 95/27, March 1995.

Fischer, David Hackett. *The Great Wave: Price Revolutions and the Rhythms of History.* Oxford University Press, 1996.

Foreman-Peck, James, and Mark Casson (ed.). *Historical Foundations of Globalization.* ISPN, 1998.

Gisselquist, David. *The Political Economics of International Bank Lending.* Praeger, 1981.

Haber, Stephen H. (ed.). *How Latin America Fell Behind: Essays on the Economic History of Brazil and Mexico, 1800–1914.* Stanford University Press, 1987.

Haber, Stephen H. *Industry and Underdevelopment: The Industrialization of Mexico, 1890–1940*. Stanford University Press, 1989.

Hamilton, Alexander. "Report on Credit." Delivered to Congress on January 14, 1790.

Hammond, Bray. *Banks and Politics in America from the Revolution to the Civil War*. 1957; reprint, Princeton University Press, 1985.

Hammond, Bray. *Sovereignty and an Empty Purse: Banks and Politics in the Civil War*. Princeton University Press, 1970.

Hart, Albert G., and Perry Mehrling. *Debt, Crisis and Recovery: The 1930s and the 1990s*. M. E. Sharpe, 1995.

Hart, John Mason. *Revolutionary Mexico: The Coming and Process of the Mexican Revolution*. University of California Press, 1989.

Hirschman, Albert O. "Inflation in Chile." In Paul W. Drake (ed.), *Money Doctors, Foreign Debts, and Economic Reforms in Latin America from the 1890s to the Present*. SR Books, 1994.

Hyndman, H. M. *Commercial Crises of the Nineteenth Century*. 1892; reprinted, Allen and Unwin, 1932.

Kahler, Miles (ed.), *Capital Flows and Financial Crises*. Cornell University Press, 1998.

Kessler, Timothy P. *Global Capital and National Politics: Reforming Mexico's Financial System*. Praeger, 1999.

Keynes, John Maynard. *Essays in Persuasion*. W. W. Norton, 1963.

Keynes, John Maynard. "War Debts and the United States" (1921). In *Essays in Persuasion*. W. W. Norton, 1963.

Keynes, John Maynard. *The Economic Consequences of the Peace*. Penguin Books, 1988.

Kindleberger, Charles P. "Financial Deregulation and Economic Performance: An Attempt to Relate European Financial History to Current LDC Issues." *Journal of Economic Development* 27, nos. 1–2 (October 1987).

Kindleberger, Charles P. *International Capital Movements*. Cambridge University Press, 1987.

Kindleberger, Charles P. *Manias, Panics, and Crashes: A History of Financial Crises*. Basic Books, 1989.

Kindleberger, Charles P. *Historical Economics*. University of California Press, 1990.

Kindleberger, Charles P. *A Financial History of Western Europe*. Oxford University Press, 1993.

Kirshner, Julius (ed.). *Business, Banking, and Economic Thought in Late Medieval and Early Modern Europe: Selected Studies of Raymond de Roover*. University of Chicago Press, 1974.

Mahon, James E. *Mobile Capital and Latin American Development*. Pennsylvania State University Press, 1996.

Marichal, Carlos. "Obstacles to the Development of Capital Markets in nineteenth-Century Mexico." in Stephen H. Haber (ed.), *How Latin America Fell Behind: Essays on the Economic History of Brazil and Mexico, 1800–1914*. Stanford University Press, 1987.

Marichal, Carlos. *A Century of Debt Crises in Latin America, from Independence to the Great Depression 1820–1930*. Princeton University Press, 1989.

McNeil, William C. *American Money and the Weimar Republic*. Columbia University Press, 1986.

Mintz, Ilse. *Deterioration in the Quality of Foreign Bonds Issued in the United States, 1920–1930*. Columbia Universty Press, 1951.

Mirowski, Philip. "The Rise (and Retreat) of a Market: English Joint Stock Shares in the Eighteenth Century." *Journal of Economic History*, 41, no. 3 (September 1981).

Mitchell, Daniel B. "Dismantling the Cross of Gold: Economic Crises and U.S. International Monetary Policy." *CIBER Working Paper Series* 99–25, 1999.

Mosse, W. E. *An Economic History of Russia 1856–1914*. I. B. Tauris, 1996.

Niven, John. *Salmon P. Chase*. Oxford University Press, 1995.

North, Douglass C. *The Economic Growth of the United States, 1790–1860*. W. W. Norton, 1966.

North, Douglass C. *Structure and Change in Economic History*. W. W. Norton, 1981.

O'Rourke, Kevin H., and Jeffrey G. Williamson. *Globalization and History: The Evolution of a Nineteenth Century Atlantic Economy*. MIT Press, 1999.

Otenasek, Mildred. *Alexander Hamilton's Financial Policies*. Arno Press, 1977.

Parsons, Burke Adrian. *British Trade Cycles and American Bank Credit: Some Aspects of Economic Fluctuations in the United States 1815–1840*. Arno Press, 1977.

Pettis, Michael. "What Hit the Emerging Markets in 1994? The Shift in Global Capital Flows." *IFR International Financing Review*, October 1994.

Phillips, Ronnie J. *The Chicago Plan and New Deal Banking Reform*. M. E. Sharpe, 1995.

Rippy, J. Fred. "Latin America and the British Investment 'Boom' of the 1820s." *Journal of Modern History* 19, no. 2 (June 1947).

Rosenberg, Emily S. *Financial Missionaries to the World: The Politics and Culture of Dollar Diplomacy, 1900–1930*. Harvard University Press, 1999.

Schubert, Eric S. "Innovations, Debts, and Bubbles: International Integration of Financial Markets in Western Europe, 1688–1720." *Journal of Economic History* 48, no. 2 (June 1988).

Schuker, Stephen. *American "Reparations" to Germany, 1919–33: Implications for the Third-World Debt Crisis*. Princeton Studies in International Finance, no. 61, July 1988.

Skiles, Marilyn. "Latin American International Loan Defaults in the 1930s: Lessons for the 1980s?" Federal Reserve Bank of New York, research paper no. 8812, April 1988.

Stallings, Barbara. *Banker to the Third World: U.S. Portfolio Investment in Latin America*. UCLA Press, 1987.

Strachey, John. *The Nature of Capitalist Crisis*. Covici Friede, 1935.

Studenski, Paul, and Herman Krooss. *Financial History of the United States: Fiscal, Monetary, Banking and Tariff, Including Financial Administration and State and Local Finance*. McGraw-Hill 1952.

Suter, Christian. *Debt Cycles in the World Economy: Foreign Loans, Financial Crises, and Debt Settlements, 1820–1990*. Westview Press, 1992.

Sylla, Richard. "Shaping the U.S. Financial System, 1690–1913: The Dominant Role of Public Finance." In Richard Sylla, Richard Tilly, and Gabriel Tortella (eds.), *The State, the Financial System, and Economic Modernization*. Cambridge University Press, 1999.

Sylla, Richard, Richard Tilly, and Gabriel Tortella (eds.), *The State, the Financial System, and Economic Modernization*. Cambridge University Press, 1999.

Sylla, Richard, and John J. Wallis. "The Anatomy of Sovereign Debt Crises: Lessons from the American State Defaults of the 1840s." *Japan and the World Economy 290*. Elsevier, 1997.

Wicker, Elmus. *The Banking Panics of the Great Depression*. Cambridge University Press, 1996.

Winkler, Max. *Foreign Bonds, an Autopsy: A Study of Defaults and Repudiations of Government Obligations*. Roland Swain, 1933.

Debt Restructuring and Burden Sharing

Aggarwal, Vinod. *Debt Games: Strategic Interaction in International Debt Rescheduling*. Cambridge University Press, 1996.

Buchheit, Lee C. "Cross-Border Lending: What's Different This Time?" *Northwestern Journal of International Law and Business* 16, no. 44 (1995).

Buckley, Ross. *Emerging Markets Debt: An Analysis of the Secondary Market*. Kluwer Law, 1999.

Conybeare, John. "On the Repudiation of Sovereign Debt: Sources of Stability and Risk." *Columbia Journal of World Business* (spring/summer 1990).

Diwan, Ishac, and Dani Rodrik. *External Debt, Adjustment, and Burden Sharing: A Unified Framework*. Princeton Studies in International Finance, no. 73, 1992.

Dooley, Michael P., "Debt Management and Crisis in Developing Countries," *Journal of Developments Economics*, Vol. 63 (2000): 45–58.

Jackson, Thomas H. "Bankruptcy, Nonbankruptcy Entitlements, and the Creditors' Bargain." In Richard A. Posner (ed.), *Corporate Bankruptcy: Economic and Legal Perspectives*, Cambridge University Press, 1996.

Macmillan, Rory. "Towards a Sovereign Workout System." *Northwestern Journal of International Law and Business*, 16, no. 1 (fall 1995).

Mudge, Alfred. "Restructuring Private and Public Sector Debt." *International Lawyer* 20, no. 3 (1986).

Mudge, Alfred. "Country Debt Restructure: Continuing Legal Concerns." In *Prospect for International Lending and Rescheduling*. 1988.

Posner, Richard A. (ed.), *Corporate Bankruptcy: Economic and Legal Perspectives*. Cambridge University Press, 1996.

Roubini, Nouriel, "Bail-in, Burden-Sharing, Private Sector Involvement in Crisis Resolution and Constructive Engagement of the Private Sector: Evolving Definitions, Doctrine, Practice and Case Law," September 2000 draft of a paper written while the author was a Visiting Scholar at the IMF.

Wynne, William H. *State Insolvency and Foreign Bondholders: Selected Case Histories of Governmental Foreign Bond Defaults and Debt Readjustments*, 1951.

Capital Structure and Corporate Finance

Calomiris, Charles. "The IMF's Imprudent Role as Lender of Last Resort." *Cato Journal* 17, no. 3 (fall 1999): 33–41.

Chang, Ganlin and Suresh M. Sundaresan, "A Model of Dynamic Sovereign Borrowing: Effects of Reputation and Sanctions," preliminary draft presented at Columbia University Graduate School of Business, revised, September 2000

Collin-Dufresne, Pierre, Robert S. Goldstein, and J. Spencer Martin. "The Determinants of Credit Spread Changes." *Working Paper Series 99–15*. Charles A. Dice Center for Research in Financial Economics, 1999. Columbus, Ohio.

Crockett, Andrew. *The Theory and Practice of Financial Stability*. Princeton Studies in International Finance, no. 203, 1997.

De Long, J. Bradford, Andrei Schleifer, Lawrence H. Summers, and Robert J. Waldmann, "Noise Trader Risk in Financial Markets." *Journal of Political Economy* 98: 4 (August 1990): 703–38.

De Long, J. Bradford, Andrei Schleifer, Lawrence H. Summers, and Robert J. Waldmann, "Positive-Feedback Investment Strategies and Destabilizing Rational Speculation." *Journal of Finance* 45: 2 (June 1990): 374–97.

Evans, Gary, and Jose Cerritelli. "The Brady Bond and Loan Sector: Smells Like Equity, Walks Like Equity and Talks Like Equity." Baring Securities, *Emerging Markets Debt Research*, November 1994.

Greenwald, Bruce. "International Adjustments in the Face of Imperfect Financial Markets." In *Annual World Bank Conference on Development Economics*. IBRD/World Bank, 1998.

Greenwald, Bruce, and Joseph E. Stiglitz. "Asymmetric Information and the New Theory of the Firm: Financial Constraints and Risk Behavior." *American Economic Review* 80 (1990): 160–65.

Krugman, Paul. "Balance Sheets, the Transfer Problem, and Financial Crises." Official Paul Krugman website, January 1999.

Minsky, Hyman P. *Can "It" Happen Again? Essays on Instability and Finance.* M. E. Sharpe, 1982.

Minsky, Hyman P. "The Financial Instability Hypothesis: A Clarification." In Martin Feldstein (ed.), *The Risk of Economic Crisis.* University of Chicago Press, 1991.

Minton, Bernadette A., and Catherine M. Schrand, 1999. "The Impact of Cash Flow Volatility on Discretionary Investment and the Costs of Debt and Equity Financing." *Journal of Financial Economics* 54, no. 3 (December): 423–60.

Peters, Edgar. *Fractal Market Analysis.* John Wiley, 1994.

Pettis, Michael. "The New Dance of the Millions." *Challenge* 4, no. 4 (July–August 1998).

Pettis, Michael. "Latin America Needs a Bond Market." *Wall Street Journal*, September 4, 1998.

Pettis, Michael, and Jared Gross, "Delta, Kappa, and the Equity-like Features of Speculative-Grade Debt." In Michael Pettis (ed.), *The New Dynamics of Emerging Markets Investment: Managing Sub-Investment-Grade Sovereign Risk.* Euromoney Publications PLC, 1997.

Pettis, Michael, and Ricardo Fleury Lacerda. "A Divida Externa e a Crise Financeira." *Gazeta Mercantil*, June 19, 1997.

Pettis, Michael, and Brian Kim. "Where's the Value in Dot Coms: Volatility-Loving Companies in a Volatility-Hating Environment." *Global Finance*, July 2000.

Shleifer, Andrei, and Lawrence H. Summers. "The Noise Trader Approach to Finance." *Journal of Economic Perspectives* 4, no. 2 (spring 1990).

Stiglitz, Joseph E. "Information and Capital Markets." In William F. Sharpe and Cathryn Cootner (eds.), *Financial Economics: Essays in Honor of Paul Cootner.* Prentice Hall, 1982.

Stiglitz, Joseph E. "Why Financial Structure Matters." *Journal of Economic Perspectives* 2 (1988): 121–26.

Stiglitz, Joseph E., and A. Weiss. "Credit Rationing in Markets with Imperfect Information." *American Economic Review 71* (September 1981): 393–440.

Stulz, Rene. "Managerial Discretion and Optimal Financing Policies." *Journal of Financial Economics* 28: 3–28.

The Recent Sovereign and Financial Crises

Adler, Michael. "Lessons from Mexico's Roller-Coaster Ride in the First Quarter of 1994." *Columbia Journal of World Business* (Summer 1994).

Backman, Michael. *Asian Eclipse: Exposing the Dark Side of Business in Asia.* John Wiley, 1999.

Brealy, Richard. "The Asian Crisis: Lessons for Crisis Management and Prevention." *International Finance* 2, no. 2 (July 1999): 249–72.

Calvo, Guillermo. "Capital Flows and Macroeconomic Management: Tequila Lessons." March 16, 1996 draft of a paper presented at the IMF-sponsored *Seminar on Implications of International Capital Flows*, December 11–15, 1995.

Calvo, Guillermo, and Enrique Mendoza. "Petty Crime and Cruel Punishment: Lessons from the Mexican Debacle." *American Economic Review* 86, no. 2: 123–39.

Carstens, Agustin. "Foreign Exchange and Monetary Policy in Mexico." *Columbia Journal of World Business* (Summer 1994): 72–77.

Chang, Ha-joon. "Korea: The Misunderstood Crisis." *World Development* 26, no. 8 (1998): 1555–61.

Dornbusch, Rudiger. "Mexico, the Folly, the Crash, and Beyond." *Garantia Economic Letter*, January 23, 1995.

Dornbusch, Rudiger. "Private Market Responses to Financial Crises." *World Economic Laboratory Columns Archive*, October 1999.

Dunbar, Nicholas. *Inventing Money: The Story of Long-Term Capital Management and the Legends behind It.* John Wiley, 2000.

Fischer, Stanley, and Stephanie Griffith Jones. "Joining Battle over Capital Controls." *Emerging Markets Investors* 5, no. 10 (November 1998): 16.

Folkerts-Landau, David. "Testimony before a Hearing of the Committee on Banking and Financial Services." May 20, 1999.

Geithner, Timothy F., "Resolving Financial Crises in Emerging Market Enconomies", Press Release, *United States Treasury*, October 23, 2000.

Goldstein, Morris. *The Asian Financial Crisis: Causes, Cures, and Systemic Implications.* Institute for International Economics, June 1998.

Greenspan, Alan. Statement Made before the Committee on Banking and Financial Services, U.S. House of Representatives, May 20, 1999.

Henderson, Callum. *Asia Falling: Making Sense of the Asian Crisis and Its Aftermath.* McGraw-Hill, 1998.

Husted, Steven, and Ronald MacDonald. "The Asian Currency Crash: Were Badly Driven Fundamentals to Blame?" *Journal of Asian Economics*, 10 no. 4 (1999): 537–50.

Ito, Takatoshi. "Capital Flows in East and Southeast Asia." In Martin Feldstein (ed.), *International Capital Flows.* University of Chicago Press, 1999.

Kregel, J. A. "Yes 'It' Did Happen Again—A Minsky Crisis Happened in Asia." *WoPEc Working Paper Archive*, working paper no. 234, Jerome Levy Economics Institute, April 1998. Annandale-on-Hudson, New York.

Kregel, J. A. "East Asia Is Not Mexico: The Difference between Balance of Payments Crises and Debt Deflation." *WoPEc Working Pa-*

per Archive, working paper no. 235, Jerome Levy Economics Institute, May 1998. Annandale-on-Hudson, New York.

United States General Accounting Office. "International Financial Crises: Efforts to Anticipate, Avoid, and Resolve Sovereign Crises." In *Report to the Chairman, Committee on Banking and Financial Services, House of Representatives*, June 1997.

Wade, Robert. "Wheels within Wheels: Rethinking the Asian Crisis and the Asian Model." In Nelson Polsby (ed.), *Annual Review of Political Science 2000*. Annual Reviews, 2000.

Zakaria, Fareed. "Beyond Money." *New York Times Book Review*, November 28, 1999.

Economics and Policy

Bhagwati, Jagdish. "The Capital Myth: The Difference between Trade in Widgets and Dollars." *Foreign Affairs* 77 (May–June 1998).

Birdsall, Nancy. "Managing Inequality in the Developing World." *Current History* 98, no. 361 (November 1999).

Borchard, Edwin. *State Insolvency and Foreign Bondholders*. Yale University Press, 1951.

"Controversial Calls: Basel Proposals Would Affect Ratings." *Latin Finance*, November 1999.

Edwards, Sebastian. *Crisis and Reform in Latin America: From Despair to Hope*. Oxford University Press, 1995.

Edwards, Sebastian. "Capital Flows to Latin America." In Martin Feldstein (ed.), *International Capital Flows*. University of Chicago Press, 1999.

Eichengreen, Barry, and Albert Fishlow. "Contending with Capital Flows: What Is Different about the 1990s?" In Miles Kahler (ed.), *Capital Flows and Financial Crises*. Cornell University Press, 1998.

Eichengreen, Barry, and Asoka Mody. "Interest Rates in the North and Capital Flows to the South: Is There a Missing Link?" Eichengreen website, June 1998.

Feldstein, Martin (ed.). *The Risk of Economic Crisis*. University of Chicago Press, 1991.

Feldstein, Martin (ed.). *International Capital Flows*. University of Chicago Press, 1999.

Fraga, Arminio. "Capital Flows to Latin America." In Martin Feldstein (ed.), *International Capital Flows*. University of Chicago Press, 1999.

Gupta, Poonan, Deepak Mishra, and Ratna Sahay. "Output Response during Currency Crises." May 2000 draft of World Bank/IMF working paper.

Guttmann, Robert. *How Credit-Money Shapes the Economy: The United States in a Global System*. M. E. Sharpe, 1994.

Hanke, Steve, and Kurt Schuler. *Currency Boards for Developing Countries*. ICS Press, 1994.

Hausman, Ricardo, and Liliana Rojas-Suarez. *Volatile Capital Flows*. Inter-American Development Bank 1996.

Hubbard, Robin. *International Fixed Income Research: Weekly Focus*. Chase Securities, February 11, 2000.

Hudson, Michael. *Trade, Development and Foreign Debt. Vol. 1. International Trade*. Pluto Press, 1992.

Hudson, Michael. *Trade, Development and Foreign Debt, Vol. 2. International Finance*. Pluto Press, 1992.

Krugman, Paul. *Development, Geography, and Economic Theory*. MIT Press, 1997.

Krugman, Paul. *The Return of Depression Economics*. W. W. Norton, 1999.

Lapper, Richard. "Foreign Direct Investment Predominance in Latin America Is Bad Sign, Argues Senior Economist." *Financial Times*, March 23, 2000.

McKinnon, Ronald. *Money and Capital in Economic Development*. Brookings Institution, 1973.

Mundell, Robert. "Making the Euro Work." *Wall Street Journal*, April 30, 1998, p. A18.

Pakko, Michael R. "Do High Interest Rates Stem Capital Outflows?" *Economic Letters* 67 (2000).

Pepper, Gordon. "Does Debt Deflation Follow Asset Price Bubbles?" *Monthly Economic Review*, Lombard Street Research, April 1999.

Pettis, Michael. "What Hit the Emerging Markets in 1994? The Shift in Global Capital Flows." *IFR International Financing Review*, October 1994.

Roach, Stephen S. "Learning to Live with Globalization." Testimony before the Committee on Banking and Financial Services of the U.S. House of Representatives, May 20, 1999.

Rodrik, Dani. "Globalization, Social Conflict and Economic Growth." Prebisch Lecture delivered at UNCTAD, Geneva, October 24, 1997.

Rodrik, Dani. *Has Globalization Gone Too Far?* Institute for International Finance, New York, 1997.

Rodrik, Dani. *The New Global Economy and Developing Countries: Making Openness Work*. Overseas Development Council, policy essay no. 24, 1999.

Rubin, Robert. "Remarks on the Reform of the International Financial Architecture to the School of Advanced International Studies." Treasury News from the Office of Public Affairs, April 21, 1999.

Sabal, Jaime. "Financial Decisions in Emerging Markets." Manuscript.

Sachs, Jeffrey D. "Creditor Panics: Causes and Remedies." *Cato Journal* 18, no. 3 (winter 1999).

Sachs, Jeffrey D., and Andrew M. Warner. "The Big Push: Natural Resource Booms and Growth." *Journal of Development Economics*, June 1999.

Siebert, Horst. *The World Economy*. Routledge, 1999.

Stiglitz, Joseph E. *Whither Socialism?* MIT Press, 1994.

Wade, Robert. *Governing the Market: Economic Theory and the Role of Government in East Asian Industrialization.* Princeton University Press, 1990.

Wallerstein, Immanuel. *The Capitalist World-Economy.* Cambridge University Press, 1980.

Werner, Richard A. "Towards a 'Quantity Theorem' of Disaggregated Capital Flows, with Evidence from Japan." Paper presented to the Annual Conference of the Royal Economic Society, April 1993.

Index